Library and Archives Canada Cataloguing in Publication

Title: Humanity at its Worst: genocide, mass atrocities, and violations of human rights in the 21st century / Dr. Mario Silva, Ph.D.

Names: Silva, Mario, 1966- author.

Description: Includes bibliographical references and index.

Identifiers: Canadiana (print) 20200158007
              Canadiana (ebook) 2020015804X

ISBN 9781771614924 (softcover) ISBN 9781771614931 (PDF)
ISBN 9781771614948 (HTML) ISBN 9781771614955 (Kindle)

Subjects: LCSH: Genocide. | LCSH: Atrocities. | LCSH: Terrorism.

Classification: LCC HV6322.7.S55 2020
                 DDC 364.15/1—dc23

Published by Mosaic Press, Oakville, Ontario, Canada, 2019.

MOSAIC PRESS, Publishers
Copyright © Mosaic Press 2020

Cover Design by Brianna Wodabek

ONTARIO ARTS COUNCIL
CONSEIL DES ARTS DE L'ONTARIO
an Ontario government agency
un organisme du gouvernement de l'Ontario

We acknowledge the Ontario Arts Council
for their support of our publishing program

Funded by the Government of Canada
Financé par le gouvernement du Canada

MOSAIC PRESS
1252 Speers Road, Units 1 & 2
Oakville, Ontario L6L 5N9
phone: (905) 825-2130

info@mosaic-press.com

Humanity at its Worst

Humanity at its Worst:

Genocide, Mass Atrocities, and Violations of Human Rights in the 21st Century

 **mosaic**PRESS

Table of Contents

Preface

The book will serve as an introduction to some of the most egregious events in modern history. These include mass atrocities, terrorism, and genocides that have occurred in the twenty-first century in various locations across the world. Through consideration of atrocities and genocides, this book will seek to examine the horrific acts which are the violent destruction of a community or group premised upon that group's culture, language, or race. This examination will encompass various regions of the world, including Iraq, Somalia, Syria, Myanmar, and a number of locations in the Middle East. There will also be consideration of these genocides and mass atrocities in terms of their individual manifestations.

This book seeks to bring together existing reasoning and research on these subjects to provide readers with a grounded overview of the subject matter. The book is not a "how-to guide" or a handbook on prevention. Rather, it is a basic coverage, an introductory text that can be used across a variety of institutional settings and for varied purposes to better understand these heinous acts. The primary focus will be upon genocide in the twenty-first century, with some discussion of similar events in the twentieth century.

Incomprehensible crimes committed by the Nazi regime and its collaborators during the Second World War will be examined, but this book cannot and will not seek to fully review this period, as thorough coverage of this subject has already been provided by a vast body of work. The Holocaust is justifiably the most examined event of its kind in human history, due to the Nazi regime's evil intentions and meticulously coordinated efforts to annihilate a specific group of human beings. The Holocaust was one of the most defining moments in human history. It was a crime against humanity unlike any the world had ever witnessed, and it fundamentally altered the manner in which acts of genocide are examined. The Holocaust provides many important lessons that can be applied in order to assist in preventing such events from reoccurring.

The challenge is to ensure that these lessons are remembered, disseminated, and applied. In this way, the world can honour the memory of the many people that humanity failed to protect. The Holocaust altered humanity forever, and it was with this heavy burden in mind that I accepted the Prime Minister's diplomatic appointment to the International Holocaust Remembrance Alliance (IHRA) as the Canadian Chair in 2013. Initiated in 1988 by then Swedish Prime Minister Göran Persson, IHRA's objective is to promote Holocaust education, remembrance, and research. Currently, it has expanded from three founding members (Sweden, the United Kingdom, and the United States), to thirty-three countries. IHRA is a unique international body in that it consists of a combination of both government diplomatic representatives and non-governmental Holocaust experts—academics, museum professionals, educators, and researchers. It is governed by the principles expressed in its founding document, the Stockholm Declaration, which emphasizes the importance of upholding the "terrible truth of the Holocaust against those who deny it," and of preserving the memory of the Holocaust as a "touchstone in our understanding of the human capacity for good and evil."

Since the Stockholm Declaration, international organizations such as the Council of Europe and the Organization for Security and Co-operation in Europe have made Holocaust remembrance a fundamental part of their mission. And, in November 2005, the United Nations declared January 27th—the date in 1945 when Russian forces liberated Auschwitz—as the International Day of Commemoration in memory of the victims of the Holocaust.

This book is dedicated to assisting readers in achieving an understanding of the circumstances of people having to contend with severe adversity across the world. The accounts of genocides in this book examine the differing interpretations of genocide from the legal viewpoints, while analyzing the influence of race, ethnicity, nationalism, and gender upon genocides.

Genocide is no new concept for the twenty-first century world, and accordingly, this book unveils in a systematic manner the abysmal conditions of the victims of genocide as well as their present-day crisis. We attempt to objectively divulge layer by layer the reality of twenty-first century genocide from the corpus of the lives of the victims of the same. The book not only paints the reality of the nations infected by the epidemic of genocide, but does so in a comprehensive and orderly manner by dedicating each chapter to a singular region so that all facts come to the surface for evaluation.

The commonality as well as the uniqueness of each genocide is considered in this compilation. We begin with Darfur and end with Nigeria, crossing several territorial and temporal borders in between—be it documenting the ongoing genocide in South Sudan, recognizing the early warning signs of genocide in Central African Republic, or examining the all-embracing extent of genocide in Myanmar, which is the most recent addition to the list of twenty-first century genocides.

We even pay attention to civil war situations that could be termed no less than genocide—such as the continuing struggle of Yemen, which faces air bombings even today; or Nigeria's war with Boko Haram, a group infecting the country with its extremist presence and preying on the sections of society made most vulnerable by their age and gender.

Introduction

The history of humanity has been characterized by countless wars and struggles. Indeed, war has been the central theme for most of our history, and not, unfortunately, a rare occurrence. It is perhaps the nature of scholarly review that stories of courage and goodness are rarely told by historians. Although this book considers the darker chapters of human history, it also remarks upon the reality that compassion and goodness is inherent in most human beings. Human history is home to countless leaders, states, and groups of individuals who have fulfilled the highest expectations that could reasonably be placed upon humanity. Through states, religious institutions, and individuals have been channelled the greatest virtues of human character. And yet, the path of history has also been littered with despots, cruel regimes, and irrepressibly horrific conduct, which have cost the lives and security of tens of millions of people.

With the adoption in 1948 of the Universal Declaration of Human Rights, the foundation of international human rights law was established. Fundamentally, Article One of the Declaration states that "[a]ll human beings are born free and equal in dignity and rights." The Declaration continues to be an inspiration to the global community, as it seeks by its very existence to address injustices. Over the years, the commitments outlined in the Declaration have been translated into law, including in the form of treaties and customary international law, as well as individual domestic law. The creation of a comprehensive body of human rights law is one of the greatest results of the United Nations with the resultant prescribed treaties to which all nations can subscribe.

It has been stated that the instrumental value of international human rights law, direct or indirect, is not as self-evident as hoped. We have only to examine the clear breaches, as evidenced by the genocide in Rwanda, the ethnic cleansing in the Yugoslavia, and the genocide of the Rohingya in Myanmar. But continued atrocities do not disprove the case for international human rights law. It is a contradiction that scholars and observers of the human condition have never fully been able to reconcile, and it is certainly the foundation upon which enormous volumes of scholarship have been based. We can note that the narratives of death and destruction have traditionally overshadowed attention to a broader history of human goodness. One would hope that this is because evil and oppression are in fact egregious breaks from the majority of human history, but that unfortunately is a narrative not yet anywhere near complete or determined. While the better aspects of human nature are referenced in this book, our focus will be upon the failure of humanity to avert evil either at the state level or in relation to individual conduct.

These are the debates that instructed the remonstrations of many of the greatest philosophers in human history. Socrates stated that humanity was required to establish fundamental principles that would instruct human behaviour, and that good and evil could be measured most importantly beyond the desires of individual human beings. Plato held a more spiritual view, maintaining that human beings were imbued with a sense of good and evil even before their individual creation. Thomas Hobbes' view was much more pragmatic, maintaining that the idea of good and evil was essentially relative and that it could change. Irrespective of these views, and those of other renowned thinkers throughout history, the practical implications for humanity have been vast.

Many of the great institutions of human creation have been established to intercede on behalf of the persecuted, whether states or individuals. The League of Nations in the period following the First World War, or the United Nations that emerged from the conclusion of the Second World War, are primary examples. Yet, in both cases, disappointment—as outlined in Part III of this book—has been an integral part of the story of these institutions. Our focus will be upon the United Nations, as it occupies the chronological period of this examination.

Protecting populations from the most serious of international crimes—including genocide, crimes against humanity, terrorism, and war crimes—is the collective responsibility of the world community. It is to the shame of the world and its human institutions that these crimes continue to take place in many parts of the globe even in contemporary times. Too often, lessons learned are not solutions applied. Although calls for accountability are now the norm when such crimes are committed, impunity remains all too common.

The whole concept of war crimes examined within the context of international law was firmly established by legal proceedings such as those witnessed at the Nuremberg and Tokyo War Crimes Trials where Nazi and Imperial Japanese leaders were prosecuted for the war crimes they committed or directed during World War II. Unfortunately, as we have witnessed, many war crimes and mass atrocities are not prosecuted, often due to lack of political will. The International Criminal Court (ICC), which began functioning on July 1st, 2002, emerging from the Rome Statute, was in many ways a response to combat the impunity of those who commit such heinous crimes.

The twentieth century witnessed some of the most horrific events in human history. Tens of millions of human beings lost their lives during the First and Second World Wars. These were conflicts that were fought not on religious grounds, but over ideology, power, and hatred. The totalitarian regimes of the Nazis in Germany and of Soviet-style communism in Russia and Eastern Europe led to the bloodiest massacres of the twentieth century. These acts of sheer evil also destroyed a vibrant European Jewish community, with six million people systematically massacred by the Nazi regime and its sympathizers.

For most of the twentieth century, tens of millions of men, women, and children have been killed, tortured, burned alive, bombed, and starved by regimes who imposed death and destruction on defenceless people.

In January 2015, the world commemorated the seventieth anniversary of the liberation of the Auschwitz extermination camp. From the horrific events of the Holocaust emerged the Genocide Convention, designed to prevent future generations from repeating these acts of unimaginable evil. These mass atrocities have had various labels applied to them, ranging from "crimes against humanity" to "genocide." Irrespective of how they are labelled, it is clear that the world community has a duty to protect humanity from these violent acts, and that it must do so more effectively than history has demonstrated.

I once had the honour and privilege of meeting Eli Wiesel, a Holocaust survivor and Nobel Laureate who once said, "The opposite of love is not hate, it's indifference. The opposite of art is not ugliness, it's indifference. The opposite of faith is not heresy, it's indifference. And the opposite of life is not death, it's indifference." He went on further to state that "[t]here may be times when we are powerless to prevent injustice, but there must never be a time when we fail to protest."

All mass atrocities are illegitimate, unforgivable, and unlawful. Conflict prevention as a strategy objective faces substantial ethical dilemmas, as demonstrated by the situation of the ex-Yugoslavia or more recently the Arab rebellions characterized as the "Arab Spring."

The world must focus more upon the condemnation of the perpetrators of such crimes when evidence of a mass atrocity is identified.

The world must be more effective and timely in identifying the indicators of risks for mass atrocities, which would in turn allow for the earlier detection of potential events of this kind. This is but one approach, but alone it is simply not sufficient. A reconceptualization of consistency in politics is needed, including the checking of power between social orders.

On April 7th, 2004, then United Nations Secretary-General Kofi Annan established a "Five Point Action Plan for the Prevention of Genocide." He stated: "We must never forget our collective failure to protect at least 800,000 defenceless men, women and children who perished in Rwanda 10 years ago. ... First, we must all acknowledge our responsibility for not having done more to prevent or stop the genocide." It is imperative that organizations like the United Nations predict, prevent, or respond to major crises in a timely manner to interrupt any process that could result in the loss of innocent lives.

The word "genocide" was first coined by Polish lawyer Raphael Lemkin in 1944 in his book *Axis Rule in Occupied Europe*. It consists of the Greek prefix "genos," meaning "race" or "tribe," and the Latin suffix "cide," meaning "killing." Lemkin developed the term partly in response to the Nazi policies of systematic murder of Jewish people during the Holocaust, but also in response to previous instances in history of targeted actions aimed at the destruction of particular groups of people. Later on, Lemkin led the campaign to have genocide recognized and codified as an international crime. Genocide was first recognized as a crime under international law in 1946 by the United Nations General Assembly (A/RES/96-I). It was codified as an independent crime in the 1948 Convention on the Prevention and Punishment of the Crime of Genocide (the Genocide Convention).[1]

Ideological and religious superiority and the zeal for dominance serve as the basic excuses for carrying out genocide, ignoring all its ferocious and negative impacts on humanity at large. Genocide has the capability to pit one group against another to such an extent that hatred and a will for extermination blinds all possibility of oneness, integration, and unity. All ideals of humanitarian concern are cut short in the battle for establishing superiority of ideology and of religion.

The potential for genocide in the wake of diminishing ideals of humanity urgently necessitates international intervention. Failing to address this challenge could seriously hamper peace and prosperity across the globe. Studying as well as understanding the impacts of potential genocide in the near future could prevent these evils from spreading. The impact of genocide is not only limited to the sphere of violence and bloodshed. It has

---

[1]   https://www.un.org/en/genocideprevention/genocide.shtml

spread its demonic claws to haunt the past, present, and future existence of its victims.

Holding the potential to exterminate entire populations, genocide—especially in the twenty-first century—has hindered the growth of the people at the receiving end of its atrocious presence. All strata of the civic framework are disrupted when genocide infects a country. The sociocultural, economic, and political grounds of those victimized by genocide are hampered to a large extent. Genocide not only holds the capacity to disrupt the geographical locale whole and sole, but also to spread disorder in the educational and health domain. For the community or groups at the receiving hand of the perils of genocide, standard education and health facilities can only be a distant dream. Irrespective of age and gender, these victims face extreme physical, mental, sexual, and psychological torture. Genocide even gives rise to other issues like refugee crises, the problem of repatriation, and the question of reintegration.

The impacts of genocide are not just contained within a specific geographical locale; they trespass the boundaries of time and space to haunt the very existence of the communities facing the brunt of modern-age genocide.

Genocides and mass atrocities are dark hallmarks of human history, but so too are efforts to preclude their reoccurrence. Regrettably, the latter have continued to lack the effectiveness required of the collective global community, and it is upon this fact that world leaders and citizens of all countries must focus their energy to realize the changes that will effectively prevent future events of this kind.

Part I

Definition and Classification of Genocide

During the period of the eighty-eight years of the twentieth century, nearly 170,000,000 men, women, and children were killed, tortured, burnt alive, bombed, starved, and murdered in countless ways by regimes which have imposed death and destruction on numerous defenceless people.

Genocide will always be seen as the gravest of all forms of human rights violations, but this is not in any way to diminish other forms of mass atrocities, as all murder of innocent lives is a violation of international law. The act of genocide entails the aggressive destruction of a group, accomplished by the annihilation of the vital features of that group, whether national, ethnic, racial, cultural, or religious. The intentions are to disintegrate political and social foundations, damaging the peace, health, and even individual lives of that group.

In international law, the crime of genocide is part of the broader category of "crimes against humanity," which were defined by the Charter of the International Military Tribunal (Nuremberg Charter). The jurisprudence created by the Nuremberg and Tokyo trials and the ensuing revelations of Nazi atrocities led to the passage by the United Nations (UN) General Assembly of Resolution 96-I in December 1946, which made the crime of genocide punishable under international law; and of Resolution 260-III in December of 1948, which approved the text of the Convention on the Prevention and Punishment of the Crime of Genocide, thus creating the first UN human rights treaty.

Article 2 of the convention defines genocide as:

> any of the following acts committed with intent to destroy, in whole or in part, a national, ethnical, racial or religious group, as such: (a) Killing members of the group; (b) Causing serious bodily or mental harm to members of the group; (c) Deliberately inflicting on the group conditions of life calculated to bring about its physical destruction in whole or in part; (d) Imposing measures intended to prevent births within the group; (e) Forcibly transferring children of the group to another group.[2]

In addition to the commission of genocide, the convention also made conspiracy, incitement, attempt, and complicity in genocide punishable under international law.

The convention has enjoyed near-unanimous international support, and although the prohibition of genocide has become, according to the International Court of Justice (ICJ), a peremptory norm (*jus cogens*) of international law, the convention has its critics, as it fails to include definitions for potential genocides based on political affiliation and sexual orientation. In addition, the so-called "intentionality clause" of the convention's definition of genocide—the part that mentions the "intent to destroy, in whole or in part, a national, ethnical, racial or religious group" has also been problematic, with the most common objections being that such intent can be difficult to establish.

Some legal scholars have also argued that an approach that focuses solely on intent ignores the "structural violence" of social systems in which economic and political inequalities can lead to the total extermination of particular groups.[3] However, defenders of the intentionality clause note that it is necessary for differentiating genocide from other forms of mass killings.

The convention also stipulates that the nations have an obligation to report any instances of genocide to the UN, at which point the UN is obligated to evaluate the case and, upon determining it to be a genocide, act on stopping it.[4] The most distinct characteristic of the definition of genocide is the recognition of both the perpetrators as well as the victims. It is the communal characteristics—i.e., the ethnolinguistic or religious attributes—that define the victim status of the victimized groups across the globe.

---

[2]   https://www.ohchr.org/en/professionalinterest/pages/crimeofgenocide.aspx

[3]   Nafeez Mosaddeq Ahmed, "Structural Violence as a Form of Genocide – The Impact of the International Economic Order", Entelequia. Revista Interdisciplinar, nº 5, otoño 2007

[4]   https://mountainscholar.org/bitstream/handle/10976/16/URJ12_Bailey.pdf?sequence=1&isAllowed=y

Under most legal constructions of genocide (e.g., under the statutes for the International Criminal Tribunals for the former Yugoslavia and for Rwanda), liability for genocide extends to those who "planned, instigated, ordered, committed or otherwise aided and abetted in the planning, preparation or execution" of one or more of the aforementioned genocidal acts (ICTY Art. 7[1]).[5] In general, both public and private individuals are punishable (ICTY Art. 7[2]). Leaders can be held accountable for the criminal actions of their subordinates if they knew or should have known about the actions and failed to prevent or punish them (ICTY Art. 7[3]):[6]

Article 7: Individual criminal responsibility

1. A person who planned, instigated, ordered, committed or otherwise aided and abetted in the planning, preparation or execution of a crime referred to in articles 2 to 5 of the present Statute, shall be individually responsible for the crime.
2. The official position of any accused person, whether as Head of State or Government or as a responsible Government official, shall not relieve such person of criminal responsibility nor mitigate punishment.
3. The fact that any of the acts referred to in articles 2 to 5 of the present Statute was committed by a subordinate does not relieve his superior of criminal responsibility if he knew or had reason to know that the subordinate was about to commit such acts or had done so and the superior failed to take the necessary and reasonable measures to prevent such acts or to punish the perpetrators thereof.
4. The fact that an accused person acted pursuant to an order of a Government or of a superior shall not relieve him of criminal responsibility, but may be considered in mitigation of punishment if the International Tribunal determines that justice so requires.[7]

Intent is the most difficult element to determine. To constitute genocide, there must be a proven intent on the part of perpetrators to physically destroy a national, ethnic, racial, or religious group. Cultural destruction does not suffice, nor does an intention to simply disperse a group. It is this special intent, or *dolus specialis*, that makes the crime of genocide unique. In addition, case law has associated intent with the existence of a state or organizational plan or policy, even if the definition of genocide in

---

5   International Tribunal for the Prosecution of Persons Responsible for Serious Violations of International Humanitarian Law Committed in the Territory of the Former Yugoslavia since 1991 (ICTY)

6   https://www.law.cornell.edu/wex/genocide

7   http://www.icty.org/x/file/Legal%20Library/Statute/statute_sept09_en.pdf

international law does not include that element. Importantly, the victims of genocide are deliberately—not randomly—targeted because of their real or perceived membership of one of the four groups protected under the convention (which excludes political groups, for example). This means that the target of destruction must be the group, as such, and not its members as individuals. Genocide can also be committed against only part of a group, as long as that part is identifiable (including within a geographically limited area) and "substantial."[8]

Though similar in overall impact, war and genocide do have distinctive qualities and methodologies. While wars are being fought with modern weapons against opposing military forces, genocide is being carried out against non-combatants with low-tech weapons such as guns, fire, rape, drowning, and machetes. Genocide tears at the very fabric of what is good and decent, and it is incomprehensible that normal people can perpetrate such horrid violence on select groups or races of people on such a grand scale and justify it.[9]

After its ratification, the Genocide Convention lacked effective enforcement mechanisms. Though it contained provisions to enable the United Nations to enforce it, such enforcement needed Security Council approval. The convention stipulated that persons charged with genocide should be tried before an international penal tribunal, and eventually with the 1998 adoption of the Rome Statute and the creation of the International Criminal Court on July 1st, 2002, this came into force. The ICC jurisdiction includes the crime of genocide, and the statute adopts the same definition of the offence as found in the Genocide Convention.

The Genocide Convention was first invoked before an international tribunal in 1993, when the government of Bosnia and Herzegovina argued before the ICJ that the Federal Republic of Yugoslavia was in breach of its obligations under the convention.

The UN Security Council established separate tribunals, the International Criminal Tribunal for the Former Yugoslavia (ICTY) and the International Criminal Tribunal for Rwanda (ICTR), both of which contributed to the clarification of the material elements of the offence of genocide, as well as of the criteria establishing individual criminal responsibility for its commission. The ICTY was established by UN Security Council Resolution 827, adopted unanimously on May 25th, 1993, in order to address the crimes committed in the conflict in the former Yugoslavia; and the ICTR was established in November 1994 by UN Security Council Resolution

---

8   https://www.un.org/en/genocideprevention/genocide.shtml

9   https://scholarship.rollins.edu/cgi/viewcontent.cgi?referer=https://www.google.com/&httpsredir=1&article=1008&context=mls

955 in order to judge people responsible for the Rwandan genocide and other serious violations of international law in Rwanda, or by Rwandan citizens in nearby states, between January 1st and December 31st, 1994.

The Rwandan tribunal, for example, stated that genocide included "subjecting a group of people to a subsistence diet, systematic expulsion from homes and the reduction of essential medical services below minimum requirement."[10] It also ruled that "rape and sexual violence constitute genocide ... as long as they were committed with the specific intent to destroy, in whole or in part, a particular group, targeted as such."[11]

On the critical issue of intent, the Yugoslav tribunal also ruled that genocidal intent can be manifest in the persecution of small groups of people as well as large ones. According to the tribunal, such intent:

> may consist of desiring the extermination of a very large number of the members of the group, in which case it would constitute an intention to destroy a group en masse. However, it may also consist of the desired destruction of a more limited number of persons selected for the impact that their disappearance would have upon the survival of the group as such. This would then constitute an intention to destroy the group selectively."[12]

War Crimes

War crimes are a serious violation of international humanitarian and human rights, and constitute criminal responsibility for those involved in the intentional killing of civilians or prisoners, torturing, destroying civilian property, taking hostages, performing a perfidy, raping, using child soldiers, pillaging, and acts such as the strategic bombing of civilian populations. With the codification of the body of international customary law in the twentieth century between sovereign states, the concept of war crimes emerged. At the end of World War II and the numerous trials at Nuremberg and Tokyo, the notion of what constitutes a war crime was defined by international law. In addition, the Geneva Conventions in 1949 also added to the body of legal work on the issue of war crimes.

The Geneva Conventions represent a legal basis and framework for the conduct of war under international law. The Conventions, with their four related treaties adopted and continuously expanded from 1864 to 1949, have been ratified by every single member state of the United Nations.

---

[10]   https://casebook.icrc.org/case-study/ictr-prosecutor-v-jean-paul-akayesu

[11]   https://casebook.icrc.org/case-study/ictr-prosecutor-v-jean-paul-akayesu

[12]   https://casebook.icrc.org/case-study/ictr-prosecutor-v-jean-paul-akayesu

However, the Additional Protocols to the Geneva Conventions, which afford additional protection of international humanitarian law, have yet to be adopted by all state parties.

Warring parties are required under international humanitarian law to differentiate between combatants and civilians and to make their attacks proportional and on legitimate military targets. Any violations of this are considered war crimes.

In addition, the affected group in the "case of war crimes is identified by its status as an enemy; the targeted group in the case of genocide is identified by its racial, national, ethnic, or religious characteristics."[13] The important qualifier in post-conflict conduct reflects the understanding that genocide can and does take place during wartime.

In addition, the Nuremberg principles also a set guideline for establishing what constitutes a war crime under international law. Subsequently, the International Law Commission of the United Nations has codified the legal principles:

Principle I
Any person who commits an act which constitutes a crime under international law is responsible therefor and liable to punishment.

Principle II
The fact that internal law does not impose a penalty for an act which constitutes a crime under international law does not relieve the person who committed the act from responsibility under international law.

Principle III
The fact that a person who committed an act which constitutes a crime under international law, acted as Head of State or responsible government official, does not relieve him from responsibility under international law.

Principle IV
The fact that a person acted pursuant to order of his Government or of a superior does not relieve him from responsibility under international law, provided a moral choice was in fact possible to him.[14]

In the March 2006 Federal Court decision of Hinzman v. Canada, the Court cited the Nuremberg Principle IV, and its reference to an individual's

---

[13] https://www.britannica.com/topic/genocide

[14] International Committee of the Red Cross (ICRC) References Principles of International Law Recognized in the Charter of the Nüremberg Tribunal and in the Judgment of the Tribunal, 1950

responsibility, in its decision. Jeremy Hinzman was a U.S. Army deserter who claimed refugee status in Canada as a conscientious objector, one of many Iraq War resisters. The Federal Court ruling was released denying refugee status to the claimant. In the decision, Justice Anne L. Mactavish addressed the issue of personal responsibility:

An individual must be involved at the policy-making level to be culpable for a crime against peace ... the ordinary foot soldier is not expected to make his or her own personal assessment as to the legality of a conflict. Similarly, such an individual cannot be held criminally responsible for fighting in support of an illegal war, assuming that his or her personal war-time conduct is otherwise proper.

During my mandate as a Federal Member of Parliament for Davenport, I supported a private members' motion adopted on June 3rd, 2008 by the Canadian Parliament that recommended that the government immediately implement a program which would allow conscientious objectors to a war not sanctioned by the United Nations to be given refugee status.

War crimes, in part, are defined in the Rome Statute as:

Grave breaches of the Geneva Conventions of 12 August 1949, namely, any of the following acts against persons or property protected under the provisions of the relevant Geneva Convention:

Willful killing, or causing great suffering or serious injury to body or health
Torture or inhumane treatment
Unlawful wanton destruction or appropriation of property
Forcing a prisoner of war to serve in the forces of a hostile power
Depriving a prisoner of war of a fair trial
Unlawful deportation, confinement or population transfer
Taking hostages[15]

Ethnic Cleansing

The systematic forced removal of ethnic, racial, and/or religious groups from a given territory by a more powerful ethnic group is referred to as ethnic cleaning. The purpose, generally, is to make the territory ethnically homogeneous through methods such as forced migration (e.g., deportation or population transfer), intimidation, as well as genocide and genocidal rape.

Ethnic cleansing does not only involve the removal of an ethnic group, but is also accompanied by efforts to remove physical and cultural evidence

---

[15]   https://www.icc-cpi.int/nr/rdonlyres/ea9aeff7-5752-4f84-be94-0a655eb30e16/0/rome_statute_english.pdf

of the targeted group within the given territory. The destruction of places of worship, for example, is commonplace.

Ethnic cleaning has been happening since the beginning of recorded history, and in modern times in regions such as Africa, there have been many tribal wars in which each side has claimed the other side to be "subhuman."

During the late 1990s and early 2000s, the police and military in Indonesia organized paramilitaries to carry out the brutal murder and expulsion of large numbers of civilians in East Timor.[16]

During the Iraq Civil War, Shia and Sunni militias perpetrated ethnic cleansing on entire neighbourhoods in Baghdad. As of June 21st, 2007, the United Nations High Commissioner for Refugees estimated that 2.2 million Iraqis had been displaced to neighbouring countries, and 2 million were displaced internally, with nearly 100,000 Iraqis fleeing to Syria and Jordan each month.[17]

The mass emigration of Iraqi Assyrians from 2003 to the time of writing can be described as ethnic cleansing. Iraqi Christians—comprising less than 5% of the total population of Iraq—make up 40% of the refugees in nearby countries, according to UNHCR.[18]

The military campaign carried out by the government of Burma against the Rohingya Muslims constitutes ethnic cleansing, as well as the cultural cleansing by the Sinhala Buddhist majority of the Muslim and Tamil minorities in Sri Lanka.[19]

In the ongoing civil war in Syria, anti-government rebels are perpetrating a campaign of ethnic cleansing of the Syriac Orthodox Church.[20]

The 1994 genocide in Rwanda was also not a result of warfare, but was based on hatred of one ethnic tribe.

Atrocity Crimes

Atrocity crimes refer to the three legally defined international crimes of genocide, war crimes, and crimes against humanity. Mass atrocities

---

[16] https://www.globalsecurity.org/military/library/news/1999/09/990908-timor7.htm

[17] http://edition.cnn.com/2007/WORLD/meast/06/20/damon.iraqrefugees/index.html

[18] https://usatoday30.usatoday.com/news/world/iraq/2007-03-22-christians-iraq_N.htm

[19] https://www.nytimes.com/2015/01/03/opinion/sri-lankas-violent-buddhists.html?_r=1

[20] https://latimesblogs.latimes.com/world_now/2012/03/church-fears-ethnic-cleansing-of-christians-in-homs-syria.html

include torture, enslavement, murder, forced prostitution, sexual violence, and enforced disappearance.[21] Since the end of the Second World War, more than 30% of mass atrocities have occurred outside periods of armed conflict. In the late 70s and 80s, mass atrocities were carried out in Cambodia under the Pol Pot regime, resulting in the killing of 25% of the country's citizens. In Latin America, large-scale killing, rape, and torture has also occurred.

In 2018, the ICC decided to include crimes of aggression within its jurisdiction, therefore effectively adding a fourth atrocity crime. In addition to the 1998 Rome Statute of the ICC, these crimes are defined in the 1948 Convention on the Prevention and Punishment of the Crime of Genocide and the 1949 Geneva Conventions and their 1977 Additional Protocols.

Under international law:

> atrocity crimes are considered to be the most serious crimes against humankind. Their position as international crimes is based on the belief that the acts associated with them affect the core dignity of human beings, in particular the persons that should be most protected by States, both in times of peace and in times of war. However, the victims targeted by acts of genocide, crimes against humanity, and war crimes differ.[22]

Atrocity crimes tend to occur in countries with some level of instability or [in failing or failed states]. Consequently, measures taken to prevent these crimes are likely to contribute to national peace and stability. Atrocity crimes and their consequences can spill over into neighbouring countries[.][23]

International human rights law also places obligations on State Parties to take steps to prevent the acts it seeks to prohibit.[24]

On June 25th, 2018, United Nations Secretary General Antonio Guterres told the Assembly that atrocity crimes—genocide, war crimes, crimes against humanity, and ethnic cleansing—are not "inevitable," and called for the international community to do more to stop violence against innocent people: "At this time of extreme challenges, we must not abandon the responsibility to protect or leave it in a state of suspended animation,

---

[21]   http://www.yadvashem.org/yv/en/education/international_projects/chairmanship/mark_levene1.pdf

[22]   https://r2pasiapacific.org/files/2872/2018_indonesian_informal_translation_Framework_of_Analysis.pdf, page 1

[23]   https://r2pasiapacific.org/files/2872/2018_indonesian_informal_translation_Framework_of_Analysis.pdf, page 3

[24]   https://r2pasiapacific.org/files/2872/2018_indonesian_informal_translation_Framework_of_Analysis.pdf, page 4

finely articulated in words but breached time and again in practice,"[25] he said.

The UN Framework for Analysis For Atrocity Crimes describes its purpose and function as follows:

> The Framework contains two main analytical tools for assessing the risk of atrocity crimes: (a) a list of 14 risk factors for atrocity crimes; and (b) indicators for each of the risk factors. Among the 14 risk factors outlined, the first eight are common to all crimes, reflecting the fact that atrocity crimes tend to occur in similar settings and share several elements or features. In addition to these common factors, the framework identifies six additional risk factors, two specific to each of the international crimes—namely genocide, crimes against humanity and war crimes.[26]

The Framework lists the risk factors as follows:

Common Risk Factors

Risk Factor 1 – Situations of armed conflict or other forms of instability

Risk Factor 2 – Record of serious violations of international human rights and humanitarian law

Risk Factor 3 – Weakness of State structures

Risk Factor 4 – Motives or incentives

Risk Factor 5 – Capacity to commit atrocity crimes

Risk Factor 6 – Absence of mitigating factors

Risk Factor 7 – Enabling circumstances or preparatory action

Risk Factor 8 – Triggering factors

Specific Risk Factors
Genocide:

Risk Factor 9 – Intergroup tensions or patterns of discrimination against protected groups

Risk Factor 10 – Signs of an intent to destroy in whole or in part a protected group

Crimes against humanity:

Risk Factor 11 – Signs of a widespread or systematic attack against any civilian population

Risk Factor 12 – Signs of a plan or policy to attack any civilian population

---

[25]   https://news.un.org/en/story/2018/06/1013002

[26]   https://www.refworld.org/docid/548afd5f4.html

War crimes:

Risk Factor 13 – Serious threats to those protected under international humanitarian law

Risk Factor 14 – Serious threats to humanitarian or peacekeeping operations[27]

The Framework notes that atrocity crimes usually take place against a background of either an international or non-international armed conflict: "If armed conflict is a violent way of dealing with problems, it is clear that the risk of atrocity crimes acutely increases during these periods. Although situations of instability, or even of armed conflict, will not necessarily lead to the occurrence of atrocity crimes, they highly increase the likelihood of those crimes."[28]

Crimes Against Humanity

A crime against humanity constitutes a deliberate attack on an identifiable segment of a civilian population, typically as part of an organized campaign, resulting in widespread death or devastation among that group. Unlike war crimes, crimes against humanity can be committed during times of peace and not just during times of war. These crimes are usually either part of a government policy, or are acts that government authorities have tolerated or condoned.

Crimes against humanity has evolved over time due to the prosecution by various international courts and customary international law.

War crimes, murder, massacres, dehumanization, genocide, ethnic cleansing, deportations, unethical human experimentation, extrajudicial punishments, state terrorism or state sponsoring of terrorism, death squads, kidnappings and forced disappearances, military use of children, unjust imprisonment, enslavement, cannibalism, torture, rape, political repression, racial discrimination, religious persecution, and other human rights abuses may be considered crimes against humanity if they are part of a large-scale or systematic practice.

The crime of "crimes against humanity" is defined, by the Rome Statute, as:

[A]ny of the following acts when committed as part of a widespread or systematic attack directed against any civilian population, with knowledge of the attack:

---

[27] https://www.refworld.org/docid/548afd5f4.html

[28] https://www.refworld.org/docid/548afd5f4.html

(a) Murder;

(b) Extermination;

(c) Enslavement;

(d) Deportation or forcible transfer of population;

(e) Imprisonment or other severe deprivation of physical liberty in violation of fundamental rules of international law;

(f) Torture;

(g) Rape, sexual slavery, enforced prostitution, forced pregnancy, enforced sterilization, or any other form of sexual violence of comparable gravity;

(h) Persecution against any identifiable group or collectivity on political, racial, national, ethnic, cultural, religious, gender as defined in paragraph 3, or other grounds that are universally recognized as impermissible under international law, in connection with any act referred to in this paragraph or any crime within the jurisdiction of the Court;

(i) Enforced disappearance of persons;

(j) The crime of apartheid;

(k) Other inhumane acts of a similar character intentionally causing great suffering, or serious injury to body or to mental or physical health.

2. For the purpose of paragraph 1:

(a) 'Attack directed against any civilian population' means a course of conduct involving the multiple commission of acts referred to in paragraph 1 against any civilian population, pursuant to or in furtherance of a State or organizational policy to commit such attack;

(b) 'Extermination' includes the intentional infliction of conditions of life, *inter alia* the deprivation of access to food and medicine, calculated to bring about the destruction of part of a population;

(c) 'Enslavement' means the exercise of any or all of the powers attaching to the right of ownership over a person and includes the exercise of such power in the course of trafficking in persons, in particular women and children;

(d) 'Deportation or forcible transfer of population' means forced displacement of the persons concerned by expulsion or other coercive acts from the area in which they are lawfully present, without grounds permitted under international law;

(e) 'Torture' means the intentional infliction of severe pain or suffering, whether physical or mental, upon a person in the custody or under the control of the accused; except that torture shall not include pain or suffering arising only from, inherent in or incidental to, lawful sanctions;

(f) 'Forced pregnancy' means the unlawful confinement of a woman forcibly made pregnant, with the intent of affecting the ethnic composition of any population or carrying out other grave violations of international law. This definition shall not in any way be interpreted as affecting national laws relating to pregnancy;

(g) 'Persecution' means the intentional and severe deprivation of fundamental rights contrary to international law by reason of the identity of the group or collectivity;

(h) 'The crime of apartheid' means inhumane acts of a character similar to those referred to in paragraph 1, committed in the context of an institutionalized regime of systematic oppression and domination by one racial group over any other racial group or groups and committed with the intention of maintaining that regime;

(i) 'Enforced disappearance of persons' means the arrest, detention or abduction of persons by, or with the authorization, support or acquiescence of, a State or a political organization, followed by a refusal to acknowledge that deprivation of freedom or to give information on the fate or whereabouts of those persons, with the intention of removing them from the protection of the law for a prolonged period of time.

3. For the purpose of this Statute, it is understood that the term 'gender' refers to the two sexes, male and female, within the context of society. The term 'gender' does not indicate any meaning different from the above.[29]

Acts of Aggression

Under international law, wars of aggression are breaches of customary international law and the United Nations Charter, and are military conflicts waged without the justification of self-defence.

Wars without international legality are never sanctioned by the United Nations Security Council, although certain wars may be unlawful but not aggressive, such as the international coalition to stop the conflict in Kosovo.

Article 39 of the UN Charter stipulates that the UN Security Council is to determine the existence of any act of aggression and to "make recommendations, or decide what measures shall be taken in accordance with Articles 41 and 42, to maintain or restore international peace and security."[30]

---

[29] https://www.icc-cpi.int/nr/rdonlyres/ea9aeff7-5752-4f84-be94-0a655eb30e16/0/rome_statute_english.pdf

[30] http://legal.un.org/repertory/art39.shtml

Crimes of aggression are referred to "as one of the "most serious crimes of concern to the international community," and falls within the jurisdiction of the International Criminal Court.

Crime of aggression:

> means the planning, preparation, initiation or execution, by a person in a position effectively to exercise control over or to direct the political or military action of a State, of an act of aggression which, by its character, gravity and scale, constitutes a manifest violation of the Charter of the United Nations. ...the use of armed force by a State against the sovereignty, territorial integrity or political independence of another State, or in any other manner inconsistent with the Charter of the United Nations. Any of the following acts, regardless of a declaration of war, shall, in accordance with United Nations General Assembly resolution 3314 (XXIX) of 14 December 1974, qualify as an act of aggression.[31]

During the 2010 Kampala Review Conference by the States Parties to the Court, the crime of aggression was added as a crime under the Rome Statute of the ICC.

On 17 July 2018, the ICC added a fourth atrocity crime under its jurisdiction, following the seminal decision of States Parties to the Rome Statute on December 15th, 2017 to adopt a resolution amending the instrument. Some legal scholars have argued that now that the ICC has jurisdiction over the "crime of aggression," it may also have standing to request humanitarian intervention, also known as the "responsibility to protect" (R2P) doctrine, to end atrocities.

The agreement on the definition of "crimes of aggression" by States Parties, and the involvement of the ICC on matters related to R2P, also importantly reflect a growing international emphasis on individual criminal accountability, as opposed to more traditional notions of state accountability.

When the Rome Statue was adopted in 1998, aggression was one of the four crimes listed. However, the completion of the definition and provisions of jurisdiction were postponed for further negotiation. It wasn't until December 15th, 2017, that States Parties agreed to activate the ICC's jurisdiction over the crime of aggression. This decision came into effect on the date of the twentieth anniversary of the adoption of the Rome Statute.

For the first time since the trials in Nuremburg and Tokyo, an international court has the authority hold political leaders criminally responsible.

---

[31] https://treaties.un.org/doc/source/docs/RC-Res.6-ENG.pdf

Under paragraphs 138 and 139 of the Summit outcomes (GA Resolution 60/1) on the "responsibility to protect populations from genocide, war crimes, ethnic cleansing and crimes against humanity," states agreed that they each have a responsibility to:

Protect their own populations from genocide, war crimes, ethnic cleansing and crimes against humanity, including by preventing such crimes from happening in the first place.

To work together, as responsible members of the international community, to provide assistance to States that may lack the capacity to fulfil their responsibilities.

To use appropriate diplomatic, humanitarian and other peaceful means, in accordance with the Charter, to help protect populations from genocide, war crimes, ethnic cleansing and crimes against humanity.

Where peaceful means prove inadequate and where national authorities are manifestly failing to protect their populations from atrocity crimes, to be prepared to take collective action, in a timely and decisive manner, through the Security Council, in accordance with the Charter (including Chapter VII).[32]

It is in the context of the ICC's legal framework that when there is a humanitarian crisis there is now the legal mechanism to determine whether military intervention is needed or not.

International Criminal Law

International criminal law is a body of public international law, the intended purpose of which is to prohibit certain categories of conduct commonly viewed as serious atrocities, and to hold perpetrators of such conduct criminally accountable. Crimes such as genocide, war crimes, crimes against humanity, and the crime of aggression are covered under international criminal law. International criminal law is a subset of international law.

Generally, international law regulates rights and responsibilities of states, whereas criminal law covers crimes committed by individuals and the penal sanctions imposed on individuals. International criminal law encompasses aspects of both.

As of date, the most important institution is the International Criminal Court, as well as several *ad hoc* international hybrid courts —judicial bodies with both international and national judges. These are:

---

[32]   https://www.un.org/en/genocideprevention/documents/2017%20SG%20report%20on%20RtoP%20Advanced%20copy.pdf

- International Criminal Tribunal for the former Yugoslavia
- International Criminal Tribunal for Rwanda
- Special Court for Sierra Leone (investigating the crimes committed the Sierra Leone Civil War)
- Extraordinary Chambers in the Courts of Cambodia (investigating the crimes of the Red Khmer era)
- Special Tribunal for Lebanon (investigating the assassination of Rafik Hariri)
- Special Panels of the Dili District Court
- War Crimes Chamber of the Court of Bosnia and Herzegovina
- Kosovo Specialist Chambers and Specialist Prosecutor's Office https://genocideinbosnia.wordpress.com/tag/international-court-of-justice/ and
- International Criminal Court (ICC)

International criminal law, though not quite as widely ratified by states as international human rights obligations, is relevant to the protection of international human rights in part due to the fact that it is aimed at punishing acts which infringe on basic human rights, such as life, liberty, and security.

States have international human rights obligations to investigate and prosecute such crimes. The international criminal law conventions and tribunals may be seen as particularly necessary with regard to states that refuse to comply with these obligations.

International criminal law can be differentiated from national criminal law in that the former penalizes crimes which are exceptionally egregious, such as genocide or crimes against humanity, and those crimes that involve actions carried out by states or their agents, or are of a trans-national nature, such as piracy and terrorism.

Rome Statute of the International Criminal Court

The Rome Statute, which was adopted on July 17th, 1998 and entered into force on July 1st, 2002, is the treaty that established the International Criminal Court. As of March, 2019, 124 states are party to the statute. The statute establishes the court's functions, jurisdiction, and structure.

The International Criminal Court can only investigate and prosecute the core international crimes: genocide, crimes against humanity, war crimes, and crimes of aggression. The Court has the jurisdiction complementary to that of the domestic courts in Member States. As well, these crimes are not subject to any statute of limitations and the Security Council has authority to refer cases to the ICC even from non-member states.

As well, I would argue along with Pieter Koojimans[33] that the International Court of Justice, as the principal judicial organ of the United Nations, should provide direction and clarification on a number of questions which are of primordial importance to international law.

International Criminal Court (ICC)

The International Criminal Court is an intergovernmental body that sits in The Hague in the Netherlands to convict and prosecute those individuals who have committed high-scale political crimes such as genocide, war crimes, and crimes against humanity.

After the conflicts of the Second World War, followed by the conflicts of the Cold War, many atrocious crimes were committed that resulted in several genocides and other appalling crimes, for which many individuals were left unpunished. When the Convention on the Prevention and Punishment of the Crime of Genocide was adopted in 1948, the United Nations General Assembly recognized the need to put a stop to the monstrosities and terror by organizing a permanent legal body that would handle all these cases of hate and crime.[34]

Thus, the idea of International Criminal Court emerged. While the United Nations was negotiating on the ICC statute, many heinous crimes were being committed in the territories of Yugoslavia and Rwanda. These atrocities made a significant impact on the decision to establish the ICC in Rome. In the summer of 1998, the General Assembly convened a conference of 160 countries in Rome, which marked the establishment of the Rome Statute of the International Criminal Court.

The mandate of the court is to try any individual who is guilty of genocide, war crimes, crimes against humanity, or crimes of aggression, without any bias. A person is prosecuted regardless of their current position or current function—even if they are a minister, Head of State, or Head of Government. The ICC does not exempt anyone from criminal responsibility.

The ICC consists of four organs: the Presidency, the Chambers, the Offices of the Prosecutor, and the Registry. The Presidency consists of three judges (the President and the Vice-Presidents) who are responsible for the administration of the Court. It represents the court to the outside

---

[33] https://www.cambridge.org/core/journals/international-and-comparative-law-quarterly/article/icj-in-the-21st-century-judicial-restraint-judicial-activism-or-proactive-judicial-policy/E382E8AC6C2B97B4FE7CC744C5A997BC

[34] https://www.icc-cpi.int/iccdocs/pids/publications/uicceng.pdf

world, and is also responsible for carrying out tasks such as ensuring the enforcement of sentences imposed by the court.

The Chambers consists of eighteen judges, including the three judges of the Presidency. They are assigned to the following three divisions: the Pre-Trial Chamber, the Trial Chamber, and the Appeals Division. The responsibility of the Pre-Trial Chamber is to supervise how the Office of the Prosecutor carries out the investigation in order to ensure the integrity of the proceedings. Then they decide whether or not to issue a warrant of arrest. The Trial Chamber, composed of six judges, determines whether an accused is innocent or guilty. If the accused is found guilty, the court issues a sentence of imprisonment for a specified number of years not exceeding thirty or life imprisonment. They also order the guilty to make reparations for the damage and harm suffered by the victims. Lastly, the Appeals Chamber is composed of the President of the court and four other judges that may uphold, revise, or correct the decisions, and may even order a new trial.[35]

The Office of the Prosecutor is an independent organ of the court whose ordain is to receive and analyze information on alleged crimes within the jurisdiction of the ICC. This body is composed of three divisions: (1) the Investigation Division, which is responsible for investigating the indictment or the exculpating of the accused carefully and equally. (2) The Prosecution Division, which litigates the cases in front of the Chambers of the Court. (3) The Jurisdiction, Complementarity and Cooperation Division, which analyzes the cases in order to determine their admissibility, and helps secure the cooperation required by the Office of the Prosecutor in order to achieve its objective.

The Registry facilitates:

Rules of Procedure and Evidence.[36]

The ICC Detention Centre operates in conformity with the highest international human rights standards for the treatment of detainees, such as the United Nations Standard Minimum rules. The convicted persons do not serve their sentences at the ICC Detention Centre in The Hague as the facility is not designed to serve a long-term investigation. They are, therefore, transferred to a prison outside The Netherlands, in a state which has willingly allowed the accused to serve their sentences at their facility.

The ICC aims for a more stable, peaceful, and equitable world, and believes in post-conflict society. It is participating in a global fight against

---

[35]   https://www.icc-cpi.int/iccdocs/pids/publications/uicceng.pdf

[36]   https://www.icc-cpi.int/iccdocs/PIDS/docs/UICCGeneralENG.pdf, page 9

violence, holding the guilty responsible for their crimes and helping to prevent any such future occurrences. The court urges all countries to fight against those who have committed such heinous crimes. It is humankind's effort towards a more just world, free of violence.[37]

History of the International Criminal Court

The history of the establishment of the International Criminal Court dates back more than a century. The "Road to Rome" was extensive and often controversial. The efforts to formulate an international criminal court go as far back as 1872 with the name "Gustav Moynier," who was one of the founders of the International Committee of the Red Cross.[38] Moynier was the first person who came up with the idea of a permanent court in response to the wrongdoings and inhuman activities of the Franco-Prussian War. Following that, another serious demand for a globalized system of justice was made by the planners and drafters of the Treaty of Versailles in 1919, who envisaged an ad hoc international court of justice to try the Kaiser and German war criminals of World War I. However, it was not until after World War II that the Allies formulated the Nuremberg and Tokyo tribunals to in an attempt to try the Axis war criminals.

In 1948, the UN General Assembly (UNGA) adopted The Convention on the Prevention and Punishment of the Crime of Genocide, in which they called for criminals to be tried "by such international penal tribunals as may have jurisdiction," and asked the International Law Commission (ILC) "to study the desirability and possibility of establishing an international judicial organ for the trials of individuals who are accused of genocide."[39] However, in the initial years of the 1950s when the ILC drafted such a statute, the Cold War foiled all these initiatives, and the General Assembly abandoned the effort pending agreement on a definition for the crime of aggression and an international Code of Crimes.

In a move to combat the problems associated with drug trafficking, Trinidad and Tobago in June 1989 came up with the pre-existing plan for the establishment of an ICC, which had earlier been put down due to the Cold War. After this proposal, UNGA yet again asked the ILC to resume its pending work of drafting the statute of an international court to deal with criminal activities.

---

[37] https://www.icc-cpi.int/iccdocs/pids/publications/uicceng.pdf

[38] http://www.iccnow.org/?mod=icchistory

[39] http://www.un-documents.net/a3r260.htm

However, in the early 1990s, due to the conflicts in Bosnia-Herzegovina, Croatia, and Rwanda, the mass destruction and genocide forced the UN Security Council to set up at least two different ad hoc and temporary tribunals to try persons responsible for the atrocities. This raised the need for an international criminal court.

The final draft of the ICC statute was presented to UNGA by the ILC in 1994.[40] In it, the ILC recommended that a consultation conference be called, to which all plenipotentiaries and diplomats would be invited to discuss the treaty and pass the ICC statute. To consider the major rules and regulations as well as substantive issues in the ICC draft, the UNGA formed the Ad Hoc Committee on the Establishment of an International Criminal Court. The committee met two times in 1995 to finalize the issues concerned with the statute.

After taking into account the report developed by the Committee, the UNGA formed the Preparatory Committee on the Establishment of the International Criminal Court to formulate a consolidated and full-fledged draft copy.[41] From 1996 until 1998, at least six sessions of the UN Preparatory Committee took place at the UN headquarters in New York. During these sessions, many NGOs were invited who attended meetings under the banner of the NGO Coalition for an ICC (CICC) and provided key inputs for the statute. In January 1998, the Bureau and coordinators of the Preparatory Committee convened for an inter-sessional meeting in Zutphen, the Netherlands, to officially consolidate and reorganize the draft articles into a complete draft.

Following the draft formed by the Preparatory Committee, UNGA decided to call upon the UN Conference of Plenipotentiaries on the Establishment of an ICC at its fifty-second session to "finalise and adopt a convention on the establishment" of an International Criminal Court. From June 15th to July 17th, 1998, the "Rome Conference"[42] was held in Italy's Rome, where 160 countries took part in the negotiations of ICC, while the NGO Coalition monitored the discussions closely, distributing information across the globe regarding the developments. The NGO Coalition worked to facilitate the participation and parallel activities of as many as 200 NGOs. The discussions and debates took almost five weeks, after which at least 120 countries voted in favour of the Rome Statute of the ICC, while seven countries voted against the treaty. The nations who voted against the ICC included the United

---

[40] http://digitalcommons.law.scu.edu/cgi/viewcontent.cgi?article=1441&context=law-review

[41] http://www.iccnow.org/?mod=prepcommittee

[42] http://www.iccnow.org/?mod=rome

States, China, Israel, Iraq, and Qatar. At least twenty-one nations did not vote.

Later, the UN asked the ICC Preparatory Commission to complete the establishment and ensure a smooth functioning of the Court by negotiating and providing complementary papers. The UN assigned the Preparatory Commission to carefully go through documents, including the Elements of Crimes, the Rules of Procedure and Evidence, the Relationship Agreement between the Court and the United Nations, the Agreement on the Privileges, the Financial Regulations, as well as Immunities of the International Criminal Court.

The ICC's Rome Statute took effect on April 11th, 2002, upon ratification by sixty states, in which the statute was deposited during a special ceremony at UN headquarters. The sixtieth ratification triggered the entry into force of the statute, deposited by a number of states in conjunction. The nations who deposited their treaty instruments included Bulgaria, Bosnia and Herzegovina, Democratic Republic of Congo, Cambodia, Jordan, Ireland, Niger, Mongolia, Slovakia, and Romania. However, on May 6th, 2002, the U.S. government run by George W. Bush officially declared to the United Nations that its intention was not to ratify the Rome Statute. In addition, the U.S. also stated that it was no longer abiding by the terms and conditions of the treaty, understood by the U.S. administration's signature under the presidency of Bill Clinton in December, 2001.[43]

The ultimate treaty entered into power on July 1st, 2002. After the completion of the Preparatory Commission's mandate and the entry into force, the Assembly of States Parties (ASP) or member states held a meeting of all delegates for the first time in September 2002.

Since the International Criminal Court came into existence in 2002, it has become an essential part of international political relations, human rights systems, as well as an intergovernmental body dealing with the prosecution of criminals. By May 2013, a total of 122 countries had ratified the Rome Statute, and the ICC had taken up the prosecution of eight country situations, including four upon the request of the country in question, two upon referral from the UN Security Council, and two utilizing the prosecutor's *proprio motu* (by its own motion) authority.[44] In 2012, the ICC concluded its ever first trial.[45]

It must be kept in mind that, even though it is an important body, the ICC is still in its initial phase, and is the first organization of its kind. The ICC is dealing with complex international criminal law issues

---

43   http://mehr.org/History.htm

44   http://mehr.org/History.htm

45   http://www.lop.parl.gc.ca/Content/LOP/ResearchPublications/2002-11-e.pdf

in a manner which could not even have been contemplated fifty years ago.[46] International criminal law has developed in leaps and bounds in last fifteen years. The ICC acts like a new hybrid law and justice system, implementing a blend of international and domestic law across the globe. It is engaged in rectifying issues and problems against humanity—both new cases popping up across the world, as well as cases which have long histories or historical importance.

The International Criminal Court can be said to be a slow and sometimes expensive institution, but it is nevertheless creating a benchmark for all other international bodies in dealing with issues at the international level. The ICC may seem slow, but its work and verdicts have proven to be packed with truth and reconciliation that offers solutions to long troubling issues.

The Foundation of the Genocide Convention – Raphael Lemkin

On December 9th, 1948, the Convention on the Prevention and Punishment of the Crime of Genocide, Resolution 260, was adopted by the UN General Assembly. The Convention entered into force on January 12th, 1951. The Convention defines genocide in legal terms, and is the culmination of years of campaigning by lawyer Raphael Lemkin. As of 2019, 149 states have ratified or acceded to the treaty, most recently Benin on November 2nd, 2017.

This historic and landmark treaty was the result of the tireless campaign of one remarkable man, Raphael Lemkin. Lemkin, of Polish-Jewish descent, coined the word "genocide" near the end of the Second World War from the Greek word *genos* (meaning family, tribe, or race) and the Latin suffix -*cide* (meaning "to kill"). Lemkin spoke several languages, was the public prosecutor for the district court of Warsaw, and was also secretary of the Committee on Codification of the Laws of the Republic of Poland, which codified the penal codes of Poland. I

At an international criminal law conference organized by the Legal Council of the League of Nations, Raphael Lemkin prepared a paper on the Crime of Barbarity as a crime against international law. The idea later evolved into the concept of genocide, and was based on the what he had learned of the Armenian Genocide.

Leaving Warsaw on September 6th, 1939, he barely evaded capture by the Germans, and by the spring of 1940 he had travelled through Lithuania to reach Sweden. He eventually moved to the United States in 1941.

---

[46]   http://www.lop.parl.gc.ca/Content/LOP/ResearchPublications/2002-11-e.pdf

Although he managed to escape with his own life, he lost forty-nine relatives in the Holocaust.

After arriving in the United States, Lemkin joined the law faculty at Duke University in North Carolina in 1941. In 1943, he was appointed consultant to the U.S. Board of Economic Warfare and Foreign Economic Administration. Owing to his expertise in international law, he later became a special advisor on foreign affairs to the War Department.

His extensive writing included a book on the legal analysis of German rule in countries occupied by Nazi Germany during the course of World War II, along with establishing a definition of the term "genocide." In 1945 to 1946, Lemkin was an advisor to Supreme Court of the United States Justice and Nuremberg Trial chief counsel Robert H. Jackson.

Raphael Lemkin submitted a draft resolution for a Genocide Convention treaty to a number of countries, in an effort to persuade them to sponsor the resolution. Eventually he managed to gain the support of the United States, which placed the resolution before the General Assembly for consideration and a vote. The Convention on the Prevention and Punishment of the Crime of Genocide was formally presented and adopted on December 9th, 1948. In 1951, the Convention came into force when twenty nations ratified the treaty, thus achieving Lemkin's lifelong mission of creating a international legal instrument against genocide.

20th Century Lessons and the Genocide Convention

The twentieth century was one of the deadliest in human history, with more than 170 million people murdered by various totalitarian left- and right-wing regimes. It has also been referred to as the century of genocide. With new advancements in weaponry and electronic communications, it was easier to identify and annihilate target groups. The twenty-first century has seen the rise of religious extremism, with suicide bombings and other violence being carried out in different parts of the globe.

Since long before the word "genocide" came into the lexicon, mass murder of populations has occurred throughout recorded history. But the genocides of the twentieth century were more extensive, more systematic, and more thorough, representing the lethal, depressing culmination of large-scale violence.

The Convention has its critics, who see its definition as too narrow in scope: for example, it does not encompass in its definition what we now call ethnic cleansing, nor attacks on groups based on their sexual orientation.

In 1996, Dr. Gregory H. Stanton, President of the International Alliance to End Genocide, presented a briefing paper on the genocidal process, including what he identified as the eight stages of genocide, and how to prevent genocide during each stage. These stages include: classification (us vs. them category); symbolization (we name people); dehumanization; denial of the humanity of another group; organization (orchestration by a state and its militias and the deniability of state responsibility); polarization (extremists drive the groups apart); preparation (victims are identified and separated out because of their ethnic or religious identity); extermination (quickly becomes mass killing, and killers do not believe their victims to be fully human); and denial (the eighth stage that always follows a genocide).

Part II

The 20th Century

The twentieth century was the century of mass killings: much blood was spilled, with over 170 million people murdered. In many states, several dictatorial regimes killed on an immense scale, as thousands of civilians watched—and in many situations also collaborated in—the mass perpetration of murder. The twentieth century was violent, brutal, and bloody, and while some genocides are at least relatively well-known, such as the Holocaust and the Cambodian and Rwandan genocides, others have become mere footnotes in history.

These mass murders were carried out by both states and non-state actors—death squads, party paramilitaries, guerrillas—but primarily by states. The late scholar Rudolph Joseph Rummel, who passed away in 2014, estimated that the purposeful state killing of civilians, which he calls "democide," took the lives of 169 million people in the twentieth century. Almost one-fourth of them (38.6 million, or 22.8%) were the victims of genocide.[47] Others were victims of politicide, indiscriminate state massacres, forced labour and concentration camps, the bombing of civilians, and starvation imposed and reinforced by the state. The number of victims in the twentieth century surpasses the population of all but the five largest states in the world today.

World War I was known infamously as the Great War, and was described at the time as "the war to end all wars." It lasted from July

---

[47] https://www.ushmm.org/confront-genocide/speakers-and-events/all-speakers-and-events/genocide-and-mass-murder-in-the-twentieth-century-a-historical-perspective/genocide-and-other-state-murders-in-the-twentieth-century

28th, 1914 to November 11th, 1918, and mobilized more than 70 million military personnel, including 60 million Europeans, making it one of the largest wars in history and also one of the deadliest conflicts in history, with millions of deaths.

The war ended with Germany signing the Treaty of Versailles on June 28th, 1919. The Paris Peace Conference imposed a series of peace treaties on the Central Powers, officially ending the war, and brought harsh punitive reparations on Germany. This disastrous policy ended up giving rise years later to extremist movements in Germany, including the rise of the Nazi party. The Treaty of Versailles, Article 231, was also known as the "War Guilt" clause as the majority of Germans felt humiliated and resentful, believing they had been unjustly dealt with by the Treaty.

The Treaty also gave life to U.S. President Woodrow Wilson's "Fourteen Points," a statement of principles to be used for peace negotiations to end World War I, which brought into being the League of Nations on June 28th, 1919. Many of the tragic lessons of the flawed Treaty of Versailles, such as Article 231, were not repeated following World War II with the leadership of the United States with its Marshall Plan (officially the European Recovery Program, or ERP) to aid Western Europe, wherein the US gave over $12 billion in economic assistance to aid in rebuilding Western Europe's economies after World War II. The Marshall Plan entailed an emphasis on overhauling and modernizing regulations and processes, and fostered a major boost in productivity and interstate connectedness.[48] The Plan helped lead to the birth of the European Union, which has brought stability and peace to Europe for the last seventy-five years. The end of the Second World War also heralded the creation of the United Nations, to replace the failed League of Nations.

The horrific Second World War lasted from 1939 to 1945, and involved two major military powers—the Allies and the Axis—and more than 100 million people from more than thirty countries. It is recognized as the deadliest conflict in human history, marked by 70 to 85 million fatalities, accomplished by massacres, the genocide of the Holocaust, strategic bombing, premeditated killing by starvation and disease, and the only use of nuclear weapons in war. From these horrors came the concept of genocide, first articulated by Raphael Lemkin during the Second World War. Such crimes were tried at Nuremberg as "crimes against humanity," based on acts against civilians prohibited in the Hague Convention of 1907. The Nuremberg Trials played a key role in the newly-created United Nations' eventual adoption of the Convention for the Prevention and Punishment

---

[48]   Carew, Anthony, Labour Under the Marshall Plan: The Politics of Productivity and the Marketing of Management Science. Manchester University Press, 1987.

of the Crime of Genocide (UNGC) to apply to acts committed in peace or war against a state's own citizens or the citizens of another state.

The twentieth century has been regarded by many scholars as "the century of genocide"—from the Armenian genocide perpetrated by the Turkish government in 1915, to the much more infamous "Final Solution" of Nazi Germany, to the mass killings in Cambodia by the Khmer Rouge, and finally the genocides in the former Yugoslavia and in Rwanda.

The First and Second World Wars set a pattern to be repeated many times in different regions of the world in the second half of the twentieth century. Unfortunately, twenty-first-century genocides continue to take place on every continent, although not as of yet to the extent they did in the twentieth century. In addition, many of the acts of genocide and war crimes that occurred in the late twentieth century carried over into the twenty-first century, with several ongoing trials by the International Criminal Court and *ad hoc* United Nations tribunals.

We are still, however, at the beginning of the century, and genocides will continue to occur unless states act to prevent and stop these acts of mass murder. It is important to study the events of the twentieth century to draw lessons on how to do this.

The Holocaust

The Holocaust was Nazi Germany's attempt to wipe out the European Jewry during the course of the Second World War. Between 1933 and 1945, the Nazis murdered millions of people, many of them their own citizens, including the disabled, the mentally ill, homosexuals, political opponents, Romani (Gypsy) people, and approximately six million Jews. Some historians have estimated that as many as 14 million more from other groups were killed over a thirteen-year period ending in 1945. The fundamental motive behind all the killings was Adolf Hitler's racist philosophy and the Nazis' belief that they were the master race, superior to all.

The Nazis indiscriminately attempted to murder every single Jew—men, women, and children. Hitler persistently accused the Jews as a collective of being the cause of Germany's economic hardship. As soon as the Nazis came to power, they began persecuting Jews and other minorities. It began with the boycotting of Jewish businesses, and progressed to stripping the Jews of their rights. This led to the segregation of Jewish people, and finally to the systematic killing in gas chambers and concentration camps.

Germany tried to set up a society based on the idea of a superior Aryan race, and in 1941, Henrich Himmler, one of the leading members of the Nazi Party and one of the most powerful men in Nazi Germany, ordered the establishment of the Auschwitz-Birkenau camps to exterminate all those who did not meet the race criteria. Initially, the first prisoners were Poles following Nazi Germany's occupation of Poland in September 1939. The illegal occupation took place one week after the signing of the Molotov–Ribbentrop Neutrality Pact between Germany and the Soviet Union. Following this, the large-scale, systematic attack on the Jews began. During this dark chapter of human history, many millions of Jews were experimented on by German scientists, gassed, shot, and even burned alive.

When World War II broke out in September 1939, Nazi Germany attempted to commit total genocide against the Jews, determined to annihilate an entire group in ways never seen before in human history. In this period of brutality, the Germans and their collaborators mercilessly devastated the Jews' society in approximately four and a half years, executing as many as 6 million Jewish people. During the period of April to November 1942, the Nazis were at their most lethal stage, killing more than 2 million Jews within 250 days. Many Jewish families were forced to flee Germany and Europe for their lives. The situation was made all the more difficult due to the fact that many countries did not provide asylum to these Jewish refugees.

During the initial period of the Nazi administration, the National Socialist government built concentration camps to detain supposed and real political and ideological rivals.[49] In the years leading up to the outbreak of World War II, SS and police officials gradually imprisoned more and more people from the Roma, Jewish, and other diverse communities. To keep a regular check on the Jewish population by constant monitoring, and to facilitate their later deportation, the Nazi Germans and their associates established transit camps, ghettos, and forced-labour camps during World War II. In addition, for non-Jewish forced labour, the German authorities established several forced-labour camps in the Greater German Reich and in the German-occupied territory.

During the occupation of Poland, the Nazis established a task force called the *Einsatzgruppen*. These were Schutzstaffel (SS) paramilitary death squads who carried out mass killings, mostly by shooting, in occupied Europe. The *Einsatzgruppen* played a significant role in the extermination of huge numbers of the intelligentsia, as well as the cultural elite of Poland (which included members of the priesthood). They were integral to the implementation of the "Final Solution to the Jewish Question."[50]

---

[49] https://www.ushmm.org/wlc/en/article.php?ModuleId=10005220

[50] https://www.britannica.com/topic/anti-Semitism/Nazi-anti-Semitism-and-the-Holocaust#ref799071

In 1941, police units and Nazi SS troops executed as many as one million Jewish people, along with hundreds of thousands of others. From 1941 to 1944, Nazis authorities deported millions of Jews from areas including Germany, its occupied territories, and the states of many of its Axis allies, to the ghettos and killing centres. These killing centres were also known as "extermination camps," and in them, Jews and other people were murdered in specially-developed gassing facilities.

The killing centres were operated under the banner of the operation "The Final Solution,"[51] which included the systematic gassing of millions of Jews. The Final Solution was orchestrated primarily by the top Gestapo brass, Adolph Eichmann and Reinhardt Heidrich.[52] The Nazis established as many as twenty-four concentration camps, innumerable labour camps, and at least six specific death camps—including Auschwitz, where nearly 1,500,000 were murdered; Chelmno, where 320,000 were murdered; Treblinka, where 870,000 were murdered; Sobibor, where 250,000 were murdered; Maidenek, where 360,000 were murdered; and Belzec, where 600,000 were murdered.[53]

In terms of brutality and executions, Auschwitz[54] was the most infamous of the camps, as it was equipped with the most efficient killing methods, and was the largest of the death camps established by the Nazi regime. At Auschwitz, as many as 12,000 Jews per day were gassed to death and cremated from the end of 1941 until 1944. Hundreds of thousands of other people considered socially deviant, racially inferior, or from communities deemed threats to Nazi rule, were also executed.

Apart from killing people by putting them into gas chambers, the Nazis also carried out other forms of extreme and pervasive brutality. The Jews and other victims were put into crowded, standing-room cattle trains, where they were deprived of all basic needs such as food and water. Due to such extreme maltreatment, many died during the journey, while those who made it to the end only faced further mistreatment. These victims were stripped and later stuffed into gas chambers with no clothes on.

During the Holocaust, the most vulnerable section of society was the children. The Nazis advocated the murder of children belonging to so-called "unwanted" or "dangerous" groups, considering this to be a necessity of their racial ideology which sought to secure a racially "pure" future.

---

51   https://www.ushmm.org/outreach/en/article.php?ModuleId=10007704

52   Reinhard Heydrich was one of Hitler's most ruthless Nazis and second in importance only to Heinrich Himmler in the Nazi SS organization and the principle planner of the Final Solution. http://www.deathcamps.info/Nazis/page_3.htm

53   https://www.ushmm.org/wlc/en/article.php?ModuleId=10007398

54   https://www.ushmm.org/wlc/en/article.php?ModuleId=10005189

The Germans and their collaborators executed over a million children for these ideological reasons, including as many as a million Jewish children, tens of thousands of Romani children, Polish children, and even German children with physical or mental disabilities living in medical facilities.

As children were being targeted and killed mercilessly, women were also especially vulnerable. The Nazi regime repeatedly subjected Jewish, Romani, and Polish women to brutal harassment, as well as women with disabilities living in facilities. German physicians and medical researchers used Jewish and Romani women as subjects for sterilization experiments as well as to carry out other unethical human testing.

In Ukraine, the Nazis deployed mobile killing units to round up the Jewish men, women, and children in every town and village, and shoot them and bury them in mass graves. They murdered some 1.5 million Jews in this way. Many of these mass graves were only uncovered in 2002, when French priest Father Patrick Desbois visited the town of Rava-Ruska in western Ukraine—where his grandfather had been held in a Nazi prison camp during the war—and began to speak to local villagers. Father Desbois published a book in 2008 on the basis of these eyewitness accounts, *The Holocaust by Bullets*. It is a pathbreaking book that documents in excruciating detail how the killings occurred, as well as the location of hundreds of gravesites.[55]

One of these notorious mass killing sites is Babi Yar, a ravine in Kyiv, Ukraine, and a site where the massacres of thousands of Jews was carried out by Nazi Germany and its collaborators. The massacre at Babi Yar was the largest single massacre in the Holocaust.[56]

By mid-1945 Nazi rule was approaching its end, but the Holocaust still continued to claim lives. The numbers of Jewish and other groups had drastically declined. The German leadership started dissolving amid internal disagreements, and soon after Hitler committed suicide, Germany formally surrendered on May 8th, 1945. The German forces began evacuating the death camps in 1944, assigning camp inmates under guard to march further from the advancing enemy's front line, with the goal of preventing the Allies from liberating prisoners. These marches were called "death marches," and resulted in the loss of up to 375,000 lives. As the Allied forces moved across Europe in a chain of offensives against Germany, they began to encounter and free concentration camp detainees,

---

[55] https://www.washingtonpost.com/opinions/ukraine-is-where-the-holocaust-began-it-should-properly-memorialize-the-victims/2019/05/27/38e283e2-7e42-11e9-8bb7-0fc796cf2ec0_story.html

[56] https://www.abc.net.au/news/2017-09-12/babi-yar-melbourne-resident-one-of-survivors-nazi-massacre/8893804

as well as inmates en route by forced march from one camp to another. The forced marches continued until the first week of May 1945, and finally, the German armed forces surrendered unconditionally.

The Western Allies announced May 8th as V-E Day, whereas Soviet forces declared their "Victory Day" on May 9th, 1945. From 1948 to 1951, as many as 700,000 Jews immigrated to the newly-created Israel, including 136,000 Jewish displaced persons (DPs) from Europe, while other Jewish DPs immigrated to the United States and other countries. The criminal activities committed during the Holocaust shattered most European Jewish communities and entirely eliminated hundreds of Jewish communities in occupied Eastern Europe.

On November 1st, 2005, the United Nations General Assembly marked the sixtieth anniversary of the liberation of the Nazi concentration camps and the end of the Holocaust, by proclaiming January 27th International Holocaust Remembrance Day. United Nations Resolution 60/7 commemorates the tragedy of the Holocaust and also memorializes the liberation of Auschwitz-Birkenau, the largest Nazi concentration and death camp, on January 27th, 1945 by the Soviet Union Red Army. The International Holocaust Remembrance Alliance (IHRA), which I chaired in 2013 on behalf of the government of Canada and which consists of thirty-three member states and eight observer countries, has united governments and experts to advance and promote Holocaust education, research, and remembrance worldwide, and to uphold the commitments of the Declaration of the Stockholm International Forum on the Holocaust. The declaration consists of eight paragraphs, which emphasize the importance of education, remembrance and research about the Holocaust and states that:

> With humanity still scarred by genocide, ethnic cleansing, racism, antisemitism and xenophobia, the international community shares a solemn responsibility to fight those evils. Together we must uphold the terrible truth of the Holocaust against those who deny it. We must strengthen the moral commitment of our peoples, and the political commitment of our governments, to ensure that future generations can understand the causes of the Holocaust and reflect upon its consequences.[57]

The declaration advocates the need to uphold the "terrible truth of the Holocaust against those who deny it," and to preserve the memory of the Holocaust as a "touchstone in our understanding of the human capacity for good and evil."[58]

---

[57]   Paragraph 3, Declaration of the Stockholm International Forum on the Holocaust

[58]   https://www.holocaustremembrance.com/about-us/stockholm-declaration

The wounds of the Holocaust are still felt to this day by the few remaining survivors and their descendants. Survivors from the different Nazi torture camps found it nearly impossible to get back to their homes, as many had lost their families and been condemned by their non-Jewish neighbours and acquaintances. The late 1940s saw an exceptionally large number of refugees, prisoners of war (POWs), and many other displaced people migrating across the Europe. To bring the villains of the Holocaust in front of the world, the Allied powers held the Nuremberg Trials of 1945–1946, revealing the full extent of the Nazi atrocities. Prior to Nuremberg, the only subjects of international law were states, and what a state did to its own citizens within its own borders was its own affairs. Nuremberg fundamentally altered that belief.

The slogan "never again" has been much acknowledged by states following the Holocaust. However, as will be seen later in the book, repeating this slogan has proven to be easier than living by it, as the mass killings across the globe in the post-war era have demonstrated. It is hoped that attempting to understand the history of the perpetrators, victims, and bystanders of these crimes will help in our quest to prevent genocide in the future.

Armenian Genocide

Considered the first genocide of the twentieth century, the Armenian Genocide was a targeted mass killing of Armenian Christians, a minority group in Turkey. During a two-year period between 1915 and 1917, Ottoman Turkey murdered 1.5 million Armenian Christians due to their ethnicity and religious background. The government undertook this organized devastation against the Armenians, who numbered some two million in total, following the decline of the Ottoman Empire. Armenian men of all ages were rounded up and killed, while the women and children were forced to embark upon death marches. With the weakening of the Ottoman Empire, the movement for national identity based on ethnicity and religion became strong, as did hatred towards those who were perceived as different.

"Genocide," the word coined by Raphael Lemkin, only came into use in 1943, and it was not until the signing of the Genocide Convention on December 9th, 1948 that the word came into legal form. Notwithstanding this, the actions carried out by the Turks against the Armenians to eradicate them from their territory can only be described by most legal scholars today as genocide.

Nationalism and violent attacks from zealots who wanted a unified, pure Muslim state decimated the Armenian population that had been in the region since long before the Ottomans conquered it. Several religious leaders of the Ottoman Empire issued a proclamation of jihad against the Christians, and a systematic approach based on falsehoods about the Armenian people was used to rid Turkey of the Armenian population. The Armenian genocide happened over 100 years ago, but a similar pattern of annihilation has repeated itself time and time again across the world since then. It could be argued that the Armenian genocide served as a template for other genocides. The Holocaust was an unprecedented event in human history, but Hitler was keenly aware that the perpetrators of the Armenian genocide were never prosecuted and that the event had faded from public memory. This must have been reassuring to the Nazi commanders who carried out the mass killings that followed soon after the invasion of Poland.

The Turks did not set out to destroy all Armenians—just the ones in their territory. Hitler, on the other hand, invaded countries with the specific goal of annihilating the entire Jewish population.

The historic discrimination against the Armenians by the Ottoman Turks led many Armenians to demand more equivalent rights under the government of the Ottoman Empire in the mid-1800s. However, with the fall of the authority of the Ottoman Empire and the army losses experienced during World War I, the Ottoman government began to blame the Armenians, which resulted in the genocide.[59] The Turks governed the Ottoman Empire, which was captured across West Asia, North Africa, and Southeast Europe. Constantinople, today's Istanbul, was the centre of Ottoman government, lead by a sultan.

On April 24th, 1915, Ottoman authorities rounded up and arrested Armenian intellectuals and community leaders, the majority of whom were eventually murdered. The killing was implemented firstly through subjecting the able-bodied male population to forced labour, which was followed by the deportation of women, children, the elderly, and the infirm on death marches to the Syrian Desert. Other minorities, such as the Assyrian Christian population and the Greek Christian Orthodox population, were also victims of same genocidal policies.[60]

The Turkish leaders intended to banish the Armenians to Syria and Anatolia. The government of the Ottoman Empire seized the property of Armenians and massacred them.[61] Most of the people died due to mass

---

59 http://www.edb.utexas.edu/faculty/salinas/students/student_sites/Fall2008/2/

60 Schaller, Dominik J; Zimmerer, Jürgen (2008). «Late Ottoman genocides: the dissolution of the Ottoman Empire and Young Turkish population and extermination policies – introduction,» Journal of Genocide Research, 10 (1): 7–14 (2008).

61 http://www.armenian-genocide.org/genocide.html

starvation. Armenians were thrown out of their homes and sent towards the Mesopotamian desert with no food or water. People were undressed and forced to march under the scorching sun till they died, and those who attempted to rest were shot on the spot. Large numbers of deportees, including women and children, were killed. The survivors who reached Syria were sent to concentration camps, leading to their deaths.

The crisis of the Ottoman Empire resulted in the formation of a political group known as the Young Turks, which dominated the revolution in 1908. The squad threw people in the rivers and from the cliffs, and also burnt them alive. Children were abducted and converted to Islam.[62] In some areas, the squad raped women and treated them as slaves. Captives were obligated to assimilate to the religion and language of their captors. There was no provision by the government for feeding the frightened mass of people.

The Ottoman Empire became a powerful state during the sixteenth century. The minorities flourished with the progress of the economy, and by the nineteenth century, the empire was declining. They had lost their conquered land in Europe and Africa by 1914. The loss of power generated political and economic pressures which intensified the tensions. The aspirations of Armenians to participate in government raised the ire of the Muslim Turks who did not want to share power with minorities.

A great amount of evidence exists which proves the brutality of the killings. In 2007, the International Association of Genocide Scholars reached a consensus that the "Ottoman campaign against Christian minorities of the Empire between 1914 and 1923 constituted a genocide against Armenians, Assyrians, and Pontian and Anatolian Greeks."[63]

Leading texts in the international law of genocide, such as the one by my doctorate thesis supervisor at the Faculty of Law at the National University of Galway in Ireland—William Schabas' *Genocide in International Law*—cite the Armenian Genocide as a precursor to the Holocaust, and as a precedent for the law on crimes against humanity.

Currently in Turkey it is illegal to openly discuss the genocide of Armenia people.[64] The country denies that the word "genocide" is an accurate term for the crimes committed against the Armenians, but in recent years, they have faced increasing calls to recognize them as such. As of 2019, governments and parliaments of thirty-one countries, including

---

[62] http://warandgenocideinchlit.weebly.com/armenia.html

[63] https://www.genocidescholars.org/images/PRelease16Dec07IAGS_Officially_Recognizes_Assyrian_Greek_Genocides.pdf

[64] http://www.edb.utexas.edu/faculty/salinas/students/student_sites/Fall2008/2/

Brazil, Canada, France, Germany, Italy, and Russia have recognized the events as a genocide.

Holodomor – Ukraine

The Holodomor, also known as the Ukrainian genocide of 1932–1933, derives from the Ukrainian words "to kill by starvation or death by starvation."[65] An estimated 7 to 10 million people were starved to death by several Soviet-style agrarian reforms. Anyone who has ever read Yale historian Timothy Snyder's book *Bloodlands*, which examines the regions of modern-day Poland, Ukraine, Belarus, Russia, and the Baltic states—the area controlled by the regimes of Stalin and Hitler—can speak of the immense suffering of the people who lived under these totalitarian regimes. There are horrific accounts of people in the Kharkiv region of Ukraine who were so starving that they resorted to cannibalism. Snyder goes into great detail covering the early 1930s famine in the Ukraine under the Soviet Union. In addition to starvation, many people were executed by firing squad or forced into concentration camps.

The term "Holodomor" refers to the mercilessly-created, large-scale artificial hunger organized by Joseph Stalin's rule of Soviet Ukraine and the mainly culturally Ukrainian regions in the Northern Caucasus in 1932–1933. The President of Ukraine, Petro Poroshenko, has called for the Holodomor, the Ukrainian famine of the 1930s, to be recognized as "genocide."

The Ukrainian genocide began in 1929, with deadly deportations of Ukraine's successful farmers such as kurkuls, and the execution of Ukraine's religious scholars and ethnic leaders. The horrors culminated in the enforced famine that killed millions of people. The genocide continued for many more years, with the further ruin of Ukraine's political management and the relocation to Ukraine's deserted regions of many ethnic groups. Those who addressed the famine in public risked prosecution by the Soviet government, who consistently and blatantly denied the famine.

After the Russian Revolution, Ukraine turned into a bloody battlefield of fighting between the Bolsheviks, who became the Communist Party of the Soviet Union, Czarist whites, and Ukrainian nationalists. Roused by a national revolution in 1917–1921, Ukraine, with its rich cultural heritage, struggled to form a sovereign state in the interests of their own freedom. Ukrainian communists did not want to toe the Moscow line, which posed a serious threat to the integrity of the Soviet empire.

---

[65] Andrea Graziosi, «Les Famines Soviétiques de 1931–1933 et le Holodomor Ukrainien.» Cahiers du monde russe et soviétique, 46/3, p. 457

The peasants of Soviet Ukraine resisted Stalin's collectivization drive, and his regime reacted by strategically suppressing them in a campaign of terror intended to prevent the formation of the Ukrainian nation. This resulted in the forced exportation of grain and other foodstuffs in exchange for the imported equipment required for the USSR's enactment of Stalin's policy of rapid industrialization.

The primary goal of Stalin and his associates was to break the back-bone of the Ukrainian country by destroying the kulaks who resisted the regime, including those who were already working in collective farms. The Holodomor was directed at the peasantry as a whole, whom the Bolsheviks considered as rank and file of Ukrainian nationalist drive. This famine-genocide was combined with an enormous campaign to defeat Ukrainian values, led by Pavel Postyshev, who was sent by Moscow. During the protest against the atrocities, the prominent writer Mykola Khvylovy committed suicide.

In 1932, Ukraine had an average grain harvest of 146.6 million centres, and there was no climate risk of famine. Yet, because of challenging forced grain demand quotas that the Bolshevik state levied upon the Soviet Ukrainian rustic inhabitants, the peasants were already experiencing hunger in the spring of 1932.[66] The collections of grain were violently carried out by 112,000 special Bolshevik agents sent to extract the grain by using terror against both collectivized and liberated farmers. To reduce the opposition by peasants, a law was introduced stipulating the death penalty for anyone who violated the sanctity of socialist property. Units of young protesters from other Soviet regions were carried in to sweep through the villages and remove secreted grain, and food from farmer's houses. Starvation became extensive.

The religious harmony of the nation was also affected as priests were executed and sent to labour camps. Monasteries were shut down and church icons were destroyed. Another terrible result of the Holodomor was a tremendously high children's mortality rate. Many children died because of the lack of shelter and food. The area of Soviet Ukraine and the chiefly Kuban region of Soviet Russia were patrolled by armed units, so that individuals could not go in search of food in the adjoining Soviet regions where it was more available. The isolation of villages and the lack of food left people to consume the meat of dogs, cats, and other dead animals. There were instances of cannibalism[67] among people maddened by starvation.

The Holodomor encompassed almost all of interwar Soviet Ukraine, growing to its greatest proportions in the area extending from Kyiv to

---

[66]   https://www.britannica.com/place/Ukraine/The-famine-of-1932-33

[67]   http://un.mfa.gov.ua/mediafiles/files/holodomor-booklet.pdf

Kharkiv. It also occurred in the territories bordering Ukraine that were inhabited mostly by Ukrainians, such the Kuban and the Don region. Peasants that were caught were returned to their starving villages.

The Holodomor resulted in an extremely high number of casualties. Millions of Ukrainians died of famine, though some did manage to escape. The mass effects of famine, disease, enhanced mortality, and a falling birthrate lasted for several years. The Soviet census results showed a catastrophic decline in population as a consequence of the Holodomor. By the end of 1932, the rural population had no means of sustenance, but the authorities did not provide any deliveries to feed the villagers. In 1981, the demographer Sergei Maksudov determined that the number of dead in Soviet Ukraine was 4.5 million.

During the late 1940s and onwards in China, under Mao Ze Dong, an estimated 40 million deaths were also caused due to failed economic experiments. The Soviet dictator Joseph Stalin and Mao Ze Dong—the Stalin of China—both had a disregard for human life which led to the killing of millions of their people. Sadly, as noted by Stalin, so many just became statistics in their eyes.

The Soviet regime continued to be silent about the Holodomor and provided no assistance to the victims. However, information about the atrocities evoked a public response in Polish-ruled Western Ukraine, where many large-scale demonstrations and protests occurred in 1933. Mykola Lemyk, a member of the Organisation of Ukrainian Nationalists, assassinated Aleksei Mailov, the Soviet consul in Lviv, which highlighted the issue to public.[68] There were relief committees organized in Europe, and a memorandum was sent to the League of Nations. The issue was also taken up by the British parliament. A relief action was offered by Vienna. But the Soviet government was not in favour of getting any aid from outside the nation. Although the international press did publish some information on the famine, it did not elicit a significant public response from non-Ukrainians. Since the war, the horrors of the Holodomor have been kept alive through memorial facilities and the many vigils sponsored by the Ukrainian community throughout the world, as well as in publications by survivors.

In 2004, the parliament of Ukraine, the Verkhovna Rada, passed a resolution to classify the horrors of the Holodomor as genocide, and to have this recognized internationally. Categorizing the case of the Holodomor as a crime against humanity will hopefully lead to increased awareness by the international community about engineered famines used as tools for mass annihilation.

---

[68]   http://www.encyclopediaofukraine.com/display.asp?linkpath=pages%5CB%-5CA%5CBanderaStepan.htm

Cambodia

Between 1975 and 1979 in Cambodia, the communist group Khmer Rouge, under the leadership of the dictator Pol Pot, seized power. Their goal was to return Cambodia to an agrarian society. The Khmer Rouge renamed the country Democratic Kampuchea, and began targeting the educated (e.g., doctors and lawyers) and the religious (e.g., Christians, Buddhists, and Muslims) in the hopes of ridding the nation of outside influences. Millions died of starvation, in concentration camps, or by firing squad, resulting in a death toll of about two million. Eventually, Vietnam's communist government invaded Cambodia and removed the Khmer Rouge from power.

The Khmer Rouge Republic wanted to rid the country of those it deemed impure, including the educated, professional class and ethnic minorities. They wanted to return Cambodia to an agrarian society free of foreign intervention. They distinguished between "'new people'—those who resided in the towns and cities and comprising foreign sympathizers, the intellectuals, teachers, the middle class, and members of the Khmer Republic—and 'base people,' those that had resided in the country-side during the 1970–1975 conflict."[69]

Genocide is undoubtedly the gravest crime which lies under international criminal law. The current definition of genocide encompasses a range of atrocities, such as mass killing and rape. Genocide can involve such methods as making a group's language or religion a criminal offence. In Cambodia, the most grievous abuses are recognized under the term genocide. The Communist Party of Kampuchea, or the Khmer Rouge, was the result of the freedom struggle against the French, which was influenced by the Vietnamese. The Khmer Rouge committed an organized operation of mass killings of Cambodians.

During Vietnam's civil war, the US-backed General Lon Nol led a military coup in 1970 against Prince Norodom Sihanouk and became the self-proclaimed president of the Khmer Republic until 1975. Cambodia became a casualty of the Vietnam War, leading to an unstable government—a situation the Marxist-Leninist ideology of Pol Pot and the Khmer nationalists took advantage of. Aided by the Viet Cong and North Vietnamese troops, Pol Pot's forces advanced, and by 1975 they controlled all of Cambodia.

Under their leaders, Pol Pot, the urban population was deported to rural areas. It is estimated that as many as two million people were killed,

---

[69] James L. Pigmon, James L., "Evil: Genocide in the 21st Century" Rollins College, Spring 2011.

most of them dying due to disease and hunger. Those who refused to move were killed. There was also a ban on religion, leading to the mass killing of many Buddhist monks.

A slogan of the Khmer was "to spare you is no profit; to destroy you is no loss."[70] For their "agricultural utopia,"[71] the strategic isolation of Cambodia from the rest of the world was necessary. Pol Pot expelled foreigners and shut down embassies and the media. Businesses, educational institutions, and health centres were all closed. Communications such as telephones, mail, and money transfer were all banned.

The new rule aimed to systematically kill former army men, teachers, police officers, and religious leaders. Many were shot to death along with their families. Those suspected of opposing the regime were killed on the spot; some were tortured to death. The Muslim, Chinese, and Vietnamese minorities were also slaughtered. Speakers of foreign languages were seen as enemies of the revolution, and were taken to concentration camps for "re-education."[72] Killing pits were used for torturing them. It was the belief of the Khmer Rouge that to eradicate the bourgeois class was not enough, so an organized crushing of their existence was needed. Hundreds of thousands were exterminated. The victims were buried in mass graves, and between 1.6 and 2 million people were slain. The Pol Pot regime also committed military assaults on its neighbouring countries.

The Khmer Rouge guerrillas were in conflict with Cambodia's political reform, and their administration began to dissolve. The struggle with Vietnam led to Vietnam's invasion of Cambodia, which saw the Khmer Rouge defeated and a socialist administration established. Many members of the Khmer Rouge fled to Thailand, continuing guerrilla attacks against the Vietnamese. The Khmer Rouge continued fighting in Vietnam for another decade, bolstered by support from China and the Soviet Union. This continued violence caused the trauma, displacement, and death of uncounted Cambodians.

On December 25th, 1978, the Vietnamese Army conquered Cambodia and dethroned the Khmer Rouge regime. On January 7th, 1979, Phnom Penh declined, and a puppet government was formed with the provision of the opponents.

Due to international pressure, the Vietnamese army withdrew from Cambodia in 1989. This had been enforced by economic sanctions on Cambodia by the U.S. and by a cut off in aid from Vietnam's own supporter,

---

[70] http://www.ppu.org.uk/genocide/g_cambodia1.html

[71] https://combatgenocide.org/?page_id=68

[72] Khmer Rouge torturer describes killing babies by 'smashing them into trees' Mail Online, June 9, 2009

the Soviet Union. A provisional coalition government was formed, and in the year 1991, a peace settlement was signed between the opposing parties. At the time of the 1993 election, former ruler Prince Sihanouk was elected.

From 1995 onwards, mass graves began to be uncovered which revealed the horrifying extent of the genocide. The disinterred skulls were preserved to form memorials of the deceased in the killing fields where they died. It was not until thirty years after the genocide that the international community began to recognize the Cambodian genocide and the mass atrocities perpetrated under the Khmer Rouge.

The Extraordinary Chambers in the Courts of Cambodia was established in 1997 to try the most senior members of the Khmer Rouge responsible for violations of international law and serious crimes perpetrated during the Cambodian genocide. It is considered a hybrid court, as it was created by the government in conjunction with the United Nations but remains independent of them, with trials held in Cambodia using Cambodian and international staff.

Pol Pot was found guilty and sentenced to death. In 1993, under United Nations supervision, democratic laws were implemented in Cambodia. However, the U.S., China, and the UN Security Council had contrasting views on how to bring the Khmer Rouge to justice. The trials of the Khmer Rouge conflict offenders continue.

In 2018, two of the most senior Khmer Rouge leaders still alive today were found guilty of genocide, almost forty years since Pol Pot's brutal communist regime fell.[73] As reported by *The Guardian*, "Nuon Chea, who was second-in-command to Pol Pot, and Khieu Samphan, who served as head of state, were both sentenced to life imprisonment for genocide and crimes against humanity carried out between 1977 and 1979, in a landmark moment for the Khmer Rouge tribunals. The pair are already serving life sentences for crimes against humanity."[74]

Burundi Genocide

The Republic of Burundi, as it is known unofficially, is a country in East Africa, and a part of the African Great Lakes region. The population of Burundi consists of two main ethnic groups: the Tutsis and the Hutus. The demographics and culture of Burundi are very similar to those of its neighbour, an equally war-torn nation called Rwanda.[75] The main occupations in

---

[73] https://www.bbc.com/news/world-asia-46217896

[74] https://www.theguardian.com/world/2018/nov/16/khmer-rouge-leaders-genocide-charges-verdict-cambodia

[75] Boggs, C. (2017). *The Burundian Genocide of 1972 | Study.com*. [online] Study.com. Available at: http://study.com/academy/lesson/the-burundian-genocide-of-1972.html

Burundi are agriculture and cattle rearing, with the former being the main domain for the Hutus and the latter for the Tutsis. Violence has dominated the greater part of this nation's politics, and ethnic war and countless acts of violence have characterized the volatile relationship between the Tutsis and the Hutus. In 1972, an estimated 300,000 Hutus were massacred in six weeks. In 1993, an estimated 25,000 Tutsis were killed.[76]

After World War I, the Belgians took control of Burundi from the defeated German government and began to identify the Tutsis as superior. Systematically, all Hutu chiefs were removed from power, leaving the fate of the nation with the "elite" Tutsi. Thereafter, the Tutsis controlled the political landscape, a state of affairs which continued after independence in 1962. When the Tutsis did not relinquish their power after independence, a Hutu revolution broke out in the country.

During the time the genocide occurred, the demographics of Burundi were as such: 86% Hutu, 13% Tutsi, and 1% Twa.[77] Despite representing a minority group, Tutsis occupied all the major government positions and had dominated the sphere of power and wealth in Burundi since independence. The unrest between the two clans was palpable, and the first post-independence election started off a chain reaction which led to the 1972 genocide.

In the 1965 elections, the Hutus landed a sweeping victory, winning twenty-three out of thirty-three seats. Despite this massive victory, the king of Burundi appointed[78] a Tutsi as Prime Minister. This move angered the Hutus and led them to stage a coup. The coup failed, stopped by a then-emerging officer, Michel Micombero. Soon after Micombero overthrew the king, causing him to flee the country, Micombero became the first President of Burundi in 1966. He eventually became the *de facto* dictator, leading an aggressive campaign against the Hutus. He ran Burundi with an iron fist, removing all other parties but his own. Any sign of dissent was instantly squashed, as was the case in any other dictatorship government. Micombero was the force behind the 1972 genocide.[79]

On April 27th, 1972, the Hutus staged a rebellion, killing over a thousand people in an attempt to overthrow Micombero. This prompted him to declare martial law and launch a massive attack on Hutus across

---

[76] International Commission of Inquiry for Burundi" (PDF). United Nations. 22 August 1996. pp. 19, 75. S/1996/682. Retrieved 15 September 2017: Paragraphs 85 and 496.

[77] Lemarchand, R. (2017). *Combat Genocide Association, Burundi 1972*(online) Combatgenocide.org

[78] Lemarchand, R. (2009) *The Burundi Genocide-* From Century of Genocide, 3rd Edition, 2009 Taylor and Francis

[79] Burundi (1993–2006) Archived 15 November 2017 at the Wayback Machine. University of Massachusetts Amherst

the nation. First, the educated, elite, and powerful Hutus were killed. Then the Tutsi army proceeded to march into heavily Hutu-populated areas, killing and brutalizing hundreds of thousands of Hutu civilians. Hundreds of thousands of Hutus also fled into neighbouring countries such as Tanzania, Rwanda, and Zaire. The Tutsis claimed that 15,000 Hutus died in the violence, and because of Micombero's tight controls, the details of the brutal violence were kept hushed. However, records have now emerged showing that Hutu deaths more accurately numbered between 80,000 and 210,000.[80]

Reliable eyewitness accounts to the violence are few and far between, as Micombero tried his level best to erase all evidence of the genocide.[81] But some researchers, like Liisa Malkki, were able to document the lives of the displaced Burundi Hutus in Tanzania and collect their eyewitness accounts of the 1972 genocide. Malkki's study "Purity and Exile: Transformations in Historical-National Consciousness Among Hutu Refugees in Tanzania" in 1995 was one such study. This eyewitness account in the study sheds light on the elimination of the entire tier of educated Hutu elites and officials:

> They wanted to kill my clan because my clan was educated. The clans which were educated, cultivated, they were killed. In my clan, there were school teachers, medical assistants, agronomists … some evangelists, not yet priests, and two who were in the army. … All have been exterminated. Among those who were educated, it is I alone who remains. … There are many persons who leave Burundi today because one kills everyday. The pupils, the students. … It is because these are intellectuals—because if you do not study you do not have much maarifa [knowledge, information]. Many Hutu university people were killed. The government workers, they were arrested when they were in their offices, working. The others also in their places, for example, an agronomist, when he was walking in the fields where he works, he was arrested. Or a veterinary technician: one finds him in his place, where he works. There were medical technicians, professors. … Or the artisans in the garage, or those who worked in printing houses or in the ateliers where furniture is made. They were killed there, on the spot. … The male missionaries and the female missionaries, who were doing their work in the Churches, in the schools as professors, or in the hospitals as doctors, they were not killed on the spot. They were killed in the prison. I think that the very first who were poured into the lake were the masculine missionaries and the feminine missionaries.

80   Boggs, C. (2017). The Burundian Genocide of 1972 | Study.com. [online] Study.com. Available at: http://study.com/academy/lesson/the-burundian-genocide-of-1972.html

81   Ndimurwimo, A, L. (2014). *Human rights violations in Burundi: A case study in post-conflict reconciliation and transitional justice.* Doctors of Law. North-West University

... If you are a student, that's a reason for killing you; if you're rich, that's a reason; if you are a man who dares to say a valid word to the population, that's a reason for killing you. In short, it is a racial hate.[82]

Another heartfelt account was gathered from a rural settlement for Burundian refugees in Tanzania, called "Refugees and Pioneers: History and Field Study of a Burundian Settlement in Tanzania," by a researcher called Hanne Christensen. The eyewitness reminisces about her Burundi and the terrible violence inflicted there:

> Homeland was a beautiful place, full of gentle hills and peacefully grazing cattle. My dreams are still bound to the homeland. We left Homeland during the warfare. Our relatives were killed. My husband lost eleven brothers, I five. They were killed by guns, spears and arrows. My husband was put in jail for three months. All that time he was tied, and fellow detainees were killed in front of his eyes. He kept alive, fortunately. After the killing stopped, he was released—and we fled. I had already taken flight from our homestead. We met on the way, in a hidden place just by coincidence. I had been living in the bush for one month, and we proceeded together to the host-country. Entering a foreign country as a refugee is to suffer extreme hardship. You feel lost after having left your country. Your belongings are completely separated from you. You live in fear of starvation. You are shocked because you have witnessed the execution of others, sometimes even of your relatives and friends. You are afraid that you have become invisible to God's merciful eye. You feel totally desolate. Arriving in the area of settlement, we got scared to death. It was in the middle of nowhere. Never in our lives had we seen such thick forest, inhabited only by wild animals, snakes and big, biting flies. We slept close to one another in a big bundle in the open air under the trees, surrounded by fires. During the daylight hours we cleared the forest. We were absolutely positive that we would starve, but prayed and prayed to get courage and food.[83]

In 1976, Colonel Jean-Baptiste Bagaza overthrew Micombero.[84] However, the violence against Hutus continued, with thousands being killed. After

---

82   Malkki, L.(1995). Purity and Exile: Transformations in Historical-National Consciousness Among Hutu Refugees in Tanzania- Harvard

83   Christensen, H.(1985) Refugees and Pioneers: History and Field Study of a Burundian Settlement in Tanzania- United Nations Research Institute for Social Development (UNRISD)
     Available at: http://repository.forcedmigration.org/show_metadata.jsp?pid=fmo:3182

84   BBC News, (2017)- Timeline-BBC News [online]
     Available at: http://www.bbc.com/news/world-africa-13087604

Western intervention, there was an attempt at democracy, with Burundi getting its democratically-elected Hutu President Melchior Ndadaye. But this, too, was cut short after three months, when on October 21st, 1993 Tutsis assassinated President Ndadaye. This set off a violent domino effect,[85] and over 100,000 people were killed as Tutsis and Hutus fought against each other.[86] A United Nations report concluded in 1993 that the mass killing of 25,000 Tutsis was a genocide.

After years of a skewered power ratio where Tutsis dominated the government, army, and every other sector in the country,[87] the national and state government and parliament are now composed of both Hutus and Tutsis, split 60% to 40%. The armed forces are also now 50% Hutu and 50% Tutsi. This move comes after former South African President Nelson Mandela brokered the Arusha Peace and Reconciliation Accords and the global ceasefire agreement.[88] Amnesty International, a human rights organization, has lauded Burundi for embracing democracy. A mausoleum has been built in Bujumbura to commemorate the life of Melchior Ndadaye, the first democratically elected Hutu president. Despite this progress, however, watchdog organizations warn that Burundi is a ticking time bomb, as skirmishes there continue between the two clans.

While the genocide of 1972 is at a risk of being forgotten, the violence has left millions scarred. Similarly, 1993 has left a gaping hole in the lives of Burundians, all of whom have been tainted by the blood that flooded the streets of their beloved country. The entire world is responsible for the blatant disregard of human rights that became the norm in war-torn Burundi. It is time for the United Nations, the European Union, and the larger international community to take a stand and send protection forces to Burundi. Political dialogue and peace talks are also another must for Burundi and all its citizens. Let 1972 and 1993 serve as reminders of humanity at its worst—events never to be repeated again. Let the Tutsis and Hutus work together, be united, and most importantly live peacefully side-by-side in their homeland, Burundi.

---

[85] Mckinley Jr, J. (1997). "Rewriting Burundi's Brutal Past," *The New York Times*. Available at: http://www.nytimes.com/1997/08/14/world/rewriting-burundi-s-brutal-past.html

[86] Lemarchand, R. (2017). *Combat Genocide Association, Burundi 1972* (online) Combat-genocide.org http://combatgenocide.org/?page_id=893

[87] Hajayandi, P. (2017). Stop calling the violence in Burundi 'genocide'. *The Guardian* Available at: https://www.theguardian.com/world/2015/nov/18/burundi-violence-genocide-patrick-hajayandi

[88] Mwachiro, K. (2017). *What Burundi could teach Rwanda about reconciliation - BBC News*. [online] BBC News. Available at: http://www.bbc.com/news/world-africa-19182107

Rwandan Genocide

In the 1980s and 1990s, a group of Rwandan refugees in Uganda began a guerrilla-style war to overthrow the government of Rwanda. In early 1993, several extremist Hutu groups formed and began a campaign of large-scale violence against the Tutsis, exploiting the fears of the population to advance an anti-Tutsi agenda which became known as Hutu Power.[89] In addition, the army began arming civilians with weapons such as machetes as a form of civil defence against the rebels. These weapons were later used to carry out murders of Tutsis. Several extremists in the Rwandan government and army began actively plotting against the President in 1992, for fear of the possibility of Tutsis being included in government.

In March 1993, Hutu Power began compiling lists of "traitors," and used Radio Télévision Libre des Mille Collines (RTLMC) to broadcast racist propaganda and obscene jokes and music promoting hatred of the Tutsis. The radio station was popular throughout the country.

In October 1993, President of Burundi Melchior Ndadaye, who had been elected in June as the country's first ever Hutu president, was assassinated by extremist Tutsi army officers.[90] The assassination caused shockwaves both in Burundi and in Rwanda, and reinforced the notion among the Hutu population that the Tutsi were the enemy. This argument was used to actively persuade the Hutu population to carry out killings. The situation became critical after Rwandan-ethnic Hutu President Juvénal Habyarimina's plane crashed and the Tutsis were blamed for the crash.

The United Nations Assistance Mission for Rwanda (UNAMIR) had forces in Rwanda as part of the peace treaty that was signed with the government and rebel forces. The Mission was established by UN Security Council Resolution 872 on October 5th, 1993.[91] It was planned to assist in the implementation of the Arusha Accords, which were signed on August 4th, 1993 to end the Rwandan Civil War between the Hutu-dominated Rwandese government and the Tutsi-dominated rebel Rwandan Patriotic Front (RPF).

General Roméo Dallaire, Commander of UNAMIR, sent his "Genocide Fax" to UN Headquarters on January 11th, 1994, warning the Security Council about the Tutsis being killed. UNAMIR failed to prevent

---

[89] Yanagizawa-Drott, David (1 November 2014). "Propaganda and Conflict: Evidence from the Rwandan Genocide," The Quarterly Journal of Economics. 129 (4): 1947–1994

[90] https://www.britannica.com/biography/Melchior-Ndadaye

[91] UN Security Council (5 October 1993). "RESOLUTION 872 (1993) Adopted by the Security Council at its 3288th meeting," Security Council. p. 1.

the Rwandan genocide due to the limitations of its rules of engagement and a lack of political will from the international community. The U.S. in particular ignored the warning signs that General Dallaire reported to the United Nations, due to a lack of domestic support for engaging in any further conflict in Africa, especially after the failure of the U.S. mission in Somalia.

During the 100-day period between April 7th and July 15th, 1994, during the Rwandan Civil War, a million Tutsis and Tutsi-sympathizers were slaughtered by the Hutus. The racial divides and rivalries that led to the civil war can be traced back to the Belgian colonist rule, which placed the minority Tutsi ethnic group in the echelons of authority. The Belgians issued identification cards based on ethnicity, in essence developing a caste system in Rwanda. These identification cards were used by the Hutu to identify and kill Tutsis.

The Rwandan genocide was a war against the Tutsi population by the Hutu majority, and even with the slaughter of nearly one million Tutsi Rwandans during a 100-day period, there was no international mobilization to end the genocide.

The genocide had profound and lasting effects on Rwanda and its neighbouring countries, and led to an international movement to establish the International Criminal Court (ICC). The UN Security Council adopted Resolution 955 in November 1994 to establish an international court in order to try the people responsible for the Rwandan genocide and other serious violations of international law in Rwanda. The International Criminal Tribunal for Rwanda was later expanded through several Security Council resolutions. It completed all trial activities in 2012 and officially closed in 2015.

The tribunal had jurisdiction over genocide, crimes against humanity, and violations of Common Article 3 and Additional Protocol II of the Geneva Conventions.[92] The ICTR indicted a total of ninety-six individuals.

An important lesson of the Rwandan genocide is that the dangers of indifference and inaction—especially in the face of state-sanctioned incitement to hatred—can lead to genocide. Combatting the dangers

---

[92] Additional Protocol I & II of the Geneva Conventions were adopted by States to make international humanitarian law more complete and more universal, and to adapt it better to modern conflicts. The Geneva Conventions of 1949 afforded major improvements in the legal protection of victims of conflict. However, they apply essentially to international conflicts – wars between states. Only Article 3, common to all four Conventions, refers to internal conflicts; its adoption was itself a great step forward but the rules contained in the Article are mainly of a general nature. In addition, most of the countries that became independent after 1945 "inherited" the Geneva Conventions from the former colonial powers – the adoption of the Protocols was also an occasion for them to contribute to developing the law.

of a culture of impunity and denial is a global and not just a domestic responsibility.

Yugoslavia

The end of Cold War left an unstable situation in Yugoslavia, as long-simmering ethnic tensions finally reached their boiling point. The country of Yugoslavia became out of control as Serb nationalism grew stronger.

The first half of the 1990s proved to be the downfall of Yugoslavia, as the political upheaval and conflict along ethnic lines gained pace, disrupting the lives of thousands. The Socialist Federal Republic of Yugoslavia, formed after World War II, comprised six republics: Bosnia, Serbia, Croatia, Slovenia, Montenegro, and Macedonia, all of which consisted of different ethnic groups. After the provinces of Slovenia and Croatia declared independence, a civil war followed, claiming several thousand lives. Of all the republics, Bosnia was the most ethnically heterogeneous, with 18% Catholic Croatians, 35% Orthodox Serbs, and 43% Muslims. All of these groups suffered brutally in the conflict.[93]

Yugoslavia was led by Joseph Broz Tito, who was able to hold the country together through various dictatorial means, and was able to control ethnic segregation, maintaining a unified Yugoslav identity.[94] After his death in 1980, many disputes and ethnic tensions were reignited, and the republics began to break behind the new political ethnic lines. The ambitious motives of succeeding politicians such as Serbian Slobodan Milošević[95] left the region's future divided. Milošević was president of Serbia from 1989 to 1997 and president of Yugoslavia from 1997 to 2000. He pursued Serbian nationalist policies that contributed to the breakup of the socialist Yugoslav federation, and involved Serbia in a series of conflicts with the successor Balkan states.

Milošević used the patriotic feelings of the Serbs to his advantage, making changes to the constitution according to the Serb ideology. Politicians ignited the flame of nationalist fervour and turned the Serbs, Croats, and Bosnians against each other and each other's ethnic values.

With his motive of creating a "Greater Serbia," Milošević began propagating a feeling of hatred among the diverse groups of Yugoslavia, which spurred the six constituent republics to pursue independence. Soon, Yugoslavia began to separate, with Slovenia and Croatia being the

---

[93] http://worldwithoutgenocide.org/genocides-and-conflicts/bosnian-genocide

[94] http://endgenocide.org/learn/past-genocides/the-bosnian-war-and-srebrenica-genocide/

[95] http://worldwithoutgenocide.org/genocides-and-conflicts/bosnian-genocide

first republics to declare independence. Problems followed as the tensions between the Croats, Serbs, and Muslims began to rise. Amid these tensions, the Bosnian Serb leader Radovan Karadzic and his Serb Democratic Party withdrew from their governance and set up their own Serbian National Assembly in 1992.[96]

Milošević's forces invaded Croatia, accompanied by Serbs, in the name of protecting the "Serbian minority." They attacked the city of Vukovar, executing more than eighty Croatian men and burying them in mass graves. A ceasefire was brokered between the Serbs and Croats fighting in Croatia by the end of 1991.[97]

Following this, the Bosnian Serbs decided to settle on a dominant Serbia, two days after the United States and the European Community declared Bosnia's independence in May 1992. With the support of Milošević and the army, they attacked Bosnia's capital, Sarajevo. They attempted to ethnically cleanse the entire population of Bosnians. Rapes and sexual violence, concentration camps, mass executions, and forced displacements[98] became prominent, constituting a genocide.

The United Nations was unable to request a military intervention due to Russia and China's opposition at the Security Council, with the exception of humanitarian aid. The attempts by the European Union at mediation were also unsuccessful.[99] Eventually, the UN tried to make safe places, but remained unsuccessful at peacemaking. The Bosnian government tried to defend the territory with the help of the Croatian army, but by then Bosnian Serbs were in control of three-quarters of the country. Several peace attempts between the Croatian-Bosnian federation and the Bosnian Serbs proved unsuccessful when the Serbs refused to relinquish any territory.

Free from the fear of any government body's involvement in the chaos, the Bosnian Serbs committed murder against the minorities in the region. However, despite reports of secret camps, mass killings, and the destruction of Muslim mosques and historic architecture in Bosnia, there was widespread indifference to the events and the genocide.

In July 1995, Bosnian Serbs attacked Srebrenica and began bombarding it. The UN peacemakers asked for support from the North Atlantic Treaty Organization (NATO) but were denied; therefore, Srebrenica fell

---

[96]   http://www.history.com/topics/bosnian-genocide

[97]   http://www.history.com/topics/bosnian-genocide

[98]   http://endgenocide.org/learn/past-genocides/the-bosnian-war-and-srebrenica-genocide/

[99]   http://endgenocide.org/learn/past-genocides/the-bosnian-war-and-srebrenica-genocide/

to the Serbs in just one day. In the course of four days, around 8,000 men and teenage boys were brutally murdered. After the mass killings at the end of July 1995, cover-up procedures took place, including re-burials in secondary mass graves.[100]

The international community did very little to prevent the horrendous mass murder of Bosnians and Croats. The UN was hesitant to engage in the conflict in Bosnia for fear of disturbing the neutrality between nations and groups, but also due to Russia's support of Serbia. Russia, as one of the five permanent members of the UN Security Council, has the veto power to block any resolution of engagement by the United Nations. After Serb forces took the town of Zepa, including the bombing of a crowded Sarajevo market, the international community finally responded to the war.

NATO began a military operation against Yugoslavia during the Kosovo War, with air strikes lasting from March 24th to June 10th, 1999.[101] The bombings continued until an agreement was reached that led to the withdrawal of Yugoslav armed forces from Kosovo, and the establishment of United Nations Interim Administration Mission in Kosovo (UNMIK), a UN peacekeeping mission in Kosovo.

NATO countries attempted to gain authorization from the UN Security Council for military action, but were opposed by China and Russia. They then launched a campaign without UN authorization, which many legal scholars have described as a humanitarian intervention. Serbia described the NATO campaign as an illegal war of aggression against a sovereign country, in violation of international law because it did not have UN Security Council support. With a few exceptions, the UN Charter does not allow military interventions in other sovereign countries without the approval of the Security Council.

Yugoslavia (Serbia) filed a complaint at the International Court of Justice (ICJ) at The Hague against ten NATO member countries in 1999, alleging that the military operation violated Article 9 of the 1948 Genocide Convention and international humanitarian law. In June 1999, the ICJ-ruled majority vote also determined that the NATO bombing was an instance of "humanitarian intervention" and thus did not violate Article 9 of the Genocide Convention.[102]

---

[100] http://www.icty.org/specials/srebrenica20/?q=srebrenica20/

[101] "Operation Allied Force – Operation Allied Force in Kosovo," Militaryhistory.about. com. Archived from the original on November 19, 2012.

[102] Review of the ICJ Order of June 2, 1999 on the Illegality of Use of Force Case Archived February 18, 2011, at the Wayback Machine Anthony D'Amato: Leighton Professor of Law, Northwest University, June 2, 1999, Accessed January 13, 2014

In addition, in May 1993, the UN Security Council passed Resolution 827, creating the International Criminal Tribunal for the Former Yugoslavia (ICTY) at The Hague, Netherlands. This was the first tribunal formed to prosecute genocide. Initially, the ICTY was slow in prosecuting the criminals who took part in the genocide, but over the next two decades, the ICTY convicted more than 160 individuals, including prominent politicians, military figures, and police leaders. Radovan Karadzic and the Bosnian Serb military commander General Ratko Mladic were among those condemned for genocide and other crimes against humanity at the ICTY.[103]

The ICTY was established to prosecute serious crimes committed during the Yugoslav Wars, and to try their perpetrators. The ICTY[104] had jurisdiction over four clusters of crimes committed on the territory of the former Yugoslavia since 1991: grave breaches of the Geneva Conventions, violations of the laws or customs of war, genocide, and crimes against humanity. The maximum sentence it could impose was life imprisonment. Various countries signed agreements with the UN to carry out custodial sentences.[105] A total of 161 persons were indicted, with the final indictments issued in December 2004.

The ICTY ruled in 2001 that the 1995 Srebrenica massacre was a genocide, with presiding judge Theodor Meron stating, "The appeals chamber ... calls the massacre at Srebrenica by its proper name: genocide. Those responsible will bear this stigma, and it will serve as a warning to those who may in future contemplate the commission of such a heinous act."[106] However, in a move that caused consternation among the families of the Srebrenica dead:

> the appeals chamber of The Hague-based court overturned the conviction of a Bosnian Serb general who led troops into the UN-protected enclave where more than 7,000 Muslim boys and men were killed. Instead, Radislav Krstic, who in 2001 became the first man found guilty of genocide over the worst atrocity in Europe since World War II, saw his conviction reduced to aiding and abetting the genocide.[107]

---

[103] https://www.icty.org/en/press/radovan-karadzic-and-ratko-mladic-accused-genocide-following-take-over-srebrenica

[104] Officially named the International Tribunal for the Prosecution of Persons Responsible for Serious Violations of International Humanitarian Law Committed in the Territory of the Former Yugoslavia since 1991

[105] https://www.icty.org/x/file/Legal%20Library/Statute/statute_827_1993_en.pdf

[106] https://www.icty.org/en/press/address-icty-president-theodor-meron-potocari-memorial-cemetery

[107] https://www.globalpolicy.org/component/content/article/163/29298.html

In 2007, the ICJ announced that Serbia had breached the Genocide Convention by not preventing the massacre, which the court stated the republic "could and should" have.[108]

On July 11th, 1995, within weeks of Srebrenica's capture, some 7,000 Muslim men and boys were murdered by the forces led by Krstic and Bosnian Serb military leader Ratko Mladic. Both Mladic and his wartime leader Radovan Karadzic were charged with genocide for their crimes. Krstic challenged the ICTY's conviction by arguing that the number of victims of the ethnic cleansing was not significant enough for the killings to be classified as genocide. The war in Bosnia claimed the lives of 200,000 people. It also harmed the reputation of the UN, whose peacekeeping forces had failed to avert the violent killings.[109]

Slobodan Milošević was convicted by the ICTY for war crimes and other crimes against humanity in Kosovo in 1999; war crimes and other crimes against humanity in Croatia in 1991 and 1992; and genocide in Bosnia in 1992 and 1995. Milošević served as his own defence lawyer. His trial was delayed multiple times due to his poor health. He pled not guilty to all sixty-six counts of war crimes, crimes against humanity, and genocide. Ultimately, he was found dead in his cell in 2006, months before his trial was due at The Hague.

During the Bosnian War, human rights violations occurred in many forms, including forced relocations, rape, castration, imprisonment in concentration camps, killings, and curfews. Many survivors lost their family members without a trace, not even finding their remains. The bodies that were found were unrecognizable due to their condition.

Without recognition of the crimes committed, there can be no reconciliation. While the victims' trauma cannot be erased and the events that sabotaged their lives cannot disappear, victims can be given closure for what they experienced if the atrocities and their horrifying effects are acknowledged. The ICTY convicts those responsible for heinous crimes and also acts as an aid for people to raise their voices against any atrocity that they have witnessed. In the case of the Bosnian War, it became a haven where victims could plead their cases in the open, without needing to be afraid of the violent officials. The ICTY also helped in maintaining accurate historical records of the war.

In April 2015, the ICC in The Hague found Vojislav Seselj, leader of the Serbian Radical Party, guilty of war crimes. The 1999 crisis and NATO intervention generated public attention to the issue of humanitarian military intervention—a topic that will be later dealt in the book—

---

108   https://www.globalpolicy.org/component/content/article/163/29298.html
109   https://www.globalpolicy.org/component/content/article/163/29298.html

and to questions about the adequacy of the UN-centred international legal system. A general doctrine of humanitarian intervention has gained momentum since the Kosovo crisis.

Kurdish People

The violent crimes committed towards the Kurds by Iraq constituted a systematic effort to wipe out an entire ethnic minority. From 1980 to 1988, a brutal war was waged against the Kurdish minority in northern Iraq, claiming almost 100,000 lives. Villages were destroyed, and Kurdish children, women, and men were killed indiscriminately.[110]

The Kurds or Kurdish people are an ethnic group whose history is as rich as it is old. After the Arabs, Turks, and Persians, they are the fourth largest ethnic and linguistic group in the region. Globally, their numbers are estimated at 30 million to 45 million; an exact number is unknown, as they have dispersed throughout the world. Some scholars have argued that they are the largest ethnic group without a state of their own. Around 25 million Kurds live in the region that overlaps eastern Turkey, northern Syria, northern Iraq, and northwestern Iran.[111] Even though Kurds make up a large part of the population in these countries, they are constantly discriminated against, and at times are not even allowed to speak their language in public.

Al-Anfal means the spoils of war, and this was the name of the military campaign headed by Saddam Hussein's cousin, Ali Hassan al-Majid, who systematically attacked the Kurds in northern Iraq between 1980 and 1988.[112] Since the Iranians were supporting the Kurds and vice versa, Iraq's response to this was unsurpassed bloodshed and violence. In this campaign, chemical weapons were a major instrument used by Iraq, beginning with crude chemical weapons and moving on to mustard gas and finally the highly-lethal sarin gas and other nerve agents. Entire villages and crops were set ablaze. During this time, nearly 90% of Kurdish villages and more than twenty towns and cities were destroyed. According to the Human Rights Watch, more than a million Kurds were killed during this Anfal campaign.[113] Saddam Hussein justified his actions by stating that the Kurdish men had "betrayed the country and ... the covenant" by siding with the Iranians in the Iran–Iraq war.[114]

---

[110] https://www.hrw.org/reports/1991/IRAQ913.htm

[111] The Kurdish Population by the Kurdish Institute of Paris, 2017 estimate.

[112] https://scholarship.kentlaw.iit.edu/cgi/viewcontent.cgi?article=4175&context=ck-lawreview

[113] https://www.hrw.org/reports/1991/IRAQ913.htm

[114] https://www.refworld.org/docid/47fdfb1d0t.html

From February 21st to March 18th, 1988, the first stage of the Anfal campaign began in Dolli Jafayty Marg, where the Iraqi military dropped chemical weapons. Similar attacks were carried out in the second stage of the Anfal campaign in the Qaradakh district; thousands subsequently died. As well, nerve agents like sarin gas were deployed on the Garmyan district from March 31st to April 14th, 1988, during the third stage of the attack. T he fourth stage of the chemical bombardment began in the Askar district, where villages named Goptapa, Shwan, Qala, Swaka, Dashti Koya were bombarded with poisonous gas.[115] The Iraqi military began its fifth, sixth, and seventh stages of the Anfal campaign from May 24th to August 31st, bombarding the Shaqlawa and Rewandiz districts. The eighth and final stage of the campaign began on August 25th and ended on September 6th in the Badinan district.[116]

One town that has become significant in the Kurdish Genocide is Halabja, where on March 16th, 1988 an attack was carried out that resulted in the day being remembered as "Bloody Friday." Iran's revolutionary guards and Kurdish fighters had occupied the town for a few days, and in retaliation the Iraqi military flew their aircrafts over Halabja, first dropping rockets and then chemical bombs. Thousands were killed. Survivors of the attack recall a sickly-sweet smell; many could smell apples, while others smelled rotten eggs—smells which were indicative of cyanide and mustard gas poisoning.[117] People who had woken up that morning to a beautiful spring day died in the most horrific manner known to man.

Nearly 5,000 civilians were killed that day, and more than 10,000 were injured. The chemical bomb managed to flush out all the citizens of the town, who were then taken to mass execution sites in the desert.[118] Some were mowed down while others were shot dead by automatic assault rifles. These tactics used by the Iraqi military killed thousands of Kurds. It has been decades since the attack, but its effects linger in the form of a higher percentage of miscarriages, cancer, heart disease, respiratory illness, and eye and skin problems.

Heartbreaking images emerged soon after the attacks, taken by Iranian journalists who spread the pictures in Iranian newspapers. Soon British journalists and others discovered the mass graves filled with bodies of those who died in chemical attacks, and the world became aware of the unspeakable brutality committed against the Kurds. Despite this glaring

---

[115] https://www.hrw.org/reports/1993/iraqanfal/ANFALINT.htm

[116] https://www.hrw.org/reports/1993/iraqanfal/ANFALINT.htm

[117] https://www.refworld.org/docid/47fdfb1d0.html

[118] https://www.refworld.org/docid/47fdfb1d0.html

evidence, Saddam Hussein repeatedly denied his part in the crimes, throwing blame on the Iranians. Nevertheless, Halabja was a turning point in the Iraqi conflict, although it took other attacks like the Dolli Jafayty Marg attacks for the international community to speak out against the crimes being committed by Hussein, his cousin, and others. The members of the United Nations were guilty bystanders for watching this brutality and not imposing sanctions or taking military action against Saddam Hussein.

Human Rights Watch termed these events "genocide in part" under the definition of the 1948 Genocide Convention. Allegations about enormous abuses against the Kurds by government security forces had been circulating in the West since long before the events of 1991, but the phenomenon of the Anfal, as well as the horrific details that emerged, has seared itself into the popular consciousness. The Kurds have been fighting an armed struggle for over a half-century against the central government of Iraq.

Following the U.S.-led coalition to overthrow the government of Iraq, Saddam Hussein went into hiding and was eventually captured by U.S. forces on December 13th, 2003. The Coalition Provisional Authority voted to create the Iraqi Special Tribunal (IST), consisting of five Iraqi judges, on December 9th, 2003, to try Saddam Hussein and his aides on charges of war crimes, crimes against humanity, and genocide.[119] The IST prosecuted Saddam Hussein, his cousin Al-Majid, and his other co-defendants, and all were convicted of genocide and crimes against humanity. Hussein, Al-Majid, and two more co-dependents were sentenced to death by hanging, while the rest were sentenced to a lifetime of imprisonment.

The legal obligation to act on the basis of information that was being provided by several international human rights NGOs, to punish the perpetrators of the violence and prevent its recurrence, needs to be pursued either through the ICJ or through the UN Security Council. The Security Council is required under the Genocide Convention to prevent genocidal action.

The Iraqi Kurds must be permitted to live in peace and security. They must be free to speak their language, practice their customs, and associate as Kurds. The United States led an international coalition in March 2003 to overthrow the government of Saddam Hussein. The international community, having participated in this mission, therefore has a collective responsibility to do all it can to protect the Kurdish community.

The U.S. military forces remained in Iraq until their withdrawal in 2011, but still have large military bases in Iraq. Unfortunately, in September

---

[119] Sachs, Susan (10 December 2003). «Iraqi Governing Council Sets Up Its Own Court for War Crimes,» The New York Times.

2019, President Donald Trump of the United States abandoned military support for the Kurdish-held region of Syria. Kurds were allies in the fight against the Islamic State (ISIS) and lost 11,000 fighters in the U.S.-led campaign. Following U.S. withdrawal, Turkey, which also has a large Kurdish community that it treats with hostility, invaded northern Syria on October 9th, 2019. Turkish President Recep Tayyip Erdoğan's bloody incursion into northern Syria is a campaign that, according to Ahmed, has so far killed at least 250 Kurds, including a large number of children, and forced 300,000 to flee their ancestral homes. Another 300 people have disappeared.

The 21st Century

For centuries, wars have claimed millions of innocent lives while also defining boundaries, cultures, and the future of human civilizations. Despite the creation of the United Nations and the codification of international law against acts of aggression, genocide, and mass atrocities, the twenty-first century has yet to bring about a period without conflict.

Due to the creation of the ICC, which began functioning on July 1st, 2002—the date that the Rome Statute entered into force—the world community now has an international tribunal with the jurisdiction to prosecute individuals for international crimes of genocide, crimes against humanity, war crimes, and crimes of aggression. This is a major step forward to combat impunity.

Notwithstanding the positive development of the ICC, we have witnessed in the last two decades conflicts in many nations of Africa, from Sudan to the Congo, and also in the Middle East and Asia—most notably in Afghanistan, Iraq, Syria, Yemen, and Pakistan, with religious persecution and the cleansing of religious minorities such as the Yazidi, Rohingya Muslims, and Christians—with little accountability for those responsible for these atrocities.

Power is a strong concept that changes its meaning and importance depending on its use, as it holds both the capacity for empowerment and disempowerment. Competition for economic, political, social, and cultural superiority has never been a distinct phenomenon for the human race. For ages, the politics of power have trapped the human race in a vicious cycle of violence attained by the pursuit and imposition of supremacy. The binary understanding of the world has divided the human race into two extremes and has created a hierarchy of beliefs that aligns power to one group by demeaning the other to an extreme degree.

This binary understanding of the world that divides it into black and white terms precludes the possibility of existence of any grey areas, thus creating a polarized setup. In the list of nations falling victim to this polarization, especially in the so-called modern world of the twenty-first century, Darfur in Sudan is the first victim of twenty-first century genocide. The preceding century witnessed a vast range of devastating genocides across the globe, but the politics of power did not find closure with the end of the century. In fact, they have transmitted along the axes of time and space to haunt the present century of the modern world.

Darfur

The first genocide of the twenty-first century began in 2003 in Darfur with the mass slaughter and rape of the Darfuri people in Western Sudan. Sudan is a massive country in Africa; the Darfur region is in Western Sudan, with an estimated population of seven million people. Unfortunately, unrest and violence persist today, with an estimated 500,000 people killed and nearly 3 million displaced persons. The killing is being carried out by a group of government-armed and funded Arab militias known as the Janjaweed, who are systematically destroying Darfurians by burning villages, murder, rape, torture, and polluting water sources. These militias are rivals of other rebel groups such as the Sudan Liberation Movement/Army (SLM/A) and the Justice and Equality Movement (JEM).[120] The conflict between the northern and southern regions of Sudan eventually led to the south's independence from the north in April 2018, and the creation of South Sudan as the newest country in the United Nations. The Darfur region is predominantly Muslim, and these Muslims are in conflict with the ethnically-different African groups of the nation. Janjaweed is an ethnic Arab group which is attacking the people who live in the Darfur region.

The conflict between the northern and southern part of Sudan paved way for civil war, which resulted in the still-ongoing genocide in Darfur, the western Sudanese region. With a predictable pattern being followed, the rivalry for dominance and power has devastated many lives in Darfur since 2003—the year that marks the beginning of not only the Darfur genocide, but of modern genocide in general. Despite the Muslim dominance in the region, the existence of several ethnic and tribal practices has augmented the difficulties and complexities of the region, helping the cycle of violence Darfur to continue.

It is important for the world community to recognize the Darfur genocide so as to prevent any similar events from occurring in the near future. The United States government has officially acknowledged the Sudan crisis as the first genocide of the twenty-first century.

---

[120] http://worldwithoutgenocide.org/genocides-and-conflicts/darfur-genocide

Conflict in Darfur is not just confined to political motives, but encompasses economic, religious, and ethnic factors as well. The main conflict in Darfur has been between the ethnic Arab groups, chiefly being nomadic herders, and the African groups (mainly Maasalit and Zaghawa), the pastoral groups.[121] The non-Arab people, especially the Fur people, have been consistently targeted for attacks. When competition for meagre resources comes into play, the politics of power and dominance automatically take centre stage, and in the case of Darfur, the same petty politics of the ballroom have translated into an extensive genocidal cycle in the region. Discrimination and inequality in the sociocultural, economic, and political spheres of life have impacted the everyday existence of the people of Darfur to date.

After Sudan's independence from Britain in 1956, two lengthy civil wars broke out in the country, which lasted for most of the remaining twentieth century. These conflicts stemmed from the north's economic, political, and social dominance over the largely non-Muslim, non-Arab, southern Sudanese people. The exploitation of the south's resources by the north played a large role.[122] According to World Without Genocide:

> [a]s nomads began to compete for grazing land, traditional reconciliation measures were no longer able to settle disputes, causing the region to become increasingly militarized. The complexities of desertification, famines, and the civil war raging between North and South Sudan contributed to a rise in regional tensions during the 1980s. Similarly, as oil was discovered in Western Sudan, the Sudanese government and international contributors became increasingly interested in the land in Darfur.[123]

Faced with discrimination, the ethnic African groups realized the need for retaliation and rebelled against the Khartoum-based regime of Sudanese President Omar al-Bashir in 2003, which led to the enduring tensions between the different ethnic groups in the Darfur region of Sudan. The violence inherent in the rebellious movement against the Sudanese military attracted the attention of Omar al-Bashir, who extended full-fledged support both economically and politically to the Arab militias called Janjaweed (which loosely translates to "devils on horseback").

The targeted atrocities inflicted on the civilians of Darfur with the intention of wiping them out in the name of ethnic cleansing have surpassed

---

[121]   https://hmh.org/library/research/genocide-in-darfur-guide/

[122]   Silva, Mario, *After Partition : The Perils of South Sudan*, University of Baltimore Journal of International Law Vol. III, No. I, 2014-2015

[123]   http://worldwithoutgenocide.org/genocides-and-conflicts/darfur-genocide

the limits of extremism. All sorts of arms and equipment were provided to the Janjaweed to carry out the genocide against the Darfurians. Women have always been a soft target for the politics of power in conflicts across the globe. Darfur is no exception in terms of using women as a weapon of war. In the process of systematic genocide, women—especially of the African tribes—have been subjected to unimaginable violence, ranging from brutal rape, to abduction, to forced labour. Millions were victims of mass murder and targeted air strikes, and another large segment of the population lost their lives in the cruel aftermath of the violent attack, wherein water and food resources were polluted due to the dumping dead bodies into them. Civilians were also unable to access basic health care, which led to widespread death from disease and starvation, on top of the extrajudicial killings and outright murder.

Dissatisfaction among civilians, who had faced the brunt of the attacks during the civil war, turned into an armed rebellion, which continued to rage even after the signing of the Comprehensive Peace Agreement in 2005. The retaliation was a return to the unbalanced distribution of power and resources in the country that adversely affected the people of Darfur. According to World Without Genocide:

> Darfur remained underdeveloped and marginalized at the federal level, lacking infrastructure and development assistance. This neglect, combined with allegations that the government was arming Arab tribesmen (Janjaweed) to raid non-Arab villages, was cited as the justification for a February 2003 rebel attack on a Sudanese Air Force Base at El Fasher, North Darfur.[124]

The rebellion of the civilians of Darfur was unacceptable to the authoritarian regime of President Omar al-Bashir, who ordered and supported a systematic attack on the civilians. The attack in its nature as well as its impact has translated into a devastating and prolonged twenty-first-century genocide which has violated a range of human rights of the people of Darfur and neighbouring areas.

Recognition of any crime is the first step towards fighting back in both spirit and action, and for such a heinous crime like genocide, especially in the modern era, international recognition of the crime is essential. The ongoing conflict in Darfur was declared a genocide by United States Secretary of State Colin Powell on September 9th, 2004, in testimony before the Senate Foreign Relations Committee. On February 18th, 2006, President George W. Bush called for doubling the number

---

[124] http://worldwithoutgenocide.org/genocides-and-conflicts/darfur-genocide

of international troops in Darfur.[125] On September 17th, U.K. Prime Minister Tony Blair penned an open letter to the European Union, in which he asserted that E.U. members should "play a central role in mobilizing world opinion on [the] issue" and "strongly call upon government of Sudan and non-signatories alike to stop immediately the violence in northern Darfur."[126]

In January 2005, UN Secretary General Kofi Annan established the International Commission of Inquiry on Darfur pursuant to Security Council Resolution 1564. The Commission concluded that there was reason to believe that war crimes and crimes against humanity had been committed. On March 31st, 2005, using its authority under the Rome Statute, the UN Security Council referred the situation in Darfur to the Prosecutor of the International Criminal Court in Resolution 1593. In 2008, the ICC Prosecutor submitted an application for the issuance of a warrant of arrest for Omar al-Bashir, and in March 2009, Pre-Trial Chamber I issued a warrant for his arrest on "charges of war crimes and crimes against humanity"—the first instance of a warrant being issued by the ICC to a sitting head of state.[127] That decision was appealed by the Prosecutor, given that genocide was not added to the charges. The Appeals Chamber concluded, on July 12th, 2010, that "there are reasonable grounds to believe that Omar al-Bashir acted with specific intent to destroy in part the Fur, Masalit and Zaghawa ethnic groups."[128] They delivered a second warrant of his arrest, including three counts of genocide pertaining to the crimes committed against the ethnic groups of Fur, Masalit, and Zaghawa. In 2010, the ICC indicted President al-Bashir for the crime of genocide. Sudan is not a party to the Rome Statute, but the Prosecutor warned that al-Bashir could be arrested if he enters international airspace.[129] However, the Arab League has shown solidarity with al-Bashir.

On May 5th, 2006, a peace agreement called the Abuja Agreement—also known as the Darfur Peace Agreement—was signed by the government of Sudan, along with a faction of the SLM/A, a Sudanese rebel group active in Darfur comprising members of three indigenous ethnic groups in Darfur, and led by Minni Minnawi. The agreement was eventually rejected

---

[125] http://www.washingtonpost.com/wp-dyn/content/article/2006/02/17/AR200602 1701935.html

[126] http://news.bbc.co.uk/2/hi/uk_news/politics/5353348.stm

[127] http://www.coalitionfortheicc.org/cases/omar-albashir

[128] http://law.emory.edu/eilr/content/volume-33/issue-1/comments/navigating-scylla-charybdis-international-criminal-court-power-play.html

[129] Atkeson, Edward B. *The New Legions: American Strategy and the Responsibility of Power* (Rowman and Littlefield, 2011)

by two other smaller groups and a rival faction of the SLM/A led by Abdul Wahid al Nur.[130] The agreement addressed national and state power-sharing, the demilitarization of the Janjaweed and other militias, integration of SLM/A and JEM troops into the Sudanese military and police, a system of national economic redistribution to support Darfur's economy, as well as a referendum on the future status of Darfur.[131]

With the collapse of the Abuja Agreement, a new initiative was initiated by the international community, which led to the Doha Agreement, or the Darfur Peace Agreement, in 2011 between the government of Sudan and the Liberation and Justice Movement. The Peace Agreement established a compensation fund for victims of the Darfur conflict, and established a new Darfur Regional Authority to oversee the region until a referendum was conducted.

In April 2016, a referendum on the permanent status of Darfur within Sudan was held, though it was subject to a boycott, with several protests and accusations of vote-rigging. The final results were in favour of the retention of the status quo.

In early 2008, the UN Security Council authorized a hybrid United Nations–African Union mission (UNAMID) which deployed up to 26,000 peacekeepers in the Darfur region to keep a check on the extent of the violence engulfing the area. Despite this directive, nevertheless, just 9,000 were sent, and regrettably, they lacked the necessary equipment to carry out their mission.

According to Jan Eliasson, the former UN special envoy to Darfur, several issues contributed to the slow deployment, including hesitation by the international community about sending equipment and reluctance by the Sudanese government to accept peacekeepers from specific countries. These were combined with other logistical problems, like a lack of water, lodging, and roads.[132]

The violence in the Darfur region is not only related to ethnic tensions. Economic factors also play a major role, as the region has been bestowed with the natural resources of oil and gold. The intention to take hold of the region's resources can be seen as an important factor leading to the massacre of the local people of the Darfur region. According to World Without Genocide:

[a]s 2013 began, there was violence between Abbala/Reizegat and Beni Hussein tribes over goldmines. This left thousands displaced and

---

130 United Nations. «UNAMID Background.» Retrieved 5/3/2019

131 United Nations. «UNAMID Background.» Retrieved 5/3/2019

132 https://www.pbs.org/newshour/politics/africa-july-dec08-origins_07-03

many dead. Conflicts between communities in Central Darfur spread to South Darfur, displacing tens of thousands of people in April 2013.[133]

The violence in the region that started in 2003 has seen no closure to date: in the passing decades, the level of violence has only increased. In 2016 and 2017, several refugee camps for internally displaced Darfuris were attacked by Arab forces. As hundreds of thousands of people flee Darfur to escape the violence, tensions have increased in nearby Chad[134] as well as the Central African Republic, whose borders have been inundated by these refugees.[135]

The genocide in Darfur has been carried out by the government in order to deprive civilians of their basic human rights and use the region's utilities for selfish economic and political motives. The initial 2003 rebellion of the ethnic black Africans was a retaliation against the nation's government, who consistently denied them their social, economic, and political rights as well as the profit-sharing of the natural resources. The main rebel groups—the SLM/A and the JEM—have demanded an end to the economic disparity between Arabs and black Africans in Sudan, as well as equal representation in the government.

Several international organizations have condemned the brutality carried out by the Sudanese government against the Darfur people. A 2004 Human Rights Watch report noted that the "government of Sudan is responsible for 'ethnic cleansing' and crimes against humanity in Darfur, one of the world's poorest and most inaccessible regions."[136] British Prime Minister Gordon Brown, in a speech before the General Assembly of the United Nations, called the Darfur crisis "the greatest humanitarian disaster the world faces today."[137] Amnesty International alleged that the Sudanese government used chemical weapons against civilians, and according to the

---

[133] http://worldwithoutgenocide.org/genocides-and-conflicts/darfur-genocide

[134] The most recent Chadian Civil War began in December 2005. Since its independence from France in 1960, Chad has been swamped by the civil war between the Arab-Muslims of the north and the Sub-Saharan-Christians of the south. As a result, leadership and presidency in Chad drifted back and forth between the Christian southerners and Muslim northerners. When one side was in power, the other side usually started a revolutionary war to counter it.

[135] The Central African Republic, an African country wedged mainly between the Democratic Republic of the Congo, South Sudan, and Chad, has been embroiled in a civil war ever since 2013 when the country's Christian President François Bozizé was overthrown by a coalition of Muslim groups.

[136] https://www.hrw.org/reports/2004/sudan0504/2.htm

[137] https://www.nytimes.com/2007/08/01/world/africa/01nations.html

United Nations, 2.6 million people were displaced by the conflict. Over three million are still seriously impacted by it.[138]

Despite the issue of an arrest warrant for Sudanese President Omar al-Bashir for crimes against humanity on March 4th, 2009 by the ICC and a warrant for his arrest on charges of genocide in July, 2010, he was shielded for years by national and international allies who have benefitted directly or indirectly from the crisis in Darfur.

From December 2018 onwards, Bashir faced large-scale protests which demanded his removal from power. This led to his being ousted in a military coup d'état on April 11th, 2019.

Currently the UNAMID is in in place, but in 2017 the United Nations decided to reduce the number of peacekeepers. With the conflict still active, UNAMID has expressed deep concern about attacks at internally displaced persons (IDP) camps in Central Darfur state.[139] Sadly, the marginalization and forced displacement of the people of Darfur has formed the first twenty-first century genocide.

The collective international failure to stop the genocidal violence and resulting humanitarian catastrophe in Sudan calls into question whether the international community has the political will and capabilities to deter or stop mass atrocities. Mobilizing domestic and international political support, as well as leveraging diplomatic, economic, and even military intervention, are necessary to stop mass atrocities. The limitations on the current international legal regime with regard to the use of military force—that is, international humanitarian law regulating the resort to armed intervention—have caused many legal scholars to question whether it is appropriate and effective in deterring and stopping mass atrocities. As we have seen in the case of Yugoslavia, the legal system that gives the five permanent Security Council members veto power can prevent a UN humanitarian intervention, even in cases where there is strong international support for one.

Iraq

The humanitarian crisis in Iraq could have been easily avoided following the collapse of the authoritarian leader Saddam Hussein had the United States not led a coalition to overthrow the government.

The Iraq War was a protracted armed conflict that began in 2003, with an estimated 151,000 to 600,000 Iraqis killed in the first three to

---

[138] http://worldwithoutgenocide.org/genocides-and-conflicts/darfur-genocide
https://www.nbcnews.com/news/world/sudan-crisis-amnesty-report-cites-evidence-government-used-chemical-weapons-n656121

[139] https://news.un.org/en/story/2018/05/1010661

four years of conflict. The conflict went on for most of the next decade as an insurgency emerged opposing the occupying forces and the Iraqi government.[140] In 2009, the U.S. officially withdrew. However, American soldiers remain on the ground fighting in Iraq. The invasion occurred as part of President George W. Bush's declared war against international terrorism following the September 11th, 2001 terrorist attacks that killed over 2,977 people[141] by the Islamic terrorist group al-Qaeda led by Osama Bin Laden.

In 2004, Abu Musab al-Zarqawi, a Jordanian jihadist, established the terrorist group al-Qaeda in Iraq (AQI), and in 2006, al-Qaeda under al-Zarqawi attempted to start a sectarian war against the majority Shia community in Iraq. Zarqawi was killed on June 7th, 2006 by U.S. air strikes. Following his death, Abu Ayyub al-Masri took his place as leader of AQI, and announced the creation of the Islamic State of Iraq (ISI). Abu Omar al-Baghdadi was established as leader of ISI, and the group later renamed itself the Islamic State in Iraq and the Levant (ISIL or ISIS). In January 2014, ISIS took control of Falluja.[142]

ISIS began a deadly campaign of kidnappings, killings, displacement of millions of people, and destruction of important historical sights, and ultimately took control of the cities of Mosul and Tikrit.

That same year, ISIS announced "the creation of a caliphate (Islamic state), and also announce[d] a name change to the Islamic State (IS). In May 2015, the terrorist group took control of Ramadi, the largest city in western Iraq, and Palmyra, an ancient Syrian city that is a UNESCO World Heritage Site."[143]

Since IS ascended to power, many thousands from Iraq's ethnic and religious minorities have been murdered, tortured, raped, displaced, and forced into sexual enslavement by the jihadist group. Well over two million Iraqis and Syrian refugees have fled to the Kurdistan Region of Iraq.

Yazidis and Christians have been particularly targeted by the Islamic State campaign of destruction. Iraqi Christians, who have lived in the region

---

140   "Iraq War," Encyclopædia Britannica, Retrieved October 27th, 2012.

141   The September 11th, 2001 attacks (also referred to as 9/11) were a series of four coordinated terrorist attacks by the Islamic terrorist group al-Qaeda against the United States on the morning of Tuesday, September 11, 2001. The attacks killed 2,977 people (not counting the 19 hijackers who also died), injured over 6,000 others, and caused at least $10 billion in infrastructure and property damage. In addition, people have died of 9/11-related cancer and respiratory diseases in the months and years following the attacks.

142   https://www.cnn.com/2014/08/08/world/isis-fast-facts/index.html

143   https://www.cnn.com/2014/08/08/world/isis-fast-facts/index.html

since the beginning of Christianity and who numbered around 1.3 million in the year 2000, are now estimated to have a population as low as 250,000.

In the midst of the ongoing Syrian civil war, ISIS took control of northern parts of Syria. On February 11th, 2015, U.S. President Obama asked the U.S. Congress to formally authorize use of military force against ISIS.[144] The United States' legal rationale for its military actions in Syria was that they were, in large part, a response to the challenges facing the government in Iraq to control the terror attacks and drive ISIS out of the region. A letter written by Samantha J. Powers, U.S. Ambassador to the United Nations, notes that:

> Iraq has made clear that it is facing a serious threat of continuing attacks from ISIL coming out of safe havens in Syria. These safe havens are used by ISIL for training, planning, financing, and carrying out attacks across Iraqi borders and against Iraq's people. For these reasons, the Government of Iraq has asked that the United States lead international efforts to strike ISIL sites and military strongholds in Syria in order to end the continuing attacks on Iraq, to protect Iraqi citizens, and ultimately to enable and arm Iraqi forces to perform their task of regaining control of the Iraqi borders. ISIL and other terrorist groups in Syria are a threat not only to Iraq, but also to many other countries, including the United States and our partners in the region and beyond. States must be able to defend themselves, in accordance with the inherent right of individual and collective self-defense, as reflected in Article 51 of the UN Charter, when, as is the case here, the government of the State where the threat is located is unwilling or unable to prevent the use of its territory for such attacks.[145]

On November 13th, 2015, Kurdish forces, backed by coalition air power, liberated the Iraqi town of Sinjar from ISIS. The terrorist group continued a series of attacks and suicide bombings, such as the one carried out on July 3rd, 2016, when a suicide car bomb detonated in a busy shopping area in Baghdad. At least 292 people were killed in the attack, and 200 more were injured. It was Iraq's deadliest single attack since 2003.

On March 15th, 2016, the U.S. House of Representatives voted unanimously to classify ISIS's attacks on religious minorities as crimes against humanity and acts of genocide. The European Parliament has also declared

---

https://www.cnn.com/2014/08/08/world/isis-fast-facts/index.html

145 Letter from Samantha J. Power, Representative of the United States of America to the United Nations, to Ban Ki-moon, Secretary-General of the United Nations (Sept. 23, 2014), available at https://www.justsecurity.org/15436/war-powers-resolution-article-51- letters-force-syria-isil-khorasan-group/ [https://perma.cc/2Z37-LHPC]

the crimes committed by the Islamic State to be acts of genocide against Christians and Yazidis and other religious and ethnic minorities.

The actions carried out by the United States and its allies to eradicate ISIS from the territories of Iraq and Syria had international support as well as legal precedents as has been clarified by the jurisprudence of the International Court of Justice, which has "repeatedly held that unless the acts of non-state actors are attributable to the territorial state, use of force against non-state actors in that state is unlawful."[146],[147] This is principally due the fact that when

> a terrorist organization is physically located within the territory of another State that is not in effective control of its operations, the right of self-defence collides with two other fundamental principles of international law: the sovereign equality of states and the renunciation of force in international relations. ... [A] state cannot be held responsible for the acts of all whose activities originate in its territory.[148]

The Iraq government, to an extent, cannot be held responsible for the acts carried out by ISIS against the Yazidi and Christian communities.

The Islamic State not only targets religious minorities within its held territory, but also incites attacks against those considered apostates, Christians, Jews, and Hindus worldwide.[149]

The Iraqi military claimed to have "fully liberated" all of Iraq's territory of "ISIS terrorist gangs" on December 9th, 2017.[150] However, the Pentagon issued a report on August 6th, 2019 saying that ISIS was "re-surging."

---

146 Scharf, Michael P., "How the War Against ISIS Changed International Law," *Case Western Reserve Journal of International Law* 48, no. 1-2 (2016): 36.

147 See generally Nicaragua v. U.S., 1986 I.C.J. 14 (holding that the United States unlawfully used force against another state); Dem. Rep. Congo v. Uganda, 2005 I.C.J. 169, at 28-166 (holding unlawful use of force and violation of territorial sovereignty). Under the International Court of Justice's jurisprudence, attribution requires that the territorial State have "effective control" of the non-state actors. This standard comes from the Nicaragua Case, where the Court was presented with the question of whether the actions of Nicaragua in supporting rebels in El Salvador through the provision of weapons was sufficient to justify military action by the United States in collective self-defence with El Salvador. The Court stated that sending "armed bands" into the territory of another State would be sufficient to constitute an armed attack, but "the supply of arms and other support to such bands cannot be equated with an armed attack."

148 Scharf, Michael P., "How the War Against ISIS Changed International Law," *Case Western Reserve Journal of International Law* 48, no. 1-2 (2016): 36.

149 https://www.counterextremism.com/content/isiss-persecution-religions

150 https://www.kbzk.com/cnn-world/2019/01/21/isis-fast-facts/

This was less than five months after Trump declared that the terror group's caliphate there had been defeated.

As we shall see in the next few chapters, the ongoing conflict in Iraq and Syria had serious consequences due to the mass atrocities that were carried out against the Christian and Yazidi communities.

ISIS War Crimes

The so-called Islamic State of Iraq and al-Sham is a "predominantly jihadist group seeking to implant civil strife in Iraq and the Levant (region spanning from southern Turkey to Egypt and including Syria, Lebanon, Israel, the Palestinian territories, and Jordan) with the ... aim of establishing a caliphate—a unitary, transnational Islamic state based on the principles of Sharia."[151,152] As discussed in the previous chapter, the group emerged in the wake of the United-States-led invasion to overthrow Saddam Hussein and al-Qaeda in Iraq, and the insurgency that followed provided it with lush ground to wage a terrorist campaign against coalition forces and their domestic allies. The terrorist group captured billions of dollars' worth of oil fields, refineries, bank assets, and antiquities, and became one of the greatest threats to peace and stability in the region.

The Islamic State of Iraq became involved in the Syrian civil war with Abu Muhammad al-Joulani, an ISI member, establishing the main jihadi group in the conflict.[153] Joulani received funding and support from the ISI and Abu Bakr al-Baghdadi.[154] Abu Bakr al-Baghdadi succeeded Abu Omar as leader of ISI in 2010, and by 2019, he had become the world's most wanted jihadist. Baghdadi was killed on October 26th, 2019 by U.S. forces in a special joint operation with the Kurds in northwest Syria.[155]

Since the withdrawal of U.S. forces in late 2011, the group has increased its attacks on mainly Shiite targets in what is seen as an attempt to reignite conflict between Iraq's Sunni[156] minority and the dominant Shiite group. According to United Nations statistics, the total number of

---

[151] https://www.newdelhitimes.com/isis-building-navy123/

[152] Sharia or Islamic law is a religious law forming part of the Islamic tradition. It is derived from the religious precepts of Islam, particularly the Quran and the Hadith.

[153] https://www.counterextremism.com/about

[154] https://www.theguardian.com/world/2014/jun/11/isis-too-extreme-al-qaida-terror-jihadi

[155] https://www.theguardian.com/world/isis

[156] Sunni is the larger of the two main branches of Islam, which differs from Shia in its understanding of the Sunna, its conception of religious leadership, and its acceptance of the first three caliphs.

civilian casualties (including police) in Iraq inflicted by ISIS in 2013 was the highest since 2008, with 7,818 killed and 17,981 injured, compared to 6,787 killed and 20,178 injured in 2008.[157]

The activities of ISIS and its explicit agenda of spreading a unitary Islamic state globally have inevitably led to a comparison with al-Qaeda. Though the ideology of the two organizations is almost the same, and both groups have found "tenuous common cause" in military engagements like Iraq, "their relations have been characterized by distrust, open competition, and outright hostility."[158]

According to the Centre for Pakistan and Gulf Studies:

> [i]n April 2013, overt enmity between ISIS and al-Qaeda broke out in full when ISIS leader Abu Bakr al-Baghdadi announced that he was extending the Islamic State of Iraq into Syria and changing the group's name to the Islamic State of Iraq and al-Sham.[159]

The major cause of the dispute between al-Qaeda and ISIS was over the question of the former merging with Jabhat al-Nusra, an al-Qaeda affiliate with more indigenous legitimacy in Syria, in April of 2013.[160] Al-Qaeda's top leader, Ayman al-Zawahiri, opposed the merger of the two jihadi groups based in Iraq and Syria. "In his letter, Zawahiri said Baghdadi was 'wrong' to declare the merger without consulting or even alerting al-Qaeda's leadership. He added that Syria was the 'spatial state' for al-Nusra, headed by Abou Mohammad al-Joulani, while Baghdadi's rule would be limited to Iraq."[161] Baghdadi "rejected Zawahiri's ruling and questioned his authority," regardless of his group's pledge of allegiance to al-Qaeda.[162]

Despite their organizational differences, the two groups' objectives are broadly the same. In a report by Reuters dated July 9th, 2014, it was highlighted that ISIS's plans for the establishment of a caliphate and, subsequently, a Sharia-driven government, were in the works years ago by an al-Qaeda group operating in Yemen. Reuters reported that it

---

[157] Anthony Cordesman and Sam Khazai, *Iraq in Crisis* (Center for Strategic and International Studies, 2014), 1.

[158] https://www.washingtoninstitute.org/policy-analysis/view/the-war-between-isis-and-al-qaeda-for-supremacy-of-the-global-jihadist

[159] http://cpakgulf.org/2014/11/18/

[160] https://www.defenseone.com/threats/2014/01/everything-you-need-to-know-about-al-qaeda-iraq/76679/

[161] https://www.aljazeera.com/news/middleeast/2013/06/2013699425657882.html

[162] https://www.defenseone.com/threats/2014/01/everything-you-need-to-know-about-al-qaeda-iraq/76679/

was shown an abandoned al-Qaeda notebook in Yemen that mapped out the "blueprint" for establishing an Islamic state. With the name Abu al-Dahdah al-Taazi written in red calligraphy on the first page, the notebook is evidence of what a local Yemeni governor described as a leadership camp for al-Qaeda in the Arab Peninsula (AQAP).[163] According to the *Daily News*:

> the abandoned notebook features notes on weapons maintenance, topography, and elaborate diagrams for creating different ambushes. It also identifies the three stages of guerrilla warfare needed to create an Islamic state—a similar blueprint to the one ISIS seems to be following in Iraq and Syria. ... It covers everything from the principles of a raid—'Surprise, firepower, a sacrificial spirit, quick performance'—to the ultimate goal: 'Establishing an Islamic state that rules by Islamic Sharia law.'[164]

Security experts now suspect that ISIS may turn out to be a greater threat for global security than the bin-Laden-led al-Qaeda in the previous decade. Robert Ford, one of the foremost experts on the affairs of the Middle East and the former American ambassador to Syria, remarks that ISIS represents an immediate threat to the United States as it has the necessary financial and human resources to attack the U.S. and its allies in places like Europe and the NATO countries, as well as friends in the region.[165] Experts point out that ISIS has capabilities that exceed even the "wildest dreams of the original founders of al-Qaeda."[166]

After capturing Mosul and raiding the its government reserves, ISIS now has a sum of over $400 million at its disposal. Some military experts have argued that ISIS now has funds adequate to execute the 9/11 attacks at least 800 times over.[167] Today, ISIS membership is estimated in

---

[163] http://www.nydailynews.com/news/world/abandoned-al-qaeda-notebook-features-blueprint-creating-islamic-state-article-1.1858534

[164] Daily News (2014), Abandoned Al Qaeda notebook found in Yemen features blueprint for creating Islamic state, July 8m URL: http://www.nydailynews.com/news/world/abandoned-al-qaeda-notebook-features-blueprint-creating-islamic-state-article-1.1858534.

[165] Chotiner, Issac (2014), A Middle East Expert Explains Assad's Dangerous Charm, ISIS's Plans, and the Future of the Region
An Interview With Robert Ford, the Former Ambassador to Syria, July 10, *New Republic, URL:* https://newrepublic.com/article/118623/qa-robert-ford-former-ambassador-syria-iraq-isis-iran.

[166] https://www.hsdl.org/?view&did=760214

[167] https://www.hsdl.org/?view&did=760214

the thousands, a number which is likely similar to al-Qaeda at its peak. Experts also point out that, while al-Qaeda was mostly successful in "bringing Arab Muslims from the Middle East to fight in wars in their own region or in South Asia,"[168] the magnitude of ISIS's terror network runs far deeper. "Unclassified reports, and ISIS's own videos, confirm that it is having unprecedented success in attracting Muslim men from the West to go and fight Jihad."[169] Apart from security experts, a United Kingdom newspaper, *Express*, in its July 3rd, 2014 edition, cites the pronouncements of one double agent (a former Jihadi turned MI5 agent) Morten Storm, that Sunni Muslim extremists storming Iraq are a bigger threat to Britain than al-Qaeda, and that "the West needs to wake up to the threat of fighters returning from Syria and Iraq."[170]

There is an urgent need for the international community to check ISIS' power in Iraq. In the crisis engulfing Iraq, the international community led by the United States and the European Union should strive to give Iraq an inclusive government. This is the best means of reducing the influence of terrorism and extremism, and restoring normalcy in Iraq.

ISIS is engaging in unprecedented acts of crimes against minorities. As Seth J. Frantzman puts it, "ISIS is made up not only of locals but of a global alliance of bigots who believe in religion-based genocide of minorities whom they call 'kuffar' or 'unbelievers.'"[171] The terrorist group follows a pattern of extermination so as to eradicate the seeds of "other" and establish a "pure Islamic" order for regional and religious dominance, with the belief in the principles of conservatism and dogmatism. Take, for example, the ongoing massacre of the Yazidis, as we shall see further in this book: they were attacked because of the differences in their faith and philosophy.

The philosophy of the Islamic State too is based rigidly on binary principles; they do not accept diversity or variance of any sort. The core of ISIS' principles is a reliance on Salafi jihadism. Salafism is an ideology and movement that calls for the return to the golden age of Islam, and advocates the religion to be practiced in the same form as it was during the era of Mohammad and his companions. In Arabic, "salaf" means

---

168 https://www.breitbart.com/national-security/2014/07/09/why-isis-is-more-dangerous-than-al-qaeda-and-what-america-must-do-about-it/

169 https://www.hsdl.org/?view&did=760214

170 Express.co.uk (2014), Isis is a bigger threat than Al Qaeda, reveals double agent, June 3, URL: http://www.express.co.uk/news/world/486399/Al-Qaeda-Isis-Double-Agent-9-11-Attack-Terrorist-Fighters-Sunni-Muslim-Syria

171 https://www.jpost.com/Opinion/Terra-Incognita-The-21st-century-is-the-century-of-Islamist-religious-genocide-503547

"predecessors; forebears, ancestors, forefathers."[172] The Salafist movement developed primarily in the nineteenth century when the proliferation of European values was seen as a direct threat to the original religious beliefs of Islam. This is a puritanical interpretation of Islam, according to which all non-believers in Islam are apostates.

The strong dichotomy of "us" versus "them," or the "believers" contrasted with "non-believers," is at the core of the ISIS mentality and ideology. The followers of the Islamic State valorize the puritanical interpretation of the world, and believe religious cleansing to be a moral and religious obligation. Their intense solidarity and fraternity have far-fetched impacts, and pose a threat to the global order. At the root of Salafi doctrine lies the concept of "Tawhid," the unity of God or monotheism—i.e., there is no other divine entity but God. According to the concept of Tawhid, not only the private life of the individual but the organization of the state should be strictly based upon the principles of Islamic law, and this is only possible when an Islamic state, or caliphate, comes into existence.[173]

Ever since its rise and solidification, ISIS has posed a major international security concern as the stories of its violent operations and brutality have spread like forest fires. But what brought the brutal extent of ISIS to the international fore was its attack on the Yazidis, beginning in 2014, with its intent of exterminating the community as a whole. Since then, ISIS has become synonymous worldwide with extremism, violence, brutality, and terrorism. ISIS has never held back from expressing its intent—be it in its rhetoric of provocative Islam or in its manifestation of violence. Theological justification for acts of barbarity against the so-called religious and ethical minorities, or the ones not complying with their cherished notion of Islam, is merely an excuse for the solidification of the Islamic State in the battle of power politics and dominance.

ISIS' conflict with the Yazidis is part of its overarching warfare against the hegemony of the West in religious and political dominance, as well as its ideological stand of solidifying the hold of the Islamic religion across the globe by consolidating the Islamic State. ISIS gives far too much importance and sanctity to the teachings of Jihad and Al-wala' wa'l-bara.' "Al-wala' wa'l-bara'" literally translates to "loyalty and disavowal," and describes the obligations of Muslims. These obligations call for a strict

---

[172] Alvi, H. (2014). The Diffusion of Intra-Islamic Violence and Terrorism: The Impact of The Proliferation of Salafi/Wahhabi. Middle East Review of International Affairs, 18(2), 38-50. Retrieved from http://www.rubincenter.org/wp-content/uploads/2014/07/v18n02a05_alvi_PDF.pdf.

[173] Westphal, J. (2018). Violence in The Name of God? A Framing Processes Approach to The Islamic State in Iraq And Syria. Social Movement Studies, 17(1): 19-34.

adherence to the principles of Islam and the principle of Tawhid,[174] along with loyalty to the community (Ummah). Al-wala' wa'l-bara' rejects all those who do not abide by Islamic laws in either their private or public life.[175]

The persecution of the Yazidis and Christians in the name of religious purification is not new to the region. Forced conversion in the Islamic world is not considered inhuman, unethical, or unjust. The Yazidis are not a "people of the book";[176] therefore, they are not protected under Islamic law.

ISIS' annihilation and persecution is not limited to the Yazidi population. The Iraqi Christians and the majority Shiite Muslims are other two archetypical enemies of the Islamic State. Other religious minorities in northern Iraq, such as the Kaka'is, a religion related to Yezidism, and the Shabak, a cultural group with some distinctive religious characteristics, are also in the jihadist group's hitlist.[177]

The Yazidis have been the target of similar mass hatred many times in the past, but the recent attack by ISIS left them only with the option of fleeing or dying. It is not an easy task to uproot an entire community from the land of their birth and send them towards the unknown.

In an interview with *Foreign Policy*, Maria Fantappie, Senior Advisor on Iraq at the International Crisis Group said, "Despite having been freed from ISIS presence ... the region de facto remains an occupied district where competing Iraqi and foreign agendas play out by coopting Yazidis into rival armed groups."[178] She added that "the continued presence of the groups in the area is preventing reconstruction, demining, and the safe return of Yazidis to their homes."[179]

A report by the International Crisis Group[180] published in February, 2018, notes that the Shiite Hashd al-Shaabi (Popular Mobilisation Units,

---

174   Tawhid is the indivisible oneness concept of monotheism in islam. Tawhid is the religion's central and single-most important concept, upon which a Muslim's entire faith rests. It unequivocally holds that God is One and Single; therefore, the Islamic belief in God is considered Unitarian.

175   Ibid

176   Jews and Christians are considered people of the book.

177   https://www.theatlantic.com/international/archive/2014/08/the-yazidis-a-people-who-fled/375964/

178   https://foreignpolicy.com/2018/11/23/isis-may-be-gone-but-iraqs-yazidis-are-still-suffering-sinjar-ezidxan-pmu-nadia-murad/

179   https://foreignpolicy.com/2018/11/23/isis-may-be-gone-but-iraqs-yazidis-are-still-suffering-sinjar-ezidxan-pmu-nadia-murad/

180   https://www.crisisgroup.org/middle-east-north-africa/gulf-and-arabian-peninsula/iraq/186-saudi-arabia-back-baghdad

PMUs) allied with Tehran, has gained territory from the Islamic State in Syria and has caused serious concerns as to its plans of action in Iraq.[181] The PMU has been directed by the Iranian government to exercise strong presence in and around the Sinjar area, as it would provide Iran with greater strategic control over Syria and Iraq. To wait for future action by the PMU would be the extension of the vulnerability of the Yazidi population.

Many Yazidis fear returning to their villages that were once controlled by ISIS, and are not yet convinced of the claimed defeat and complete eradication of the Islamic State. The Yazidis are being instructed by the Iraqi government to return to Sinjar, but their sense of insecurity prevents them from trusting again. With the decreased Yazidi population due to ISIS' brutal campaign against them, their insecurity and fear of returning to their villages is justified. We explore this further in the next chapter.

Yazidis – Religious and Ethnic Cleansing

The terrorist campaign waged by ISIL/ISIS in August 2014 led to the Yazidis being systematically targeted in a genocidal fashion. Although many other ethnic and religious groups were victims of ISIS' campaign of brutality, the atrocities faced by the Yazidis—one of the religious and ethnic minorities tracing its history mainly in the Middle East—presents the sad reality of the inhumanity at its worst.

To comprehend the abysmal suffering of the Yazidis, it is important to know who they actually are and what have they done to attract the attention of the extremist ideology which has manifested in violent attacks on them.

Yazidis predominantly belong to the Kurdish community, and are a heterodox religious minority that has primarily inhabited northern Iraq—though some live in northern Syria and the southeast of Turkey, as well as in parts of Iran. There are also established Yazidi communities in the Caucasus region, and a growing European diaspora.[182] Tracing the origin of the Yazidis is difficult, as uncertainty and ambiguity engulf the religion's history and traditions. The faith, being heterodox in nature, has an intrinsic structure and monotheistic principles. It incorporates elements of Christianity, Zoroastrianism, Islam, and other monotheistic religions, while integrating several folk traditions. Debates surround the name "Yazidi," with various scholars and researchers having distinct views on its origins. Some scholars have proposed that it comes from the Old Iranian "yazata" (divine

---

[181]   https://foreignpolicy.com/2018/11/23/isis-may-be-gone-but-iraqs-yazidis-are-still-suffering-sinjar-ezidxan-pmu-nadia-murad/

[182]   http://www.cais-soas.com/CAIS/Religions/iranian/yazidis.htm

being), while others hold that it derives from the name of the Umayyad Caliph Yazid I, who is venerated by Yazidis.[183] As well, the Yazidi religion includes:

> elements of ancient Iranian religions as well as elements of Judaism, Nestorian Christianity, and Islam. Although scattered and probably numbering only between 200,000 and 1,000,000, the Yazidis have a well-organized society, with a Chief Sheikh as the supreme religious head and an Emir, or prince, as the secular head.[184]

Most scholars have come to the conclusion that the Yazidi faith finds its roots in areas of the Kurdish mountains of northern Iraq, where "pockets of devotion to the fallen Umayyad dynasty persisted long after the death of the last Umayyad Caliph, the half-Kurdish Marwan II, in 750."[185] The religion saw its evolvement in the region with the successors of the Umayyad dynasty settling in the area and practicing their mystical faith while creating a sort of hierarchical order among its followers.

Known among other religious groups for their conservatism and insular nature, the Yazidis are declining significantly in the Middle East and elsewhere. Geographically speaking, northern Iraq has been the nucleus of their population, and they have long been inhabiting the area around Mount Sinjar, about eighty kilometres (fifty miles) west of Mosul near the border with Syria.

It is not only religious identity but also linguistic distinctiveness that can be a significant factor in defining a community, as well as a marker for marginalization and exclusion. Yazidis, already at the receiving end of persecution for abiding by a faith deemed "devil-worshipping" by Islamists, were doubly marked by their linguistic uniqueness.

The highly insular community of Yazidis has a strong communal sense and a strict hierarchical caste order. The individual's identity is closely intertwined with that of the community at large. The Yazidis tend to avoid mixing with other communities, and to date have also been avoiding formal education and military services.

With the strengthening of religious and cultural practices among the Yazidis, the community attracted the criticism of the Islamic order when the Yazidis departed from the Islamic norms. The beginning of the fifteenth century paved way for the conflicted world order among the Yazidis and the neighbouring Muslim rulers, who claimed to uphold

---

183 https://www.britannica.com/topic/Yazidi

184 https://www.britannica.com/topic/Yazidi

185 https://www.britannica.com/topic/Yazidi

the mantel of purification of religion, and considered the religious practices of the Yazidis to be against Islam—thus considering them apostates.

The number of followers of the Yazidi faith is declining due to widespread massacres and an increasing number of conversions, either voluntarily or imposed. But the seeds of this decline can be traced back to the Yazidis' loss of political influence after the thirteenth century.

The concentration of the Yazidi population in the late nineteenth and early twentieth centuries in the Caucasus region—in countries such as Georgia and Armenia—speaks of the political displacement carried out under the name of religious purification. "The Yazidis, also targets of militant Sunnism, suffered at the hands of Kurdish tribal leaders such as Moháammed Beg of Rowanduz (1832) and Bedir Khan Beg (1840s), as well as Ottoman officials, such as 'Omar Wahbi Pasha."[186] The Yazidis' existence, even before ISIS, has always been fraught with life-or-death decisions—whether to inhabit their traditional spaces and be murdered, or to flee to avoid persecution. The late twentieth century marked an increase in Yazidi displacement, as most of the Yazidis, especially those residing in Turkey, migrated to Germany.

The Yazidis have faced mass massacres several times throughout history—sometimes in religiously motivated conflicts, and sometimes in imbibing the troubled water of politics. Repeatedly, they have been the target of extremist ideologies that measure the value of a person by scanning it through a fundamentalist prism.

The contemporary reality of the Yazidis has not departed much from its disturbing past. The ISIS attack on August 3rd, 2014 in the town of Sinjar, Iraq—with the primary goal of wiping out its whole Yazidi population—was a recent addition to the list of massacres carried out against the Yazidi people.

The town of Sinjar, which is thirty-two kilometres (or twenty miles) from the Syrian border, lies south of the Sinjar mountains, and was devastatingly attacked by ISIS forces on August 3rd, 2014, with thousands of Yazidi civilians murdered. Survivors fled, taking refuge in the hills of Mount Sinjar. The geostrategic importance of the mountain range is clear. With its advantageous height of 1,463 metres (or 4,800 feet), it was also used by former Iraqi dictator Saddam Hussein "to launch missiles into Israel during the Gulf War in the 1990s."[187]

The ethnic cleansing of the Yazidis carried out under ISIS' mantle of religious purification or "jihad" has forced the displacement of the

---

[186] http://www.cais-soas.com/CAIS/Religions/iranian/yazidis.htm

[187] https://foreignpolicy.com/2018/11/23/isis-may-be-gone-but-iraqs-yazidis-are-still-suffering-sinjar-ezidxan-pmu-nadia-murad/

community. The siege and merciless destruction of Sinjar also resulted in ISIS gaining full control of the area, giving them a land corridor and supply route. Scholars debate whether the motivation for the attack was primarily religious in nature, as a political motive seems clear: the seizure of this territory provided the Islamic State with better control of Syria and Iraq.

Life for the Yazidi population came to a standstill when ISIS seized the city of Sinjar and the surrounding villages in the timeframe of few hours, abducting and killing the Yazidis who could not flee. Those who took refuge in the rugged terrain of Mount Sinjar were besieged by ISIS for several days, and had to endure harshness from the coercion of the ISIS armed forces as well as the cruelty of the nature. They were forced to tolerate temperatures of over 50 degrees Celsius (or 122 Fahrenheit), along with a shortage of water, food, and medical care.[188] More than 1,700 people died due to lack of food and water. It is estimated that the number of people who fled was about 130,000, and those not lucky enough to escape at the right time were murdered in their own homes or held hostage.[189]

During the ISIS assault on Mount Sinjar, Yazidi husbands were separated from their wives, and women from their families, with many women raped by the terrorists. Young girls and middle-aged women faced the worst forms of torture by ISIS. Their horrific stories present a disturbing picture of the attack and its aftermath. Elderly women, deemed incapable of providing any sort of sexual pleasure, met the same fate as the Yazidi men: many were shot and dumped into the mass graves.[190]

Statistics on the Yazidi people who have lost, and continue to lose, their lives are difficult to determine with accuracy. However, reports by several non-profit organizations note that between 2,500 and 5,000 Yazidis have been killed by ISIS and over 6,000 have been kidnapped. Of the abducted persons, more than 3,000 women and about 400 children between four to ten years of age are still held captive.[191] Considering the extent of the atrocities, it became necessary for international community to intervene to help the Yazidis. The United States began conducting air strikes and air-dropping humanitarian aid on August 8th, 2014, and "between August 9th and August 13th, Kurdish forces opened a safe corridor, allowing most

---

188 https://www.foreignaffairs.com/articles/syria/2017-06-08/isis-yazidi-genocide

189 https://www.nytimes.com/2014/08/10/world/middleeast/chased-onto-iraqi-moun-tain-there-is-no-water-nothing.html http://www.slate.com/blogs/atlas_obscura/2013/07/26/lake_nyos_killed_1746_when_it_released_a_huge_pocket_of_co2.html https://science.howstuffworks.com/environmental/earth/geophysics/lake-nyos.htm

190 https://www.ohchr.org/Documents/Countries/IQ/UNAMI_OHCHR_POC_Report_FINAL_6July_10September2014.pdf

191 https://www.foreignaffairs.com/articles/syria/2017-06-08/isis-yazidi-genocide

of the surviving Yazidis to flee through Syria into the Kurdistan region of Iraq."[192] Despite these international efforts, a great number of Yazidis are still suffering to date.

ISIS has never attempted to shield its intentions to exterminate the religion and people they claim to be "infidels." In fact, they have been quite vocal about their philosophy and intentions, openly declaring in their English-language magazine, *Dabiq*, their "intent to destroy the 'pagan' Yazidi minority through killing, enslavement, and forced conversion."[193] But although their intentions have long been out in the open, the full extent of their genocidal violence remains obscured.[194]

Often, the publication of magazines or the release of videos on social sites is carried out by ISIS to attract new recruits and terrorize civilians. ISIS even operates its own websites and sends signals through the encrypted application Telegram to potential targets whom they deem vulnerable enough to be easily moulded by the jihadist mentality.[195] ISIS employs tactics of psychological warfare and the mass brainwashing of young boys with their version of jihad.

Despite ISIS' clear genocidal intent against the Yazidis, the world turned a blind eye to their genocide. The Convention on the Prevention and Punishment of the Crime of Genocide is widely supported by the majority of UN members, and states have a duty to protect innocent people from acts of genocide. Yet little was done to protect this vulnerable minority.

The August 3rd, 2014 attack of Sinjar did not receive substantial media coverage. Only after prolonged attacks and hardship did the plight of the Yazidi attract the attention of the international media. The situation in the region of Sinjar is still precarious, given the weak central government of Iraq with little no political voice in the Parliament of Iraq.

The incidents of ISIS brutality and the torments faced by the Yazidis have been recognized as crimes against humanity. Although ISIS has been largely defeated and has lost much of its territory, the Yazidis' scars from their persecution by the extremist forces are still strongly felt.

As ISIS' motive for the genocidal attack was based on deep-seated religious hatred, they employed cruel tactics in their quest to destroy the Yazidi people, including the enslavement of Yazidi women. ISIS knew well that impregnating Yazidi women would mean that the children produced

---

192 https://www.foreignaffairs.com/articles/syria/2017-06-08/isis-yazidi-genocide

193 https://www.foreignaffairs.com/articles/syria/2017-06-08/isis-yazidi-genocide

194 https://www.foreignaffairs.com/articles/syria/2017-06-08/isis-yazidi-genocide

195 Mia Bloom, Hicham Tiflati, and John Horgan, "Navigating ISIS's Preferred Platform: Telegram," Terrorism and Political Violence 31, no. 6 (2019): 1242–1254.

would not be welcomed home into the Yazidi community, as under Yazidi tradition only children born to Yazidi parents can be considered Yazidi.[196]

According to a 2018 report by the International Federation for Human Rights, "[m]ore than 6,800 Yazidis are said to have been held captive, 4,300 of whom have allegedly escaped or been bought back. 2,500 members of the community are still believed to be 'missing.'"[197] Per another estimate, approximately 6,700 females[198] were forced into domestic and sexual servitude across eastern Syria and western Iraq, while thousands of men and older women were executed.[199] As of November, 2017, it was estimated that almost 400,000 Yazidis remained displaced.[200] In the words of Muhammad al-Khuza'ee, spokesman for the Iraqi Red Cross, the abducted Yazidi women "were taken as spoils of war and exposed at a market for sale."[201]

Most of the torture has been inflicted in an attempt to force the female populace to convert to Islam. The violence acts as a war stratagem to overpower the entire community, to indoctrinate and perpetrate fear, to destabilize the family and community structures, and most significantly, to taint the purity of the bloodline of the insular community. Even after the claimed defeat of ISIS, still more than 3,430 women and children from the Yazidi community are being held captive, according to current figures.[202]

The women who resisted were killed, while some committed suicide.[203] Stories from victims have shown that girls and women were sold like cattle[204] at slave markets or on specialized websites through applications such as Telegram and Signal. "One online resale chat group called 'The Great

---

[196]   https://www.independent.co.uk/news/world/middle-east/yezidis-sinjar-massacre-rape-iraq-isis-fighters-children-a9037126.html

[197]   https://reliefweb.int/report/iraq/sexual-violence-against-yazidis-isil-foreign-fighters-should-be-prosecuted-genocide-and

[198]   https://www.nationalreview.com/2017/07/brave-ladys-fight-against-isis-vian-dakhil-yazidi-parliamentarian/

[199]   https://www.passblue.com/2017/08/01/building-a-case-for-prosecuting-the-gendered-genocide-of-yazidi-women/

[200]   https://blogs.lse.ac.uk/wps/2018/10/12/to-address-the-plight-of-yazidi-women-we-must-look-beyond-the-notion-of-wartime-sex-slaves/

[201]   https://www.nazandbegikhani.com/info/why-isis-s-treatment-of-yazidi-women-must-be-treated-as-genocide-630.html

[202]   https://www.visapourlimage.com/en/festival/exhibitions/le-corps-des-femmes-yezidies-comme-champ-de-bataille

[203]   https://www.nazandbegikhani.com/info/why-isis-s-treatment-of-yazidi-women-must-be-treated-as-genocide-630.html

[204]   https://www.cnn.com/2014/10/30/world/meast/isis-female-slaves/index.html

Mall of the Islamic State' had up to 754 members. Here, ISIL fighters could buy women or children, with detailed descriptions of their age or physical appearance, as well as weapons or cars."[205]

Yazidi women have been the target of the extremist mentality because of their vulnerability both on religious grounds and gender lines. The persecution of women has often been used as a weapon of war.

The International Criminal Tribunal for Rwanda (ICTR) was the international court established in November, 1994 by the United Nations Security Council in Resolution 955 in order to judge people responsible for the Rwandan genocide and other serious violations of international law in Rwanda. The ICTR convicted Jean-Paul Akayesu for using rape as form of genocide.[206] During his trial, the ICTR asserted that sexual violence, such as rape, fell under paragraph B of the Convention on the Prevention and Punishment of the Crime of Genocide, as the rapes had been perpetrated with the singular intention of destroying, partially or wholly, a particular group.

Despite many being reluctant to share their plights, various Yazidi women who managed to escape their horrendous incarceration by ISIS have spoken out on behalf of the unheard voices. Sharing a violent experience almost equals reliving it, but several brave women have come forward with their horrific stories. Solav, for example, is a 19-year-old Yazidi girl, who said:

> They put us in trucks and drove us to a big building, before transferring us to a hall across the road. Then their seniors came and started condemning our religion and asking us to convert to Islam[.] ... They separated me along with other young ones and ordered us to stay there while taking away the elderly women[.] ... The man I was given to raped me several times and then left me in the room on my own. I was shaking from pain and fear in that hot room, my entire body sweating. Suddenly, another man came and did what he wanted to do despite me crying and begging him, kissing his foot to leave me alone.[207]

Solav now lives with her relatives in a newly-established displaced persons camp in Iraq's Duhok region.[208] The scars of beating and physical torture

---

[205] https://reliefweb.int/report/iraq/sexual-violence-against-yazidis-isil-foreign-fighters-should-be-prosecuted-genocide-and

[206] De Brouwer, Anne-Marie, Supranational Criminal Prosecution of Sexual Violence: The ICC and the Practice of the ICTY and the ICTR, 2005.

[207] https://www.nazandbegikhani.com/info/why-isis-s-treatment-of-yazidi-women-must-be-treated-as-genocide-630.html

[208] https://www.nazandbegikhani.com/info/why-isis-s-treatment-of-yazidi-women-must-be-treated-as-genocide-630.html

may be fresh, but these women's valour in coping with them has brought them international attention.

A large number of children are also the victims of the violent coercive force of ISIS. The abduction of small boys has mainly been done with the goal of turning them into the next generation of terrorists, forcing them to convert and fight the jihadist cause. According to British charity worker Sally Becker, more than 1,700 children are still missing, and if targeted efforts are not carried out to rescue them, they will fall prey to trafficking for the slave and organ industry.[209]

Through killings, torture, degrading treatment, enslavement, and inhumane mental harm, ISIS has pursued a campaign to extinguish the Yazidis. This brutal crusade has resulted in a slow death of the Yazidi culture, achieved by several cruel tactics, including the conversion of Yazidi adults; the reduction of the Yazidi birth rate, accomplished by separating the women from the men and inflicting mental trauma; and the separation of Yazidi children from their families in order to raise them as ISIS soldiers.

The conduct of ISIS clearly reveals their intention to extinguish the Yazidis of Sinjar. With over 3,200 Yazidi women and children still being held by ISIS, along with the sexual enslavement of Yazidi women and the jihadist training and indoctrination of Yazidi boys in regions of Syria, it is clear that ISIS' intent is to destroy the basic identity of the Yazidi people and to erase Yazidi children's ties to their religion.

The August 2014 attack on Sinjar, home to the majority of the Yazidi population, was well organized. Hundreds of ISIS armed forces seized towns, and faced no major resistance from the defenceless population. U.S. President Barack Obama asked the American military to provide help to the trapped Yazidis, and there were airdrops of water and other necessary supplies by American, French, British forces. Planes for the airdropping were shot by ISIS fighters. On the ground level, thousands of Yazidis were captured on roads while they were attempting to flee. Besides the attack on Sinjar, other intentional mass killings of Yazidis took place in Syria, in the Kocho and Qani villages. These genocidal attacks and mass atrocities have done serious physical and psychological damage to the Yazidi people. The rapes and sexual violence have brought indescribable suffering to the victims and to their families.

ISIS still continues to commit genocide and war crimes against the Yazidis. The kind of genocide enacted against the Yazidis is annihilation accomplished not only by killing the community but also by seeking their

---

[209] https://www.theguardian.com/world/2018/sep/09/yazidis-isis-only-bones-remain-fear-returning-home

physical devastation. There have been various recommendations by the Commission to the United Nations and Government of Syria and Iraq for the protection and care for the Yazidi community.

Article I of the Genocide Convention lays out the responsibility to punish the crime of genocide. A systematic procedure to investigate the case for crimes against the Yazidis should be set up. There must be investigation and prosecution of ISIS members who are involved in these crimes. Immediate steps should be taken to protect the mass Yazidi grave sites in order to preserve the evidence of ISIS' crimes. Some amount of funding to support the social workers in Syria would be a great help. Taking steps to protect the existing Syrian Yazidi people and to preserve the historical record will help to provide the survivors with an opportunity to heal.

Due to the numerous conversions and sexual slavery and the malicious campaign to eradicate the Yazidi people and their culture, the Office of the United Nations High Commissioner for Human Rights in a March 2015 report has described the persecution of the Yazidis as genocide.

On August 13th, 2014, the United Nations declared the Yazidi crisis a highest-level "Level 3 Emergency,"[210] stating that the declaration would "facilitate mobilization of additional resources in goods, funds and assets to ensure a more effective response to the humanitarian needs of populations affected by forced displacements."[211]

Twenty-five-year-old Nadia Murad of the Sinjar district was the Nobel Peace Prize 2018 co-winner. According to *Foreign Policy*, she was "recognized for her efforts to end sexual violence as a weapon of war," and was "among the estimated 6,500 Yazidi women and girls abducted and sold into sexual slavery when the Islamic State attacked in 2014. She managed to escape and make her way to Germany, where she now lives as a refugee and runs Nadia's Initiative, an advocacy organization."[212]

In her interview with *Foreign Policy*, Murad said, "We suffered but didn't give up. We were not helped and rescued when ISIS attacked, but I hope this recognition means that the international community will help us recover from this genocide and will prevent such attacks against other communities like us in the future."[213] Murad pledged to give all of the

---

[210] UN Declares a 'Level 3 Emergency' for Iraq to Ensure More Effective Humanitarian Response." United Nations Iraq. 14 August 2014.

[211] UN Declares a 'Level 3 Emergency' for Iraq to Ensure More Effective Humanitarian Response." United Nations Iraq. 14 August 2014.

[212] https://foreignpolicy.com/2018/11/23/isis-may-be-gone-but-iraqs-yazidis-are-still-suffering-sinjar-ezidxan-pmu-nadia-murad/

[213] https://foreignpolicy.com/2018/11/23/isis-may-be-gone-but-iraqs-yazidis-are-still-suffering-sinjar-ezidxan-pmu-nadia-murad/

prize money to her organization, which provides aid for women and other minorities in Iraq.[214] She hopes that the award "will convince the Iraqi government as well as other countries to form a special task force to rescue the estimated 3,000 remaining Yazidi women and girls still held captive," as her organization fears the Yazidis could be completely exterminated from the region if real steps are not taken to help the community recover.[215]

Women will continue to be at risk as long as they are deprived of full access to education and political power. Forgetting, ignoring, or moving on is not a luxury afforded to the Yazidis—Yazidi women in particular.

In the words of Gayle Tzemach Lemmon, the Yazidis today "confront grief over the missing members of their community, a lack of mental health services for those returning after the trauma of enslavement, mass displacement as homes remain out of reach, and a shortage of economic opportunities which exacerbates all the other ills."[216] Many seeking asylum are denied access, and many still face detention after the defeat of ISIS. The contemporary situation of Yazidis seeking refuge across the globe merits examination.

Ignoring or not providing a proper response to the plea of those being persecuted worsens their suffering. With the breach of all humanitarian ideals by ISIS in the case of the Yazidis, it has become imperative for national and international organizations to take consolidatory steps toward helping the Yazidis emerge from their perilous situation.

The most important way to help the Yazidis is to recognize the crimes directed towards them as crimes against humanity, and to identify these crimes under international law. Genocide is a crime against humanity, and the nature of the massacre carried out by ISIS was nothing less than a genocide. The UN Independent International Commission of Inquiry determined that ISIS' violence against the Yazidis indeed constitutes a case of genocide, as defined by the 1948 Convention on the Prevention and Punishment of the Crime of Genocide as "acts committed with intent to destroy, in whole or in part, a national, ethnical, racial or religious group."[217]

Defining the horrific incidents of violence and massacre of the Yazidis as genocide was further accomplished by the findings of the investigation

214 https://thehill.com/blogs/blog-briefing-room/410892-nobel-peace-prize-winner-pledges-to-give-away-entire-award-to-sex

215 https://foreignpolicy.com/2018/11/23/isis-may-be-gone-but-iraqs-yazidis-are-still-suffering-sinjar-ezidxan-pmu-nadia-murad/

216 https://www.cnn.com/2018/07/31/opinions/pence-yazidi-survivors-need-support-lemmon-opinion/index.html

217 https://www.fidh.org/en/region/north-africa-middle-east/iraq/sexual-violence-against-yazidis-isil-foreign-fighters-should-be

led by the UN team that proved several cases of violation of humanitarian ideals, especially towards the Yazidi women who faced the brunt of ISIS' extremist ideology. The UN Security Council adopted a resolution in September 2017 to bring those responsible for ISIS war crimes to justice. The need to bring the perpetrators under the jurisdiction of international law was accelerated when the case was championed by Nobel Peace Prize winner Nadia Murad and international human rights lawyer Amal Clooney.

Due to the efforts of the United States, a team led by British lawyer Karim Asad Ahmad Khan was employed to Baghdad in October. But due to government technicalities, the team is still struggling to facilitate a full-fledged investigation. The Iraqi government resisted calls for the UN probe, and the head of the investigative team stated that significant effort had been exerted to ensure Baghdad's cooperation. Ahmad Khan stated to the council that "the realisation of our investigative activities is dependent on securing the cooperation, support and trust of all elements of Iraqi society."[218]

On September 21st, 2017, as part of the goal to counter terrorism, the UN Security Council adopted Resolution 2379, authorizing "the creation of an independent team to investigate crimes committed by ISIL in Iraq[.]" This team was "designed to investigate and preserve evidence relating to genocide, war crimes, and crimes against humanity ... to aid in bringing charges against those responsible for such atrocities."[219]

According to the resolution passed by the United Nations, the authorized investigators in the matter of the Yazidi genocide would collect evidence on war crimes, genocide, or crimes against humanity, so that the evidence could aid in charging the ISIS militants in the trials to be held in Iraqi courts. To date, the investigation team has discovered more than 200 mass graves encompassing up to 12,000 bodies in Iraq that could act as sufficient proof for the Yazidi genocide. The United States has allocated US$2 million to support the work of the investigative team, known as the United Nations Investigative Team to Promote Accountability for Crimes Committed by Islamic State in Iraq and the Levant (UNITAD), in investigating and promoting accountability for crimes committed by Daesh, an Arabic acronym for ISIS.[220]

As confirmed in recent UN Security Council Resolution 2379, ISIS has perpetrated crimes including:

---

[218] https://www.france24.com/en/20181204-un-team-begin-probe-crimes-iraq-early-2019

[219] https://ecr2p.leeds.ac.uk/r2p-in-brief/iraq/

[220] https://www.straitstimes.com/world/united-states/un-team-to-begin-probe-of-isis-crimes-in-iraq-in-early-2019

murder, kidnapping, hostage-taking, suicide bombings, enslavement, sale into or otherwise forced marriage, trafficking in persons, rape, sexual slavery and other forms of sexual violence, recruitment and use of children, attacks on critical infrastructure, as well as its destruction of cultural heritage, including archaeological sites, and trafficking of cultural property.[221]

Despite the Islamic State's loss of captured territory, the Yazidis are still living a perilous existence. The contemporary reality of the Yazidis presents a bleak picture of desperation, displacement, vulnerability, and instability.

The war with ISIS displaced almost 6 million Iraqis, or 15% of the population. By September 2018, the number of displaced persons had dropped to 1.9 million, the lowest level since November 2014. Four million Iraqis have now returned home—but not the people of Sinjar. Rania Abouzeid explains:

> Key challenges for post-conflict stabilisation in Sinjar's towns and villages persist in rebuilding communities (and the idea of community); providing security and basic services; addressing public grievances; seeking accountability and justice; fostering local reconciliation; and helping people return home, to live in peace, dignity, and safety with their neighbours (as well as with their emotional and physical scars). ... Failure to address the challenges will likely result in continued instability, social unease, villages that remain empty and derelict, permanent camps for the displaced, and rising migration. ... The Mines Advisory Group, a British de-mining non-governmental organisation (NGO), has been working in Sinjar city and areas north of the mountain for more than three years. It describes the contamination there as 'extensive.'[222]

The Yazidis are being pressured to return to their town of origin with claims of the defeat of ISIS in the region. But for the Yazidis, who are still haunted by the trauma of the past atrocities at the hand of ISIS and because of the neglect of the central government of Iraq, a return to Sinjar is not the solution to their problems. Iraq's government has said it needs "$88 billion to rebuild after the war on ISIS. An international donor conference in February in Kuwait only managed to secure $30 billion in pledges. Germany promised €500m and the European Union €400m."[223]

---

[221] https://www.forbes.com/sites/ewelinaochab/2018/05/26/we-can-do-more-to-help-yazidis-and-other-victims-and-survivors-of-religious-persecutions/

[222] https://www.ecfr.eu/publications/summary/when_the_weapons_fall_silent_reconciliation_in_sinjar_after_isis

[223] https://www.ecfr.eu/publications/summary/when_the_weapons_fall_silent_reconciliation_in_sinjar_after_isis

According to the State Department:

> the United States announced in October that it was giving more than $178 million to support vulnerable communities in Iraq, specifically focusing on religious minorities, bringing the total amount of U.S. assistance for vulnerable communities to nearly $300 million since the 2017 fiscal year. But despite such shows of support, reconstruction in Sinjar is sluggish and a deeply skeptical Yazidi community is still too terrified to return, nervous that they'll be targeted again.[224]

UN Women reported that on August 1st, 2018:

> ahead of the fourth anniversary of the ISIS attack on the Yazidi community in Sinjar, UN Women Executive Director Phumzile Mlambo Ngcuka, UN Special Representative of the Secretary-General on Sexual Violence in Conflict Pramila Patten, and Free Yezidi Foundation Executive Director Pari Ibrahim participated in a panel discussion to mark and remember the genocide victims.[225]

During the discussion, Ngcuka stated:

> We must invest in empowering civil society, especially women's organizations working at the front line of the response to the needs of women and girl refugees and IDPs, whose efforts could otherwise go unnoticed. The UN Trust Fund is doing this successfully and the Free Yezidi Foundation is a testimony to it, but we need strong and wider partnerships on board.[226]

The Free Yezidi Foundation is a grantee of the UN Trust Fund to End Violence against Women. The organization supports female Yazidi survivors in the Kurdistan Region of Iraq, by operating a women's centre providing "trauma therapy and counselling, along with language classes and other empowerment interventions."[227]

The suffering of the Yazidi women drew the attention of international organizations to the community at large. The humanitarian aid provided by

---

[224] https://foreignpolicy.com/2018/11/23/isis-may-be-gone-but-iraqs-yazidis-are-still-suffering-sinjar-ezidxan-pmu-nadia-murad/

[225] https://untf.unwomen.org/en/news-and-events/stories/2018/08/event-yazidi-genocide-remembrance

[226] https://untf.unwomen.org/en/news-and-events/stories/2018/08/event-yazidi-genocide-remembrance

[227] http://www.unwomen.org/en/news/stories/2018/8/news-event-yazidi-genocide-remembrance

international communities, especially the UN, acted as the stepping stone in the journey of improvement, inclusion, aid, and human rights for the Yazidi community. In order to achieve the global goals of peace and security, we must respect the rights and security of all people, especially those from marginalized and vulnerable communities living a perilous existence.

The vulnerability of the Yazidis must be kept in mind by the countries who, in the wake of the defeat of ISIS, are denying asylum to Yazidi refugees. To date, the Yazidis fear for their lives in returning to Iraq. The right to asylum must keep in mind the vulnerability of the community and respect their right to exist.

According to Sareta Ashraph and Makrina Finlay:

> [f]or the 1951 Refugee Convention, the notion of a well-founded fear of 'persecution' is the touchstone for protection. Article 1 of the Genocide Convention sets out the duty to 'prevent and punish' genocide, but whereas the content of the duty to punish is further fleshed out, the duty to 'prevent' is left hanging as a vague promise. ... The debates and resolutions that unfolded over the next decades centred around the notion of the 'responsibility to protect' (R2P). While the question as to the upper-limits of responsibility hovered on the controversial question of humanitarian intervention, less attention was given to the role of asylum protection as a means for preventing genocide, and protecting its victims.[228]

Though many nations across the globe, including the United States, have acknowledged the atrocities committed by ISIS against the Yazidis as genocide, some nations are yet to do so. According to Ahmed Khudida Burjus of Yazda, an organization which supports victims of the Yazidi massacre, "many countries, UN and international organisations have recognised the genocide, [but] EU countries are refusing the asylum applications of so many Yazidis."[229] Both the U.S. Holocaust Memorial Museum and the Commission of Inquiry on Syria "determined that ISIS was committing genocide, as well as crimes against humanity and war crimes, in its multi-pronged attack on Yazidi women, children, and men."[230]

The combined efforts of both the 1951 Refugee Convention and 1948 Genocide Convention, with their strengthening effect on asylum law, present

---

[228] http://opiniojuris.org/2018/08/15/asylum-and-the-duty-to-protect-the-yazidis-from-genocide/

[229] https://www.aljazeera.com/indepth/features/yazidis-seek-church-asylum-europe-empathy-refugees-wanes-180828221815711.html

[230] http://opiniojuris.org/2018/08/15/asylum-and-the-duty-to-protect-the-yazidis-from-genocide/

the need to categorize the Yazidis as a "vulnerable group" in dire need of an increase in the degree of protection given to them, in order to safeguard the rights of this ancient religion for the sake of their existence and to protect them from intersectional layers of discrimination. Despite these efforts, many Yazidis at present are facing detentions and being denied asylum rights.

In 2014, out of the several nations, Germany was most active in providing humanitarian aid to Yazidi refugees. Many important members of the Yazidi community—including the late Mir Tahseen Said Beg, who died recently, and Nadia Murad, the co-winner of Nobel Peace Prize in 2018—took refuge in Germany. The acceptance rate for Yazidis claiming asylum in Germany is currently around 83%, but this is a large drop from the 97.4% of Yazidi asylum requests granted by the country in 2015.[231] The denial of asylum by the German authorities is based on European Union regulations, which state that asylum-seekers are required to remain in the first safe E.U. country that they are fingerprinted in.

Out of humanitarian concern, several church authorities in Germany admitted numerous Yazidis to their convents, and have been overwhelmed by the requests for refuge. In 2017, German churches successfully stopped some 1,478 planned deportations, and in the first three months of 2018, they stopped or delayed more than 500 cases.[232] In an interview with Al Jazeera, Sister Stephanie, a German nun, said, "We'll protect them because it's clear that these people are refugees who have been through everything. We would take hundreds if we had hundreds of beds."[233] Al Jazeera further explains:

> In 2015, an agreement rooted in tradition was signed between the church and the German Federal Office for Migration and Refugees. Under the deal, the state must tolerate church asylum while notices of deportation are reconsidered. Churches, in turn, have to notify the authorities about each case they take on. The practice of seeking sanctuary in a church is a centuries-old tradition across Europe and was written into medieval canon and common law in England between the 12th and 16th centuries. In Greek and Roman societies, temples could also harbour those in fear for their lives.[234]

---

[231] https://www.aljazeera.com/indepth/features/yazidis-seek-church-asylum-europe-empathy-refugees-wanes-180828221815711.html

[232] https://www.aljazeera.com/indepth/features/yazidis-seek-church-asylum-europe-empathy-refugees-wanes-180828221815711.html, and https://www.dw.com/en/german-churches-preventing-deportations/a-43932284

[233] https://www.aljazeera.com/indepth/features/yazidis-seek-church-asylum-europe-empathy-refugees-wanes-180828221815711.html

[234] https://www.aljazeera.com/indepth/features/yazidis-seek-church-asylum-europe-empathy-refugees-wanes-180828221815711.html

In the United Kingdom, the Yazidis are identified as Iraqis in the asylum process, and no separate or special identity is bestowed upon them to distinguish and acknowledge their sufferings at large. According to Ashraph and Finlay:

> [d]urable solutions must ensure the integrity of the people at risk. Individuals need to be accepted and protected as a community, and the notion of a safe and sustainable return to the country of origin needs to take into consideration the extent to which the 'return' allows the 'population' to maintain their identity as a group. A forced return to an IDP camp in a different geographic area might be consistent with the 'safe' return of the individual, but not the sustainable return of the protected population, and the protection of a people 'as such.'[235]

It important to recognize the various NGOs and faith groups who are working on the plight of the Yazidi refugees. It is up to international community to do all it can to safeguard the peace and security for their ancestral home.

Christian Persecution

The twenty-first century has seen the pervasive persecution of Christians in predominately Muslim states, and in the case of ISIS this persecution has risen to the level of genocide. In many parts of the Middle East, there has been an exodus of Christians over the past two decades, according to a 2019 report commissioned by British Foreign Secretary Jeremy Hunt. As *The Guardian* explains, "[m]illions of Christians in the region have been uprooted from their homes, and many have been killed, kidnapped, imprisoned and discriminated."[236] Hunt's report states that "the inconvenient truth" is that "the overwhelming majority (80%) of persecuted religious believers are Christians."[237]

Recent attacks on churches in Pakistan, where eighty-five people died when two suicide bombers rushed the Anglican All Saints Church in Peshawar in 2013,[238] and in Kenya, where an assault on a Catholic church in Wajir left one dead and two injured, have horrified us all.

The Spectator points out:

---

[235] http://opiniojuris.org/2018/08/15/asylum-and-the-duty-to-protect-the-yazidis-from-genocide/

[236] https://www.theguardian.com/world/2019/may/02/persecution-driving-christians-out-of-middle-east-report

[237] Ibid.

[238] https://www.theguardian.com/world/2013/sep/23/pakistan-church-bombings-christian-minority

According to the International Society for Human Rights, a secular observatory based in Frankfurt, Germany, 80% of all acts of religious discrimination in the world today are directed at Christians. Statistically speaking, that makes Christians by far the most persecuted religious body on the planet.[239]

Between 2006 and 2010, Christians faced discrimination—either in *de jure* or *de facto* form—in 139 nations.[240] In addition, approximately 100,000 Christians have been killed every year for the past ten years, in what the Center for the Study of Global Christianity at Gordon-Conwell Theological Seminary in Massachusetts calls a "situation of witness."[241] This can only be described as a slow genocide in places such as Iraq and Pakistan.[242] On October 31st, 2010, Islamic militants stormed the Syriac Catholic cathedral of Our Lady of Salvation in Baghdad, killing a total of fifty-eight people, including the two priests celebrating Mass.[243] Most of the casualties were believed to have resulted when the gunmen detonated two suicide vests after Iraqi commandos blew off the doors and stormed the building. The Iraqi television station received a call from the Islamic State of Iraq, claiming responsibility for the attack and demanding the release of prisoners in Iraq and Egypt.[244]

Since the beginning of the 2003 U.S.-led invasion of Iraq, over sixty-five Christian churches have been bombed and attacked. Before the invasion, Iraq boasted a flourishing Christian population of at least 1.5 million. However, today the number of Christians is estimated at less than 400,000.[245]

Testifying before the United States House Foreign Affairs Committee in May 2015, Sister Diana Momeka of the Dominican Sisters of St. Catherine of Sienna from Mosul, Iraq, said the following:

> There are many who say, 'Why don't the Christians just leave Iraq and move to another country and be done with it?' To this question we would

---

[239] https://www.spectator.co.uk/2013/10/the-war-on-christians/

[240] Ibid.

[241] Ibid.

[242] https://www.foxnews.com/world/nearly-1-million-christians-reportedly-martyred-for-their-faith-in-last-decade

[243] https://www.spectator.co.uk/2013/10/the-war-on-christians/, and https://www.csmonitor.com/World/Middle-East/2010/1101/After-Baghdad-church-attack-Christians-shocked-but-say-we-still-have-a-mission-here

[244] https://www.csmonitor.com/World/Middle-East/2010/1101/After-Baghdad-church-attack-Christians-shocked-but-say-we-still-have-a-mission-here

[245] https://www.state.gov/wp-content/uploads/2019/05/IRAQ-2018-INTER-NATIONAL-RELIGIOUS-FREEDOM-REPORT.pdf

respond, 'Why should we leave our country—what have we done?' The Christians of Iraq are the first people of the land. You read about us in the Old Testament of the Bible. Christianity came to Iraq from the very earliest days through the preaching and witness of St. Thomas and others of the Apostles and Church Elders. While our ancestors experienced all kinds of persecution, they stayed in their land, building a culture that has served humanity for the ages. We, as Christians, do not want or deserve to leave or be forced out of our country any more than you would want to leave or be forced out of yours. But the current persecution our community is facing is the most brutal in our history.[246]

The most limited yet most severe form of repression of Christians in Muslim-majority countries is active persecution perpetrated by government and terrorist groups. This is most clearly evidenced by the actions of ISIS against religious minorities in Iraq and Syria. But in many Muslim countries, apostasy is also punishable by death. There are many Christian converts who have been incarcerated in jails from Afghanistan to Pakistan for professing their Christian faith.

One recent report claims that after 2,000 years of continued existence, Christianity could be nearly eradicated from large swathes of the Middle East in the next five years.[247]

A 2013 Pew research report notes that 77% of the world at the time was experiencing some form of religious discrimination. The Pew report is subdivided into two categories: (1) Government Restrictions on Religion, and (2) Social Hostilities Due to Religion. Actions are then ranked according to the classifications Very High, High, Moderate, and Low. The report notes of the two most restrictive categories, Very High and High:

- 70%, or thirty-one out of forty-four Muslim majority countries have Very High or High government restrictions on religion.
- 48%, or twenty-one out of forty-four Muslim majority countries have Very High or High social hostilities due to religion.
- After accounting for overlap between the two categories, 81%, or thirty-six of the forty-four Muslim majority countries, currently maintain either significant social hostilities or government restrictions on religion. Of all groups, the Christian community is the most significantly impacted religious minority community as it is the second largest religious grouping in thirty-one of these thirty-six countries.[248]

---

[246] https://docs.house.gov/meetings/FA/FA00/20150513/103454/HHRG-114-FA00-Wstate-MomekaS-20150513.pdf

[247] Ibid.

[248] Elijah M. Brown, "Persecution of Christians in Muslim-Majority Countries," *Journal of Ecumenical Studies* 51, no. 2 (2016).

These restrictions can be seen in numerous "inhibiting laws, policies, and structural practices,"[249] such as:

- Lack of constitutional protection for freedom of religion and sometimes constitutional wording actively restricting freedom of religion
- Interference during religious worship
- Limitations or prohibitions on public preaching
- Limitations or prohibitions on evangelism
- Limitations or prohibitions on conversion
- Limitations on the publication and distribution of religious literature
- Exclusion of foreign missionaries
- Harassment and intimidation of those who adhere to Christianity
- Different court systems, limited access to the court system, and failure by the government to prosecute individuals who commit crimes against Christians
- Denunciation by the government as a "sect" or "cult"
- Different set of tax obligations from the Muslim majority
- Physical abuse, imprisonment, displacement from homes
- Lack of access to employment in certain sectors
- Attending schools where all individuals are required to participate in education related to Islam
- Mob violence
- Honor killings
- Restrictions on marital choices[250]

Blasphemy laws, such as those in Pakistan, "are another example of structural discrimination with the potential to flare into active persecution," according to Elijah M. Brown.[251] Section 295-C of the 1986 Pakistan Penal Code states that any person who makes "derogatory remarks" with regard to the Holy Prophet, whether "spoken or written … directly or indirectly" shall be punished "with death, or imprisonment for life, and shall also be liable to fine."[252] This law has been used as a tool to arrest and silence Christians accused of speaking against the Prophet Muhammad. Also, Section 298 of the Penal code states:

Whoever, with the deliberate intention of wounding the religious feelings of any person, utters any word or makes any sound in the hearing of

---

[249]   Ibid.

[250]   Ibid.

[251]   Ibid.

[252]   https://www.oecd.org/site/adboecdanti-corruptioninitiative/46816797.pdf

that person or makes any gesture in the sight of that person or places any object in the sight of that person, shall be punished with imprisonment of either description for a term which may extend to one year or with fine, or with both.[253]

Blasphemy laws are found all over the world, but most numerously in Muslim-majority countries. In Pakistan, these laws are often used to suppress the rights of religious minorities. Perhaps the most egregious abuse of blasphemy laws occurred in 2014 in Pakistan with the case of Asia Bibi, who languished on death row for six years after a questionable application of the blasphemy law. Although she was eventually released from prison, she was kept under armed guard at her home and was unable to leave the country until May 7th, 2019, when she departed for Canada.[254]

According to Brown:

Additional examples of ways in which constitutions, laws, policies, and practices leave Christians and other religious minorities in an insecure situation include:

- Repression related to clothing, such as when in July and August 2015, fifteen Christian women were arrested in Khartoum, Sudan for wearing trousers and skirts, which was deemed to be "immoral" because it did not conform to Sharia law.[25]
- Confiscation of personal property such as a recent report noting that, since 2003, seventy percent of the homes that belonged to Christians in Baghdad have been illegally confiscated and resold by members of the government.[26]
- Economic limitations such as in Kurdistan in northern Iraq, where Catholic nuns have reported difficulty accessing their bank accounts and withdrawing money for failure to be accompanied by a male.[255]

Brown continues:

In 2013 the Pew Research Center surveyed individuals in twenty-three countries related to Muslim perspectives on religion, politics, and society, and found in part:

- On average, sixty-four percent of the population of Muslim majority countries favor enshrining Sharia as the law of the land.

---

[253] Ibid.

[254] https://www.khaleejtimes.com/international/pakistan/aasia-bibi-breaks-silence-on-death-row-ordeal

[255] Brown, "Persecution of Christians in Muslim-Majority Countries."

- In Muslim majority countries, forty-three percent believe that Sharia should apply to all citizens of the country, even non-Muslims.
- In the thirteen Muslim-majority countries included in this particular survey, on average forty-seven percent of the population indicated support for the death penalty for those who convert from Islam.[256]

Sociologist Rodney Stark argues that irrespective of the religion, religious monopolies like the ones that exist in Muslim-majority countries create societies where religious freedom is curtailed and religious minorities suffer negative impacts. Religious monopolies also lead to more public corruption.[257]

Huma Haider explains that "[t]he tremendous changes in the political order in the Middle East since 2003, and the rise of violent extremist ideologies, have adversely impacted on Muslim-Christian relations."[258] Christians throughout the Middle East experience various forms of persecution and discrimination, including violence and harassment and targeted attacks.

In Egypt, tensions between Muslims and Christians are not new, but the situation deteriorated during the uprising against the Mubarak regime and the rise to power of the Muslim Brotherhood, who led large-scale targeted, sectarian attacks against the Copts.

The Copts, the largest Christian community in the Middle East, face "numerous forms of quotidian discrimination" and have been traditionally barred from positions of leadership.[259] The Carnegie Endowment of International Peace report notes that:

> [e]veryday forms of prejudice no doubt contribute to a climate of insecurity. ... [W]hen Copts want to construct or renovate their places of worship, an essential practice for freedom of belief and religious equality, they face a political minefield rather than a simple administrative process. ... [T]he broader phenomenon of anti-Coptic discrimination in everyday affairs ... weigh[s] heavily on current discussions of a 'road map' to a stronger and more egalitarian Egypt.[260]

Egyptian officials, lacking the political resolve to defend citizens' legal rights,[261] have added to the sense of Coptic insecurity.

---

256 Ibid.

257 Ibid.

258 Huma Haider, "The Persecution of Christians in the Middle East," https://opendocs.ids.ac.uk/opendocs/handle/20.500.12413/13055.

259 https://carnegieendowment.org/files/violence_against_copts3.pdf

260 https://carnegieendowment.org/files/violence_against_copts3.pdf

261 https://carnegieendowment.org/files/violence_against_copts3.pdf

In 2015, ISIS attacked thirty-five Assyrian Christian villages in the north-eastern Al-Hasakah governorate. They kidnapped 253 Assyrian Christians, including many women and children, and destroyed eleven churches. These attacks led to the migration of the remaining villagers,[262] and few Assyrian Christians have returned.

In Saudi Arabia, the small Christian population is constantly harassed, and their inequality under the law is clear:

> [P]enalties for crimes against Muslims are much harsher than for those committed against non-Muslims. ... [T]here are limitations on all forms of expression of the Christian religion, including a complete ban on public display of crosses and other Christian symbols and on public acts of worship by non-Muslims. There are reports of frequent crackdowns on private Christian services. ... Government-provided school textbooks have been found to continue to teach hatred and intolerance toward non-Muslims, including references to anti-Christian and anti-Jewish bigotry.[263]

In Iran, proselytizing—"the act of attempting to convert someone from one religion, belief, or opinion to another"[264]—is punishable by death. Similarly, apostasy—"the abandonment or renunciation of a religious or political belief"[265]—is also punishable by death, not just in Iran but in many Muslim countries. To date, there are many Christians in prison for converting from Islam to Christianity.

In Iran, there are widespread raids on the private homes of Christians, and detentions and arbitrary arrests of Christians. The Christian population, which comprised 0.9% of the country's population in 1970, has been reduced to 0.35% today.[266] Given the many human rights violations faced by Christians in the region, many have sought to leave. According to Haider, "The drastic decline in the number of Christians in the Middle East is considered to be part of a longer-term exodus related to general violence in various countries, lack of economic opportunities in the region, and religious persecution."[267] Haider goes on to explain that:

---

262 https://assets.publishing.service.gov.uk/media/59786a0040f0b65dcb00000a/042-Persecution-of-Christians-in-the-Middle-East.pdf

263 https://assets.publishing.service.gov.uk/media/59786a0040f0b65dcb00000a/042-Persecution-of-Christians-in-the-Middle-East.pdf

264 https://www.lexico.com/en/definition/proselytizing

265 https://www.lexico.com/en/definition/apostasy

266 https://assets.publishing.service.gov.uk/media/59786a0040f0b65dcb00000a/042-Persecution-of-Christians-in-the-Middle-East.pdf

267 https://assets.publishing.service.gov.uk/media/59786a0040f0b65dcb00000a/042-Persecution-of-Christians-in-the-Middle-East.pdf

[i]n March 2016, then U.S. Secretary of State, John Kerry, officially recognized that ISIS' atrocities against Christians, Yazidis, Shi'a Muslims, and other religious minorities in areas under its control amount[ed] to genocide, crimes against humanity, and ethnic cleansing. This recognition was supported in resolutions of the U.S. House of Representatives and Senate. The UK Parliament also subsequently acknowledged ISIS' genocide against Christians. The U.S. Commission on International Religious Freedom (USCIRF) made a finding of genocide in December 2015. A report by the Knights of Columbus, which also documented the Darfur genocide, gathered information from several hundred of the Nineveh Christian survivors in Kurdistan in March 2016. It concludes that ISIS is committing genocide against Christians and other religious groups in Syria, Iraq and Libya.[268]

In Burma, people belonging to the strongly-Christian Chin and Karen ethnic groups are considered dissidents by the regime and are frequently imprisoned, tortured, murdered, and made to endure forced labour. Thousands of Burmese Christians are believed to have been killed in government-led military offensive strikes.[269]

In Nigeria, the militant Islamic movement Boko Haram is held responsible for almost 6,700 deaths since 2014, including 800 fatalities last year alone.[270] The movement doggedly targets Christians and their churches. In some cases, Boko Haram seems set on driving Christians out of certain regions of Nigeria.[271]

In North Korea, approximately 25% of the country's 200,000 to 400,000 Christians are "believed to be living in forced labour camps for their refusal to join the national cult around founder Kim Il Sung."[272]

Following the civil war that ended in Sri Lanka in 2009, the minority Christians, Hindus, and Muslims have suffered attacks by Sinhalese Buddhist nationalists. On Easter Sunday, April 21st, 2019, three churches in Sri Lanka were targeted in a series of coordinated terrorist suicide bombings. The Islamic State claimed responsibility for the attacks that

---

[268] https://assets.publishing.service.gov.uk/media/59786a0040f0b65dcb0000 0a/042-Persecution-of-Christians-in-the-Middle-East.pdf

[269] John L. Allen, *The Global War on Christians: Dispatches from the Front Lines of Anti-Christian Persecution* (Crown Publishing Group: 2013), 5, **or** https://www.spectator.co.uk/2013/10/the-war-on-christians/

[270] http://visionofhumanity.org/app/uploads/2017/11/Global-Terrorism-Index-2017.pdf http://visionofhumanity.org/app/uploads/2017/11/Global-Terrorism-Index-2017.pdf)

[271] https://www.spectator.co.uk/2013/10/the-war-on-christians/

[272] https://www.spectator.co.uk/2013/10/the-war-on-christians/

killed 258 people and injured around 500.[273] According to Angelus News, "Cardinal Malcolm Ranjith of Colombo alleged that the government could have done more to prevent the bombings, and told ACN that 'five training camps for jihadists have been found.'"[274]

Freedom of religion is a basic human right as expressed in the Universal Declaration of Human Rights, the International Covenant on Civil and Political Rights (ICCPR) Article 18, and the Declaration on the Elimination of All Forms of Intolerance and of Discrimination Based on Religion or Belief. Article 18 of ICCPR states that:

> Art. 18 (1): "Everyone shall have the right to freedom of thought, conscience and religion. This right shall include freedom [...] either individually or in community with others and in public or private, to manifest his religion or belief in worship, observance, practice and teaching."
> Art. 18 (3): "Freedom to manifest one's religion or beliefs may be subject only to such limitations as are prescribed by law and are necessary to protect public safety, order, health, or morals or the fundamental rights and freedoms of others."[275]

Religious freedom remains the most problematic of all human rights, and customary international law is therefore vital in protecting religious liberties given today's hostility towards religious freedom.

2011–Present: Syrian Civil War

The Syrian Civil War is an ongoing, multi-sided, armed conflict between the Ba'athist Syrian Arab Republic, led by President Bashar al-Assad, and other domestic and foreign terrorist forces who oppose both the Syrian government as well as each other. The complexity of the scenario makes the bringing of peace to Syria an intractable task for the international community.

The conflict began on March 15th, 2011, with widespread protests in Damascus and Aleppo calling for democratic reforms.[276] When war broke out, there were four main fighting groups: "Kurdish forces, ISIS, other opposition (such as Jaish al Fateh, an alliance between the Nusra Front and

---

273   https://angelusnews.com/news/world/south-and-east-asia-now-the-hotbed-of-christian-persecution-report-finds/

274   https://angelusnews.com/news/world/south-and-east-asia-now-the-hotbed-of-christian-persecution-report-finds/

275   https://www.ohchr.org/EN/Issues/FreedomReligion/Pages/IStandardsI3.aspx

276   https://www.bbc.com/news/world-middle-east-12749674

Ahrar-al-Sham) and the Assad regime."[277] As ISIS began losing control of its territory, more complex in-fighting between the groups began.[278]

All sides of the conflict (including the Ba'athist Syrian government, ISIS, opposition rebel groups, Russia, and the U.S.-led coalition) have been accused by international organizations of major human rights violations and massacres. The conflict has also led to a large-scale refugee crisis.[279]

Among the Middle East nations, the power struggle is no new fact, but the humanitarian crisis engulfing Syria calls for urgent intervention. Syria has been engaged in civil war since 2011 with horrific loss of life and ongoing persecution that has led to the massacre of thousands of people.

According to a report by FREE-Syria:

[i]n March 2011, encouraged in part by Arab Spring movements in other countries, many Syrians took to the streets in peaceful demonstrations to demand that the regime of Bashar al-Assad implement long-promised social, political, and economic reforms be implemented. In response to peaceful demonstrations, the regime's security forces fired live ammunition on protesters, setting off a cycle of demonstrations and violence. Since 2011, the Assad regime has systematically increased the level and types of violence against Syrian civilians.[280]

The Arab Spring movement was not limited to Syria—its revolutionary energy led to popular uprisings throughout the Middle East and North Africa that toppled the authoritarian regimes of Tunisia, Libya, Egypt, and Yemen.

The non-violent demonstrations in Syria were a reaction against the detainment and torture of fifteen boys who had written graffiti in support of the Arab Spring. The protest took a stronger turn when Hamza al-Khateeb, a thirteen-year-old boy, was brutally tortured to death by government security forces.[281] The hopes of the Syrian population to translate their demands for socioeconomic and political reforms into a thriving reality were shattered by President Assad's violent retaliation to their peaceful protests. The Arab Spring protest marks the beginning of the ongoing civil war which has resulted in large-scale killing until today.

Bashar al-Assad succeeded his father, Hafez al-Assad, who ruled Syria from 1970 to 2000. Since 2000, Bashar has been the head of Syria, exercising

---

277 https://www.cnn.com/2013/08/27/world/meast/syria-civil-war-fast-facts/index.html

278 https://www.cnn.com/2013/08/27/world/meast/syria-civil-war-fast-facts/index.html

279 https://www.objectiveias.in/regional-and-global-implications-of-syrian-conflict/

280 https://www.ushmm.org/m/pdfs/FREE-Syria_Survey_Report_030818.pdf

281 https://www.aljazeera.com/indepth/features/2011/05/201153185927813389.html

an authoritarian style of power.[282] The escalating violence in Syria, and the various protests taking place, paved way for the formation of several rebel groups who aimed to overthrow the government, thus bringing about a civil war. The main rebel group, the Free Syrian Army, was formed in July 2011 by the defectors from the military. According to FREE-Syria, "In 2013, the growing militarization of the opposition and emergence of several radical armed groups had changed the dynamics of the original struggle for freedom and democracy for all Syrians."[283] The escalating violence spread into neighbouring Iraq, feeding the growth of militant groups such as ISIS. Rebel groups began seizing Syrian territory, and the government lost control of everything but a small strip of land in western Syria.

A year after the onset of the war, the civilian death toll in Syria had risen to about 40,000.[284] By five years in, an estimated 400,000 Syrians had been killed in the conflict, as reported by the UN Envoy for Syria. According to the UN High Commissioner for Refugees, roughly 5.7 million Syrians had fled the country as of March 2019, and over 6.1 million people had been displaced internally.[285] By mid-2014, some 250,000 civilians were being held "in regime jails as prisoners of conscience, most of them without access to the outside world, let alone access to due process or legal representation," and over half of Syria's pre-war population of 22 million had been "displaced internally or as refugees abroad."[286]

The beginning of the twenty-first century heralded misfortune for the Syrian people. According to World Without Genocide:

> [i]n 2006, Syria experienced its worst drought on record. Herders in the northeast of the country lost 85% of their livestock and 75% of farmers experienced total crop loss. One expert called it "the worst long-term drought and most severe set of crop failures since agricultural civilizations began in the Fertile Crescent many millennia ago."[287] Food prices skyrocketed and people were starving. Nearly 2 million Syrians who relied on agriculture for food or income lost their livelihoods. Over 1.5 million people were forced to leave their homes for cities in search of

---

282 https://repository.hkbu.edu.hk/cgi/viewcontent.cgi?article=1008&context=lib_uga-ward

283 https://www.ushmm.org/m/pdfs/FREE-Syria_Survey_Report_030818.pdf

284 https://www.ushmm.org/m/pdfs/FREE-Syria_Survey_Report_030818.pdf

285 https://edition.cnn.com/2013/08/27/world/meast/syria-civil-war-fast-facts/index.html

286 https://www.ushmm.org/m/pdfs/FREE-Syria_Survey_Report_030818.pdf

287 https://www.thenation.com/article/syria-may-be-the-first-climate-change-conflict-but-it-wont-be-the-last/

work. Syria's major cities were already experiencing overcrowding from a previous influx of 1.5 million Iraqi refugees.[288]

With this natural disaster, the burden on the urban spaces increased, bringing on an economic crisis. This migration from the countryside into the cities exacerbated poverty and social unrest.[289]

The nature of the earlier protests in Syria was more politically and economically based, but with the passing years it gained a sectarian overtone. The Syrian demography shows a majority of Sunni Muslims (nearly 50% of the population[290]), but Syria's security establishment has long been controlled by members of the minority Alawi sect (approximately 17% of the population[291]), to which President Assad belongs.[292] This contributes to civilians' and rebel factions' suspicions about the government's bias.

The strategic importance of Syria for its neighbouring nations as well as for the international community increases the likelihood of interventions. Several countries such as Iran, Saudi Arabia, and Russia have been playing a proxy game of dominance and alliance in Syria since the start of the conflict, both overtly and indirectly.

Russia has been an ally of Syria since the Cold War, and entered the Syrian conflict in 2015. According to World Without Genocide, "Russia has military bases in Syria and sells $1.5 billion worth of weapons to Syria each year, about 10% of Russian global weapons sales."[293] To this day, Russia supports Assad by carrying out military and air strikes on his behalf as well as shielding his regime against international sanctions. With the world polarized over the Syrian conflict (the U.S. supporting the anti-government regime in Syria[294] and Russia and China aligning with Assad due to their vested interests[295]) it becomes important to trace the pattern of international interests in the conflict-ridden region. The governments of Iran and Iraq—Shia-majority countries—as well as Lebanon-based Shia Islamist group

---

288   https://worldwithoutgenocide.org/genocides-and-conflicts/syria

289   https://www.businessinsider.com/heres-why-theres-a-war-in-aleppo-and-syria-2016-12

290   http://gulf2000.columbia.edu/images/maps/Syria_Ethnic_Shift_2010-2018_lg.png

291   http://gulf2000.columbia.edu/images/maps/Syria_Ethnic_Shift_2010-2018_lg.png

292   https://www.aljazeera.com/news/2016/05/syria-civil-war-explained-160505084119966.html

293   https://worldwithoutgenocide.org/genocides-and-conflicts/syria

294   https://www.washingtonpost.com/blogs/checkpoint-washington/post/how-the-us-message-on-assad-shifted/2011/08/18/gIQAfPZxNJ_blog.html

295   https://www.atlanticcouncil.org/blogs/syriasource/chinese-strategic-engagement-with-assad-s-syria/

Hezbollah, have supported the Syrian government; while Sunni-majority countries—such as Turkey, Qatar, and Saudi Arabia—have supported the anti-government rebel groups.[296] Russia and China have continually vetoed Western-backed resolutions on Syria at the UN Security Council.[297]

The brutal acts committed by Assad's government only grew more savage as he continued to consolidate his authoritative regime. In 2012, rebel fighters reached the capital of Damascus and the city of Aleppo. According to World Without Genocide, in December 2012, "the Assad regime carried out the first of many chemical weapons attacks, killing women and children and sparking international condemnation."[298] In the absence of early military intervention, on August 21st, 2013, the Assad regime launched a sarin gas attack in the Damascus suburbs, killing nearly 1,500 people and defying the U.S. President Obama administration's "red line" on the use of chemical weapons.[299] As the regime's violence against unarmed protesters escalated, the Obama administration, along with other members of the international community, called for regime change. Assad's government, emboldened by the lack of consequences for its actions, "continued to target schools, hospitals, marketplaces, and other civilian centres using internationally banned weapons such as barrel bombs, cluster bombs, and chemical weapons."[300] In eight years of civil war, more than 570,000 people have been killed on the Syrian territory.[301]

Witnessing the strengthening of the Assad regime, and perceiving its negative impact on Syrian civilians and the world at large, the U.S. intervened in Syrian politics by providing training, arms, and aid to anti-Assad groups, and leading an international coalition to bomb ISIL targets. In April 2017, the U.S. carried out:

> its first direct military action against Assad's forces, launching fifty-nine Tomahawk cruise missiles at a Syrian air force base from which US officials believe a chemical attack on Khan Sheikhoun had been launched.

---

[296] https://www.aljazeera.com/news/2016/05/syria-civil-war-explained-1605050841 19966.html https://www.politico.com/magazine/story/2016/07/obama-syria-foreign-policy-red-line-revisited-214059

[297] https://www.aljazeera.com/news/2016/05/syria-civil-war-explained-1605050 84119966.html

[298] https://worldwithoutgenocide.org/genocides-and-conflicts/syria

[299] https://www.washingtonpost.com/news/worldviews/wp/2018/04/11/chlorine-sarin-or-something-else-the-big-questions-in-alleged-syrian-chemical-weapons-attack/

[300] https://www.ushmm.org/m/pdfs/FREE-Syria_Survey_Report_030818.pdf

[301] http://www.syriahr.com/en/?p=120851

One year later, on April 14, despite Russian warnings, the US launched an attack together with France and the UK, at 'chemical weapon sites.'[302]

In September 2015, Russia launched a campaign to bomb what it called "terrorist groups" in Syria, including ISIL and anti-Assad, U.S.-backed rebel groups. Russia has also sent military advisors to reinforce Assad's defences.[303] The severe violence has seen no change to date, despite the several ceasefire agreements which have been signed in attempts to de-escalate it.

A World Bank report estimates that "as of early 2017, the conflict in Syria has damaged or destroyed about a third of the housing stock and about half of medical and education facilities, and led to significant economic losses."[304] World Without Genocide reports that "the government-backed military [has] shot unarmed civilians, carried out door-to-door arrest campaigns, and targeted medical personnel aiding the wounded."[305] It further explains that:

[h]ospitals have been targeted from the beginning of the war. Since 2011, over 450 attacks have been made on Syrian hospitals and over 800 medical professionals have been killed. So many doctors have been killed or have fled that veterinarians and dentists are often forced to perform surgeries. Organizations like the Syrian American Medical Society (SAMS) have built underground hospitals to escape the bombings. SAMS has spent more than $3.5 million on underground cave hospitals. The organization has delivered 100,000 babies and has supported nearly 400,000 surgeries.[306]

The inhuman conditions prevailing in Syria have forced civilians to flee the country. The Syrian refugee crisis has been deemed the worst across the globe since World War II. As of February 2018, the UN Refugee Agency (UNHCR) "had registered over 5.5 million refugees from Syria and estimated that there [were] over 6.5 million internally displaced persons (IDP) within Syria's borders."[307] Most of the Syrian migrants have

302 https://www.aljazeera.com/news/2016/05/syria-civil-war-explained-16050
5084119966.html

303 https://www.aljazeera.com/news/2016/05/syria-civil-war-explained-16050
5084119966.html

304 https://www.worldbank.org/en/news/press-release/2017/07/18/the-visible-impacts-
of-the-syrian-war-may-only-be-the-tip-of-the-iceberg

305 https://worldwithoutgenocide.org/genocides-and-conflicts/syria

306 https://worldwithoutgenocide.org/genocides-and-conflicts/syria

307 https://www.aljazeera.com/news/2016/05/syria-civil-war-explained-1605050
84119966.html

taken refuge in Jordan, Turkey, and Lebanon, with many of these refugees attempting to travel onward to Europe in search of improved conditions.[308] In 2016, over 360,000 refugees crossed the Mediterranean to Europe, and nearly 4,000 died en route.[309]

Syrian refugees continue to live below the poverty line, and language barriers as well as the need to earn money often prevent refugee children from getting an education, fuelling the problems of child labour and physical and mental abuse. Women and children have always been especially vulnerable to the most common "weapons of war": rape and assault. Child marriage has also increased in refugee communities, as "poverty-stricken parents marry off daughters to afford to feed the rest of their families."[310]

With the political and economic instability in Syria in 2013, ISIL/ISIS terrorists established a caliphate after taking control of the city of Raqqa and claiming it as their capital. The United States supported Kurdish forces with weapons and training, and the Kurds were successful in fighting ISIS and Assad in the north.

ISIS has lost all the territory it gained in Syria and Iraq, and the United States and its allies have declared victory over ISIS. On March 23rd, 2019, the U.S.-supported Kurdish forces blew the trumpet of victory, announcing that they had "captured the eastern Syrian pocket of Baghouz, the last populated area under ISIS rule."[311] Although many Westerners believe the Syrian conflict revolves around ISIS, the Syrian government and its allies are no less responsible for the majority of Syrian casualties.

In early October 2019, the U.S. President announced the withdrawal of U.S. troops from northern Syria and abandoned the Kurdish forces who had fought alongside the U.S. against the Islamic State for nearly five years, losing approximately 11,000 fighters.[312] In the following days, Turkey launched an offensive into north-eastern Syria, targeting Kurdish forces that control the region. The abandonment of a key ally by President Donald Trump will have serious consequences for many more years to come.

In 2019, as Syria enters the ninth year of the conflict, it is important to recognize that the Syrian conflict is much more than a subject of research and studies; it is a clear example of twenty-first century genocide. Condemned by the Arab League, the European Union, the United States and

---

308 https://www.aljazeera.com/news/2016/05/syria-civil-war-explained-160505 084119966.html

309 https://worldwithoutgenocide.org/genocides-and-conflicts/syria

310 https://worldwithoutgenocide.org/genocides-and-conflicts/syria

311 https://www.cnn.com/2019/03/23/middleeast/end-of-isis-caliphate-intl/index.html

312 https://www.theguardian.com/us-news/2019/oct/09/trump-syria-kurds-normandy

other countries, the brutal acts of violence and genocide against the many minority religious and ethnic groups in Syria have devasted the country. The torture and intimidation used on innocent civilians urgently requires action. The world should unite to fight this draconian evil and prevent its germination elsewhere in the world.

2006 Lebanon War

In 2006, Hezbollah violated international humanitarian law and committed war crimes during the Lebanon war, including attacks on civilian populations, disproportionate or indiscriminate attacks, the use of human shields, and the use of prohibited weapons. Hezbollah also stored weapons in and fired from civilian areas, and transferred weapons using ambulances—acts which are in violation of humanitarian law.

United Nations Under-Secretary-General for Humanitarian Affairs and Emergency Relief Coordinator Jan Egeland accused Hezbollah of "cowardly blending ... among women and children." He went on to state: "I heard they were proud because they lost very few fighters and that it was the civilians bearing the brunt of this. I don't think anyone should be proud of having many more children and women dead than armed men."[313]

A Human Rights Watch report released on August 3rd, 2006, said:

> Human Rights Watch found no cases in which Hezbollah deliberately used civilians as shields to protect them from retaliatory IDF attack. In none of the cases of civilian deaths documented in this report is there evidence to suggest that Hezbollah forces or weapons were in or near the area that the IDF targeted during or just prior to the attack.[314]

In the same report, Human Rights Watch wrote:

> Hezbollah occasionally did store weapons in or near civilian homes and fighters placed rocket launchers within populated areas or near U.N. observers, which are serious violations of the laws of war because they violate the duty to take all feasible precautions to avoid civilian casualties. ... In addition, Human Rights Watch continues to investigate allegations that Hezbollah is shielding its military personnel and materiel by locating them in civilian homes or areas, and it is deeply concerned by Hezbollah's placement of certain troops and materiel near civilians, which

---

[313] "UN humanitarian chief blasts Hizbullah." The Jerusalem Post. Associated Press. 25 July 2006. Retrieved 7 August 2006.

[314] "Israel/Lebanon: End Indiscriminate Strikes on Civilians." Human Rights Watch. 3 August 2006.

endangers them and violates the duty to take all feasible precautions to avoid civilian casualties. Human Rights Watch uses the occasion of this report to reiterate Hezbollah's legal duty never to deliberately use civilians to shield military objects and never to needlessly endanger civilians by conducting military operations, maintaining troops, or storing weapons in their vicinity.[315]

Hezbollah continues to launch rockets and mortars in southern Lebanon and Israel, threatening the lives of innocent civilians. Hezbollah has had a destabilizing effect on the region, and is a threat to the security and peace of both Lebanon and Israel. Israel has responded to the threats carried out by the terrorist organization, and it is now up to the international community to support Israel in the quest to rid the region of Hezbollah and reduce the influence of its proxy, Iran. War crimes committed by Hezbollah in clear violation of international humanitarian law must be punished for the stability and security of the region.

Balochistan

Balochistan is the largest province of Pakistan. Though primarily underdeveloped, it is home to 13 million people. With its independence from Britain in 1947, Pakistan began waging a war of terror against the Baloch people.

Under British rule, various territories in Pakistan had been allowed to self-govern, ruled by their respective princes. Upon independence, these self-governed territories did not meet the approval of the newly created nation, and the following year in March 1948, the new Pakistan army carried out a military campaign to extend the country's territory and bring the region under central control. Balochistan, which was called Kalat State, was secular, and struggled against the Islamist Pakistan. Later, a treaty was signed by Yar Khan, who ruled Kalat, instigating fights between the Pakistanis and Balochis.[316]

With a relatively low population density, Balochistan is rich in natural resources, but lags behind the other provinces of Pakistan in terms of economic and social development. Regional disparity is the contemporary reality of Pakistan, and Balochistan has faced the negative consequences of these disparities. Extensive economic pillages brought by political and military strategizing are the daily reality of Balochistan.

---

315 "Fatal Strikes: Israel's Indiscriminate Attacks Against Civilians in Lebanon: Summary." Human Rights Watch. August 2006. 10 December 2006.

316 Hawla, Iqbal. "Prelude to the Accession of the Kalat State to Pakistan in 1948: An Appraisal". *Journal of the Research Society of Pakistan*, 1996.

Between 1962 and 1963, and again between 1973 and 1977, there were several brutal campaigns against the Baloch people. In late 1999, when General Pervez Musharraf came to power, a new military campaign was waged to take control of the Balochistan region.

Amnesty International's annual report stated that there were enforced disappearances and extrajudicial killings in Balochistan.[317] There have been merciless killings, houses looted, and brutal rapes in every corner of Balochistan.

Pakistan has implemented many cruel attacks on the Balochistan territory. Athar Hussain, Director of the Asia Research Centre at the London School of Economics, expressed that Pakistan had used weapons which were provided by the United States to combat terrorism against the Baloch people.[318]

According to Human Rights Watch report, from 2003 onwards, more than 18,000 people have disappeared from Balochistan. In 2014, three mass graves were discovered in the district Khuzdar in Balochistan which had hundreds of dead and decomposed bodies.[319] Chemicals were used to mutilate the bodies so that nobody could identify them. Pakistan forces forced the locals to vacate the area. These mass graves created a fear among the families of missing Baloch people.

According to Pakistan's Federal Ministry of Human Rights, the large-scale extrajudicial killings were carried out by infighting among insurgent groups. However, locals claim that it was Pakistan security agencies who did the killings. It has been reported that "thousands of people have disappeared without trace in Balochistan since a separatist insurgency gained momentum in 2007."[320]

The Voice for Baloch Missing Persons (VBMP) stated in 2016 that it had "recorded 1,200 cases of dumped bodies and there are many more it has not been able to document."[321] The head of VBMP, Nasrullah Baloch, told the BBC most of the bodies were "of those activists who have been victims of 'enforced disappearances'—people who are picked up by authorities and then just go missing."[322]

---

[317] https://www.amnesty.org/en/latest/research/2017/11/pakistan-end-enforced-disappearances-now/

[318] http://swarajyamag.com/world/genocide-in-balochistan-why-pakistan-must-pay-the-price

[319] https://www.hrw.org/reports/2003/iraq0503/2.htm https://www.dw.com/en/activists-wants-un-inquiry-into-pakistan-mass-graves/a-17392230

[320] https://www.bbc.com/news/world-asia-38454483

[321] https://www.bbc.com/news/world-asia-38454483

[322] https://www.bbc.com/news/world-asia-38454483

The reports of killing and dumping bodies in mass graves were also confirmed by a 2013 report by the independent Human Rights Commission of Pakistan (HRCP), which noted "credible reports of continued serious human rights violations, including [enforced] disappearances of people, arbitrary arrests, torture and extrajudicial killings."[323]

In early 2005, a military-led operation was launched with the goal of stifling the uprising by the ethnic Baloch groups who were fighting for a larger share of the province's resources.[324] This took a toll on civilians. The increased armed conflict had negative consequences on the public health and safety of the region, with Balochis calling on the UN to provide personnel to protect them from the extrajudicial killings. Most of the bodies of those killed by Pakistan military and security forces were dumped in the regions of Quetta, Qalat, Khuzdar, and Makran, where the separatist insurgency has its roots.

The military plays a vital role in all spheres of the civic framework of Pakistan, influencing each sector of the nation. It is only with the military's support for the government that the massacres in Balochistan can be carried out. Francesca Marina, an eminent Italian scholar and the editor-in-chief of *Stringer Asia*—who has visited Balochistan several times and regularly keeps a close watch on the happenings there—described what is happening in Balochistan today as not only a violation of human rights, but a systematic massacre being carried out by Pakistan and a war leading to the extermination of a culture. She said the conditions in the region are akin to the happenings in Bosnia. "What is happening in Balochistan today is not the problem of simple human rights violations," she said. "It is genocide by Pakistan army. It is a pogrom undertaken by Pakistan against the Baloch people. More than 18,000 people have just disappeared and some of them have been founded [sic] killed or inhumanly tortured in the streets."[325]

Baloch and Sindhi scholar Zulfiqar Ali said:

Human rights violation is a general term for what is happening in Balochistan. It is indeed ethnic cleansing. Massacres of Baloch and Hazara people are there. Whole Balochistan is a victim of the interests that are invested in Gwadar and the natural resources in Balochistan. We, Bloch, reject and condemn them for the atrocities. We surely demand the international community to intervene and force Pakistan to stop this crime against humanity. No doubt, the people of Balochistan are expressing their opinion through

323 https://www.bbc.com/news/world-asia-38454483

324 https://www.bbc.com/news/world-asia-38454483

325 https://www.organiser.org/Encyc/2018/11/25/State-sponsored-Genocide-in-Balochistan-Italian-journalist-Francesca-Marina.html

peaceful or other means. It is heinous criminality in Pakistan that we the Baloch and Sindhis have witnessed after whatsoever happened in Bangladesh when billions of women and men were raped and murdered. If we have to live in Pakistan, we have to live with dignity.[326]

Pakistan continues military operations in the region, despite repeatedly facing internal calls to stop the suffering of the local population of Balochistan. As long as there is a heavy military presence in the province, extra judicial killing, intimidation, abduction, and arbitrary detention of the Baloch people will continue.

It is not only the people and resources of Balochistan that face exploitation. The environment of the region has also been adversely affected by the claimed progressive economic projects being undertaken in the name of the China–Pakistan Economic Corridor (CPEC).

The reports of the United Nations Development Programme state that Balochistan lacks basic amenities for day-to-day survival, and is at the top of the poverty chart. In Qilla Abdullah, 96% of people are living below their means, making it the poorest part of Pakistan. The World Bank report titled, "When Water Becomes a Hazard 2018" reveals that Balochistan has the highest rural poverty in all of Pakistan.

Pakistan has been able to escape international condemnation over the issue because of the support of China as well as the U.S.-backed Saudi Arabia regime. Pakistan bans the travel of international media to Balochistan and hides the horrors of mass graves, rapes, and war crimes against the Balochis, leaving them largely unreported.[327] There have been several reports that over 14,000 people are missing from Balochistan, allegedly picked up by security agencies.[328]

A Pakistani minister in Balochistan, who is the *de-jure* head of the security apparatus in the region, has declared that genocide is the only option to resolve the security crisis in Balochistan. Home Office Minister Sarfaraz Bugti made the shocking comments on November 19th, 2017 while talking to tribal elders in Pakistan House in Dera Bugti. An UNPO report summarized his words as: "To establish long-lasting peace in the region for a prosperous Pakistan, the only option is to commit a full-scale genocide against the dissidents."[329]

---

[326] https://www.organiser.org/Encyc/2018/11/25/State-sponsored-Genocide-in-Balochistan-Italian-journalist-Francesca-Marina.html

[327] https://www.organiser.org/Encyc/2018/11/25/State-sponsored-Genocide-in-Balochistan-Italian-journalist-Francesca-Marina.html

[328] https://www.business-standard.com/article/news-ani/forced-disappearance-growing-in-balochistan-says-bugti-118080400454_1.html

[329] https://unpo.org/article/20466?id=20466

The Pakistani Government has ruled with impunity and has dismissed charges of human rights violations by blaming Baloch nationals for the problems. The xenophobic attitude of Pakistan is manifested in its denying Balochis the basic rights of education, health care facilities, security, and law and order, as well as its disrespect of their cultural and ethical differences. All of this exposes the hypocrisy of Pakistan's claim of being a democratic nation.

Pakistan has deprived the Baloch people of their basic human rights. According to Human Rights Watch, "[a] climate of fear continues to impede media coverage of abuses both by government security forces and militant groups. ... In several cases, government regulatory agencies blocked cable operators from broadcasting networks that had aired critical programs."[330] Pakistan needs to meet its international human rights obligations in their totality and end the culture of ethnic cleansing and religious bigotry that has led to the deaths of thousands of its own people.

Only in 2010 did Pakistan become a party to the ICCPR. As described in Pakistan's newspaper *Dawn*:

[This was] a move that many hoped would herald greater human rights protection in the country. The government, however, never fully acknowledged the obligations it undertook under the ICCPR, and the treaty was rarely used to guide the country's laws and policies. On the contrary, senior government officials often publicly disavowed international human rights law as a 'Western' concept 'alien' to Pakistan's values. Sadly, Pakistan has seen some major reversals in human rights protection since becoming a party to the ICCPR.[331]

The International Court of Justice in *Bosnia and Herzegovina v. Serbia and Montenegro* confirmed that a state could commit genocide and that the court would arbitrate the case accordingly. The Genocide Convention therefore ensures that the twofold execution of the universal duty of Pakistan and the criminal accountability of the individuals such as General Musharraf, Nawaz Sharif, and General Raheel Sharif can be attained.

International humanitarian law ensures the provision of protection and security to people who have suffered from acts of aggression by state actors and non-state actors. The UN Security Council needs to adopt a resolution calling for UN observers in Balochistan to halt operations by the Pakistan military.

---

[330] https://www.hrw.org/world-report/2019/country-chapters/pakistan

[331] https://www.dawn.com/news/1348318

This twenty-first century crisis has manifested itself in variant forms—humanitarian crises, human rights violations, and the breach of the principles of trust and peace nationally as well as internationally—leading to a vicious cycle of violence and war. It is crucial to understand the pattern of the violence and mobilize global actions to combat it.

Balochistan suffered from repercussions of Cyclone Yemyin in July 2007, but the government of Pakistan refused to accept foreign aid for the recovery of the Baloch area. Pakistan claimed that the provincial government was proficient and prepared to deal with the calamity, despite numerous reports of lack of food, water, and health care centres in the region. Many experts have concluded that the motive behind the rejection was to hide the serious human rights violations taking place in Balochistan.

2009 Sri Lankan Civil War

The armed conflict in Sri Lanka, which began on July 23rd, 1983, was between the Sri Lankan government and the Liberation Tigers of Tamil Eelam (LTTE, or "the Tamil Tigers"). The latter's goal was the creation of an independent Tamil state, "Tamil Eelam." The conflict escalated into a large-scale civil war, and ended with the military defeating the Tamil Tigers in May 2009.[332]

During a period of over twenty-five years, the war caused significant strife for Sri Lanka's people, environment, and economy. An estimated 80,000 to 100,000 people were killed in the conflict,[333] and many atrocities were committed by both sides.

The tactics employed by the LTTE against government forces resulted in the group being listed as a terrorist organization in thirty-two countries, including the United States, India, Canada, and the member nations of the European Union. The Sri Lankan armed forces have also been accused of grave human rights abuses, systematic impunity for serious human rights violations, ethnic cleansing, and forced disappearances.

The LTTE was a terrorist group that employed tactics contrary to international law and international humanitarian law, including the use of human suicide bombers. But however brutal their tactics, the government of Sri Lanka also used disproportionate force against the civilian population and committed several human rights abuses. To date, there has been systematic impunity for the high-ranking officials responsible for the human rights violations and genocide committed against the Tamil

---

[332] https://web.archive.org/web/20090521113622/http://www.defence.lk/new.asp?f-name=20090518_10

[333] "Up to 100,000 killed in Sri Lanka's civil war: UN." ABC Australia. 20 May 2009.

people. In 2013, a UN panel conducted during the last phase of the war estimated that some 40,000 died in this time period, "while other independent reports estimated the number of civilians dead to exceed 100,000."[334]

All parties to an armed conflict must ensure respect for international humanitarian law. This obligation does not depend on reciprocity—a party must respect the requirements whether or not its opposing side does. The reasons for which the respective parties go to war are also irrelevant; all parties to an armed conflict must be held to the same standards.

The armed conflict between Sri Lanka and the LTTE is governed by international treaties and the rules of customary international humanitarian law. According to Human Rights watch, "[h]olding individuals accountable for serious violations of the laws of war is important because it may deter future violations, promote respect for the law, and provide avenues of redress for the victims."[335] Furthermore:

> [a]ll states, whether or not a party to the conflict, have a responsibility under the Geneva Conventions of 1949 to exert their influence, to the degree possible, to stop violations of international humanitarian law. ... States have an obligation to investigate serious violations that implicate members of their forces or other persons under their jurisdiction. ... All too often, states whose citizens are implicated in serious violations in the laws of war lack the will or capacity to investigate and prosecute these crimes. ... Sri Lanka's long civil war has been characterized by a climate of impunity for perpetrators of serious human rights violations.[336]

The ICC can only take on the criminal investigation and prosecution of a state if that state is a party to the ICC treaty[337]—which Sri Lanka is not. Only if the UN Security Council refers a situation to the court can the ICC assume jurisdiction. The Security Council has, under the UN Charter, the utmost stature and authority to establish an investigative mechanism. Since the Security Council has not addressed issues of accountability in Sri Lanka before, there may be no alternative but to "explore other avenues to justice."[338] National courts have the well-deserved ability to play a role

---

334 "UNHCR Overview: IDPs in Sri Lanka."

335 https://www.hrw.org/news/2009/04/27/q-accountability-violations-international-humanitarian-law-sri-lanka

336 https://www.hrw.org/news/2009/04/27/q-accountability-violations-international-humanitarian-law-sri-lanka

337 https://www.hrw.org/news/2009/04/27/q-accountability-violations-international-humanitarian-law-sri-lanka

338 https://www.hrw.org/news/2009/04/27/q-accountability-violations-international-humanitarian-law-sri-lanka

in "combating impunity for grave violations of international human rights and humanitarian law."[339] Both the Geneva Conventions as well as the Convention against Torture mandate the exercise of universal jurisdiction. Under universal jurisdiction, cases can be referred to the competence of a national court to try a person suspected of a serious international crime, such as war crimes, crimes against humanity, torture, or genocide. Many countries have laws that would permit them to do this.[340]

In May 2010, Sri Lankan President Mahinda Rajapaksa appointed a commission to examine the twenty-six-year-long civil war in Sri Lanka. The commission was mandated to look into the circumstances that resulted in the failure of the February 27th, 2002 ceasefire agreement, as well as to summarize the lessons that should have been learned from the conflict, and to facilitate national unity and reconciliation. However, after an eighteen-month inquiry, the commission sent its report to the President on November 15th, 2011. The report was criticized by the international community for its conclusion that the Sri Lankan military was not guilty of deliberately targeting civilians,[341] despite the many reports to the contrary made by international organizations. The commission instead placed exclusive blame on the LTTE for the violations of international humanitarian law. Critics charged that the Sri Lankan government was using the commission as a tool to prevent further external investigation into the alleged abuses. Given the Sri Lankan government's failure to investigate, it is time for the intentional community to mandate the United Nations to investigate and provide a full account of the mass killings.

Rohingya

The Rohingya people, who derive their name from their spoken dialect, practice Islam amongst a Buddhist majority of Myanmar. According to Yasmin Ajirniar and Johns Creek:

> [s]ince the beginnings of Myanmar's history as an independent nation in 1948, the Rohingya have faced discrimination. During the independence process, after the upheaval of the government years later, and, again following the enactment of new legislation, the Rohingya were barred

---

[339] https://www.hrw.org/news/2009/04/27/q-accountability-violations-international-humanitarian-law-sri-lanka

[340] https://www.hrw.org/news/2009/04/27/q-accountability-violations-international-humanitarian-law-sri-lanka

[341] https://web.archive.org/web/20150219004350/https://www.latimes.com/world/asia/la-fg-un-report-sri-lanka-war-crimes-20150216-story.html

from gaining citizenship and were even officially recognized as foreigners in 1962, being issued foreign identification cards. Without proper documentation or citizenship, Rohingya have been effectively ostracized, unable to participate in the government, receive education or apply for jobs. With limited options living as a stranger in their own country, many people have been forced to flee Myanmar. Recent allegations by the United Nations indicate that the Rohingya have not only experienced blatant discrimination but also become the victims of genocide carried out by the Myanmar government and bolstered by the support of other citizens. For example, the government has been reported to have opened on large groups of Rohingya, including upon children; while children have been burnt in open flames, and refugees have been targets of gang rapes.[342]

Several reports by various international NGOs, including Human Rights Watch, state that over half a million Rohingya have fled the country to neighbouring Bangladesh since the beginning of the military campaign of ethnic cleansing in August 2017.[343] "The government denied extensive evidence of atrocities, refused to allow independent investigators access to Rakhine State, and punished local journalists for reporting on military abuses."[344] The systematic discrimination against the Rohingya people conveys a threat towards other Muslims in the country—that they are unwelcome and vulnerable to attack.

Genocide is challenging our contemporary notions of universal peace and security based on the human rights of the people across the globe. It is extremely difficult for people—especially those belonging to minority communities—to survive in a nation that has failed to uphold the mantle of equality and justice. The contemporary crisis of the Rohingya Muslims has sparked concern and condemnation by many world leaders, but few have acted.

Myanmar is a Buddhist-majority nation with small Muslim and Christian religious minorities. The Rohingya are a Muslim ethnic group. There are approximately 1.1 million Rohingya living in Myanmar, though hundreds of thousands continue to flee.

The Rohingya have their own language and culture, and describe themselves as descendants of "Arab traders and other groups who have been in the region for generations."[345] They are one of the many ethnic minorities in Myanmar, and represent the country's largest Muslim group.[346]

---

342   https://www.theodysseyonline.com/21st-century-genocide

343   https://www.hrw.org/world-report/2019/country-chapters/burma

344   https://www.hrw.org/world-report/2019/country-chapters/burma

345   https://www.bbc.com/news/world-asia-41566561

346   https://www.bbc.com/news/world-asia-41566561

The Rohingya Muslims in Myanmar live mostly in the area in and around Rakhine State. They are facing a humanitarian crisis as they are denied their citizenship, freedom to travel, and access to education and basic health facilities. They are at the receiving end of worst form of persecution, which in modern times has taken a genocidal turn. The Rohingya are not able to claim their well-deserved rights because of the discriminatory 1982 Citizenship Law that officially and legally prevented this ethnic minority from claiming citizenship. The same law encourages the Myanmar authorities to hide their responsibilities in the sphere of denial. The Rohingya residing within the territorial border of Myanmar are treated as illegal immigrants from the neighbouring nation, Bangladesh.

Communal violence, arbitrary detentions, mass killings, and alleged abuses by security forces have become the norm for this ethnic minority, resulting in a perilous existence for the ethnic group. The augmented violence in Myanmar, especially in the past few years, has forced thousands of Rohingya Muslims to make dangerous and uncertain journeys out of Myanmar, thus ascertaining their refugee status across the globe.

According to the *AJC*:

[i]n October 2016, the Myanmar government blamed members of the Rohingya for the killings of nine border police, leading to a crackdown on Rakhine State villages in which troops were accused of rape, extra-judicial killing, and other human rights abuses—all allegations they denied. In August 2017, violence erupted after a Rohingya armed rebel group called the Arakan Rohingya Salvation Army (ARSA) attacked police posts and an army base in Rakhine.[347]

The army launched a military campaign "clearance operation," which United Nations Commissioner for Human Rights Zeid Ra'ad al-Hussein has called "a textbook example of ethnic cleansing."[348]

According to Médecins Sans Frontières (MSF), at least 6,700 Rohingya, including at least 730 children under five, were killed in the month after the violence first broke out.[349] The mass killing and arbitrary burning of entire villages forced the Rohingyas to flee to nearby nations in search of security.

---

[347] https://www.ajc.com/news/world/who-are-the-rohingya-muslims-things-know-about-the-world-most-persecuted-minority/MzQM06SjX8k0hGKz0t9cnM/

[348] https://www.ajc.com/news/world/who-are-the-rohingya-muslims-things-know-about-the-world-most-persecuted-minority/MzQM06SjX8k0hGKz0t9cnM/

[349] https://www.bbc.com/news/world-asia-41566561

The findings of MSF were based on interviews with several thousand Rohingya refugees in four Bangladeshi camps in late October and early November 2017.[350] *AJC* reports that "[a]ccording to the MSF news release, the Rohingya death toll following the crackdown could be as high as 13,759, including at least 1,000 children under the age of 5." MSF also claimed that "at least 2,700 people died from disease and malnutrition."[351]

All accusations of genocide have been denied by the Myanmar government in an attempt to efface criticism and responsibility. The government and security forces have refuted the reports of several international agencies who, despite the crackdown of the media, were able to collect basic data differing to a great extent from the nation's portrayal of the Rohingya situation. The government of Myanmar lists the number of fatalities at a mere 400, even in the wake of countering the so-called militants of the Rakhine province. After the ARSA attack, security forces carried out the so-called "clearance operations" that, counter to claims of their termination, have been continued to date.

The BBC reports:

Rohingyas arriving in an area known as Cox's Bazaar—a district in Bangladesh—say they fled after troops, backed by local Buddhist mobs, responded by burning their villages and attacking and killing civilians. ... Amnesty International says the Myanmar military also raped and abused Rohingya women and girls. ... At least 288 villages were partially or totally destroyed by fire in northern Rakhine State after August 2017, according to analysis of satellite imagery by Human Rights Watch. ... Human Rights Watch say[s] most damage occurred in Maungdaw Township, between 25 August and 25 September 2017—with many villages destroyed after 5 September, when Myanmar's de facto leader, Aung San Suu Kyi, said security force operations had ended.[352]

The statistics derived from the satellite images have been supported by an Amnesty International report as well. Recent satellite images showed that approximately 392 villages had been partially or wholly destroyed in northern Rakhine State. Nearly 40% of all homes in the area, totalling some 37,700 buildings, were damaged, and approximately 80% were "burned in the first three weeks of the military campaign."[353]

---

350   https://www.ajc.com/news/world/who-are-the-rohingya-muslims-things-know-about-the-world-most-persecuted-minority/MzQM06SjX8k0hGKz0t9cnM/

351   https://www.ajc.com/news/world/who-are-the-rohingya-muslims-things-know-about-the-world-most-persecuted-minority/MzQM06SjX8k0hGKz0t9cnM/

352   https://www.bbc.com/news/world-asia-41566561

353   https://www.bbc.com/news/world-45341112

This humanitarian crisis has led to the twenty-first century's fastest growing refugee crisis, which is not only affecting Myanmar but also its neighbouring countries. Because of the growing number of refugees, nations like Bangladesh and Indonesia who have been providing humanitarian aid to the Rohingyas are facing a significant burden on their nations' economies. Before August 2017, there were already some 307,500 Rohingya refugees "living in camps, makeshift settlements, and with host communities, according to the UNHCR. A further 687,000 are estimated to have arrived since ... August [2017]."[354]

According to the BBC:

> [m]ost Rohingya refugees reaching Bangladesh—men, women and children with barely any belongings—have sought shelter in these areas, setting up camp wherever possible in the difficult terrain and with little access to aid, safe drinking water, food, shelter or healthcare. The largest refugee camp is Kutupalong, but limited space means spontaneous settlements have sprung up in the surrounding countryside and nearby Balukhali as refugees keep arriving. While numbers in the Kutupalong refugee camp have reduced from a high of 22,241 to 13,900, the number living in makeshift or spontaneous settlements outside the camp has climbed from 99,495 to more than 604,000. Most other refugee sites have also continued to expanded [sic]—as of mid-April 2018, there were 781,000 refugees living in nine camps and settlements. There are also around 117, 000 people staying outside the camps in host communities. Risking death by sea or on foot, nearly 725,000 have fled the destruction of their homes and persecution in the northern Rakhine province of Myanmar (Burma) for neighbouring Bangladesh since August 2017. ... On 24 March 2017, the UN Human Rights Council agreed to form an independent fact-finding mission on Myanmar to look into 'alleged recent human rights violations by military and security forces.' ... The report names six senior military figures it believes should go on trial, including Commander-in-Chief Min Aung Hlaing and his deputy.[355]

The 440-page UN report recommends that the UN Security Council impose an arms embargo and targeted sanctions against Myanmar. The government of Myanmar rejected the report, calling the investigation "flawed, biased and politically motivated."[356]

---

[354] https://social.shorthand.com/ymuntaiwan/ugLVkBcqB3/unhrc-i-rights-of-refugees

[355] https://www.bbc.com/news/world-45341112

[356] https://www.aljazeera.com/news/2018/12/law-firm-myanmar-committed-genocide-rohingya-181204042107254.html

Al Jazeera reports that:

> [t]wo months later, the head of the UN's Fact-Finding Mission on Myanmar told the council that the Rohingya who remained in Myanmar, some of whom have been confined to grim camps since communal violence in 2012, faced an 'ongoing genocide' and severe repression. That briefing drew objections from six of the Security Council's 15 members, including China and Russia with veto.[357]

The findings of the United Nations investigation, which alleged that "the gravest crimes under international law"[358] were committed in Myanmar last August, were strictly opposed by the government of Myanmar. Examining the severity of the crackdown not just on the so-called insurgents but also on the civilians, the report said the army must be investigated for genocide against the Rohingya Muslims in western Rakhine State. As the report states, "genocide is when a person commits a prohibited act with the intent to destroy, in whole or in part, a national, ethnical, racial or religious group."[359] The presence of "intent" in the crackdown by the Myanmar army could not be overlooked.

Sadly, nations across the globe have not followed up on the UN report of genocide, and continue to do trade with the government of Aung San Suu Kyi, who was awarded the Nobel Peace Prize in 1991 for her efforts to bring Myanmar under the parasol of democracy. But her rule, unfortunately, has proven to be no different from the past military dictatorship in the country.

On October 24th, 2018, Marzuki Darusman, chair of the UN fact-finding mission on Myanmar, described the situation as "an ongoing genocide."[360] As reported by *The Guardian*:

> Darusman ... said thousands of Rohingya were still fleeing to Bangladesh, and the estimated 250,000 to 400,000 who have remained following last year's brutal military campaign in the Buddhist-majority country 'continue to suffer the most severe' restrictions and repression. ... As for the Rohingya refugees returning to Myanmar, Yanghee Lee, the UN special investigator on human rights in Myanmar, said, 'There's been a lot of

---

357   https://www.aljazeera.com/news/2018/10/investigator-myanmar-genocide-rohingya-ongoing-181025035804009.html

358   https://www.un.org/press/en/2018/sc13552.doc.htm

359   https://www.ohchr.org/Documents/HRBodies/HRCouncil/FFM-Myanmar/A_HRC_39_64.docx

360   https://www.theguardian.com/world/2018/oct/24/rohingya-genocide-is-still-going-on-says-top-un-investigator

progress in terms of economic development and infrastructure, but in the area of 'democratic space' and people's right to claim back their land ... there is no progress.'[361]

Tirana Hassan, Amnesty International's crisis response director, noted:

What we are seeing in Rakhine State is a land grab by the military on a dramatic scale. New bases are being erected to house the very same security forces that have committed crimes against humanity against Rohingya. ... This makes the voluntary, safe and dignified return of Rohingya refugees an even more distant prospect. Not only are their homes gone, but the new construction is entrenching the already dehumanizing discrimination they have faced in Myanmar.[362]

The return of the Rohingya Muslims to Myanmar seems a distant dream, but even if the aid of international forces could facilitate it, the return would be fraught with the troubled realities of ethnic prejudice and religious intolerance.[363]

In late 2018, Paul Williams of the Public International Law and Policy Group told a press conference in Washington, DC that it was clear from their intense legal review that there was, in fact, a legal basis to conclude that the Rohingya were the victims of war crimes, crimes against humanity, and genocide. The lawyers' report documented more than 13,000 instances of "grave human rights violations" in the crackdown.[364] As reported by Al Jazeera:

[o]f the 1,024 Rohingya interviewed in the PILPG report, 20% told investigators that they had been physically wounded in the attacks. Nearly 70% said they had watched their homes or villages being destroyed, while 80% witnessed the killing of a family member, friend, or personal acquaintance. ... The Myanmar armed forces ... only targeted Rohingya civilians in the attacks[.] ... The military's actions were 'highly-coordinated' and required both tactical and logistical planning.[365]

---

361 https://www.theguardian.com/world/2018/oct/24/rohingya-genocide-is-still-going-on-says-top-un-investigator

362 https://www.amnesty.org/en/latest/news/2018/03/myanmar-military-land-grab-as-security-forces-build-bases-on-torched-rohingya-villages/

363 https://www.ajc.com/news/world/who-are-the-rohingya-muslims-things-know-about-the-world-most-persecuted-minority/MzQM06SjX8k0hGKz0t9cnM/

364 https://www.aljazeera.com/news/2018/12/law-firm-myanmar-committed-genocide-rohingya-181204042107254.html

365 https://www.aljazeera.com/news/2018/10/investigator-myanmar-genocide-rohingya-ongoing-181025035804009.html

The inhumane conditions in which the Rohingya of Myanmar are currently surviving require urgent attention and prompt action.

Congo

Similar to its neighbouring country, Rwanda, the Democratic Republic of the Congo (DRC) is experiencing civil unrest that continues to destabilize the Central African country.

In 2018, residents of the DRC in the Djugu territory of Ituri saw and fell victim to unprompted and recurring attacks on mostly Hema villages. This apparent genocide is the first of its kind since the genocide in Rwanda.[366]

The Congolese civil war that lasted from 1998 to 2003and engulfed neighbouring countries such as Rwanda, Uganda, Angola, Zimbabwe and Namibia, is estimated to have caused over five million deaths (including deaths that occurred in the violent wake of the war's official end).[367] It has been called the "bloodiest conflict since the end of the Second World War."[368]

Fighting involved Mai-Mai militia and Congolese government soldiers. There are several reports of rape and killing by the army:

> The army attacks the local population as it passes through, often raping and pillaging like the militias. Those who resist are branded Mai-Mai supporters and face detention, even death. The Mai-Mai ... accuse the villagers of collaborating with the army. They return to the villages at night and extract revenge. Sometimes they march the villagers into the bush to work as human mules.[369]

On June 17th, 2019, it was reported that at least 161 people had been killed in the northeastern Ituri province of the DRC, "in an apparent resurgence of ethnic clashes between farming and herding communities."[370] The attacks predominantly targeted Hema herders, who have "long been in conflict with Lendu farmers."[371] Between 1999 and 2007, open fighting between the two groups resulted in:

---

366   https://www.vibe.com/2018/03/congo-ethnic-cleansing-facts

367   https://www.voanews.com/africa/new-study-finds-death-toll-congo-war-too-high

368   https://pdfs.semanticscholar.org/5c66/a9daeaae13693708d8c70738ce435bb9a617.pdf

369   Jonathan Clayton, "In a disease-ridden and stinking swamp, thousands hide from war," The Times, April 3rd, 2006.

370   https://www.reuters.com/article/us-congo-violence/at-least-161-dead-in-northeast-congo-in-apparent-ethnic-clashes-idUSKCN1TI1FT

371   https://www.reuters.com/article/us-congo-violence/at-least-161-dead-in-northeast-congo-in-apparent-ethnic-clashes-idUSKCN1TI1FT

an estimated 50,000 deaths in one of the bloodiest chapters of a civil war in eastern Congo that left millions dead from conflict, hunger, and disease. Tit-for-tat attacks between the two groups in late 2017 and early 2018 killed hundreds of people and forced tens of thousands more to flee their homes, but a tenuous calm had taken hold until this month.[372]

Attacks are not demographically limited to adults, as several infants and children have also been killed. As of January 2019, an estimated 13.1 million people in the Congo were in need of humanitarian assistance, UNICEF reported.[373]

As a result of the continuing conflict between the ethnic groups and between non-state actors' armed groups and the Congolese security forces, the humanitarian situation in the Democratic Republic of the Congo remains dangerous. Further complicating the issue is political uncertainty and an economic downturn. The United Nations Office of the Coordination of Humanitarian Affairs (OCHA) reported in 2019 that:

> an estimated 12.8 people are in need of humanitarian assistance and protection in 2019: this figure represents 10 per cent of the total worldwide humanitarian caseload. Those affected by this complex and widespread crisis remain exposed to pervasive human rights violations, especially sexual and gender-based violence, chronic malnutrition, and epidemics, notably cholera, measles, and the Ebola Virus Disease (EVD). Insecurity has had a devastating impact on people's capacity to access food, and 12.8 million people across the DRC are facing severe food insecurity.[374]

Many Hema people are now homeless due to the continued spontaneous attacks, and the Congolese government has not intervened to end the conflict. The forced displacement is a growing problem. According to *Vibe*, over 150,000 people have been displaced, "some having fled their homes for safety and others hav[ing] had theirs burned down. Many are fleeing to Uganda or to the town of Bunia in the Congo."[375]

The United Nations repeatedly warned the Congolese government of the early signs of ethnic cleansing back in 2017, but the government ignored, and continues to ignore, these warnings. As well, the Congolese government has yet to address the continued tribal killings. Many believe

---

[372]   https://www.reuters.com/article/us-congo-violence/at-least-161-dead-in-northeast-congo-in-apparent-ethnic-clashes-idUSKCN1TI1FT

[373]   https://reliefweb.int/report/democratic-republic-congo/unicef-drc-humanitarian-situation-report-january-2019

[374]   https://www.unocha.org/democratic-republic-congo-drc/about-ocha-drc

[375]   https://www.vibe.com/2018/03/congo-ethnic-cleansing-facts

that the cleansing was incited at least partially to "sow disorder" in order to delay national elections and to extend the rule of President Joseph Kabila, whose final term should have ended in December 2016.[376] Kabila delayed the election many times, but announced at a press conference earlier in 2018 that the next election would be held on December 23rd, 2018. After years of speculation, it was confirmed in August 2018 that Kabila would not be standing in the election, and he stepped down on January 24th, 2019, handing power to Tshisekedi. This was the first peaceful power transition in Congo since the country's independence in 1960.[377]

The ICC's inaugural case was that of the DRC in 2004. The Court opened its first ever investigation with a focus on the leaders of numerous rebel groups and armed militia suspected of crimes against humanity and war crimes.[378] In April 2002, the DRC ratified the ICC's Rome Statute. After the rigorous efforts of civil society for many years, the DRC incorporated ICC crimes into its domestic law system and formal cooperation with the Court was ultimately adopted in 2015. Along with the ICC's investigation, the local courts of the DRC have also been prosecuting cases of severe crimes in special domestic courts in eastern Congo.

Since the investigations were started by the ICC, at least seven warrants for arrests have been issued for war crimes and crimes against humanity to date. The cases have been filed against Thomas Lubanga Dyilo, Bosco Ntaganda, Matthieu Ngudjolo Chui, Germain Katanga, Callixte Mbarushimana, and Sylvestre Mudacumura. Initially, the situation in the DRC was allocated to Pre-Trial Chamber (PTC) I, which included Presiding Judge Sylvia Steiner, along with Judge Cuno Tarfusser and Judge Sanji Mmasenono Monageng. However, at present, the situation is being dealt with by PTC II, comprising Judge Cuno Tarfusser, Judge Ekaterina Trendafilova, and Judge Hans-Peter Kaul.[379]

The ICC's first trial case was of the DRC rebel Thomas Lubanga Dyilo.[380] Lubanga was charged with the war crimes of enlisting and conscripting children below the age of fifteen years old and using them in conflict situations in eastern DRC. The arrest warrant against Lubanga was issued on February 10th, 2006, and he was arrested and sent to the ICC's headquarters in The Hague on March 16th, 2006. Following the arrest, the accusations were confirmed by PTC I on January 29th, 2007.

---

[376] https://foreignpolicy.com/2018/11/27/is-kabila-using-ethnic-violence-to-stay-in-power/

[377] https://www.britannica.com/biography/Joseph-Kabila

[378] http://www.coalitionfortheicc.org/country/democratic-republic-congo

[379] http://www.iccnow.org/index.php?mod=drc

[380] http://www.coalitionfortheicc.org/cases/thomas-lubanga-dyilo

Lubanga was the founding leader of the Union of Congolese Patriots (UPC) as well as the commander-in-chief of the group's military section, the Forces patriotiques pour la libération du Congo (FPLC). The armed forces under Lubanga's control mainly included the Hema ethnic group, which was suspected of conducting severe abuses against civilians during the conflict with militias of the Lendu ethnic group over resources and land in Ituri between 2002 and 2003.[381] Following Lubanga's arrest, his second-in-command Bosco Ntaganda, a fellow ICC suspect, took over as the group's commander to carry out all activities of the UPC.[382] The ICC judges discovered that the FPLC used an extensive youth recruitment strategy employing children under the age of fifteen for war-conflicts. As soon as the militant group had finished training these children in military camps, they were deployed as armed forces in Tchomia, Bunia, Bogoro, and Kasenvi. They also participated in conflict situations in regions such as Mongbwalu, Songolo, and Kobu. In addition, the children were used as military guards, as well as for a special "Kadogo Unit" that comprised basically children, both male and female.[383]

At last, on July 10th, 2012, the ICC announced a sentence of fourteen years' jail imprisonment for Lubanga.[384] The prosecution asked for a maximum thirty-year sentence, but the judges asserted that this would be inappropriate, as Lubanga had already served six years in detention in The Hague since March 2006. The Appeals Chamber has since received many requests to reduce Lubanga's sentence, but all have so far been declined.

Bosco Ntaganda[385] is an alleged ex-deputy chief of the general staff of the FPLC. It has also been alleged that Ntaganda is the current chief of staff of the Congrès national pour la défense du people (CNDP), an armed group active in the North Kivu province of the DRC. Ntaganda is charged with crimes against humanity and war crimes allegedly committed in the Ituri region. The ICC opened his trial in September 2015. He is accused of thirteen counts of war crimes, including murder, attacking civilians, sexual slavery of civilians, rape, displacement of civilians, and attacking protected objects; as well as five crimes against humanity, including sexual slavery, murder, persecution, and forcible transfer of population. All these charges were confirmed on June 9th, 2014. At present, Ntaganda is in the ICC custody.

---

[381] https://www.icc-cpi.int/RelatedRecords/CR2015_15483.PDF

[382] http://www.coalitionfortheicc.org/cases/thomas-lubanga-dyilo

[383] https://www.icc-cpi.int/RelatedRecords/CR2015_15483.PDF

[384] https://www.icc-cpi.int/drc/lubanga/Documents/LubangaEng.pdf

[385] http://www.iccnow.org/index.php?mod=drc

Ntaganda is infamously known as "Warrior" or "Terminator" by his militant group. He is accused of being a leader of numerous armed rebel groups which are alleged to have been committing violence and atrocities in the Ituri region since the late 1990s. In 2009, Ntaganda was made a general in the Congolese army for a peace deal and lived freely in Goma, eastern DRC, even though he was announced as wanted by the ICC. He, along with many others, reportedly led a mutiny in 2012 and formed the M23 insurgent group, causing renewed conflict in the region. The following year, a split in this group reportedly led Ntaganda and his followers to flee to neighbouring Rwanda.[386]

The ICC issued an arrest warrant against Ntaganda on August 22nd, 2006, followed by a second warrant on July 13th, 2012. However, Ntaganda voluntarily surrendered on March 18th, 2013, and was transferred to the ICC's headquarters on March 22nd, 2013.

Germain Katanga[387] is a Congolese rebel leader who was convicted by the ICC in March 2014 on the charges of four counts of war crimes, including attacking a civilian population, murder, destruction of property, and pillaging, as well as one count of crimes against humanity, including murder, committed during an attack on Bogoro village in eastern DRC's Ituri in February 2003. The attack was executed by the Front des nationalistes et intégrationnistes (Allied Forces of the Nationalist and Integrationist Front, or FNI), the group led by Mathieu Ngudjolo Chui. The ICC issued a warrant of arrest against Katanga in 2007, while an arrest warrant against Ngudjolo was issued in 2008. Their trial began on November 24th, 2009.

The Trial Chamber II on May 23rd, 2014 sentenced Katanga to a jail imprisonment of twelve years. However, his detention time spent at the ICC from September 18th, 2007 to May 23rd, 2014 was deducted from his punishment.

The DRC has a total number of at least six cases, including Thomas Lubanga Dyilo, Bosco Ntaganda, Germain Katanga, Mathieu Ngudjolo Chui, Callixte Mbarushimana, and Sylvestre Mudacumura.

In Lubanga's case, he was found guilty of the war crimes of enlisting and conscripting children under the age of fifteen years and using them to participate actively in hostilities (child soldiers). The ICC sentenced him on July 10th, 2012 to a total of fourteen years' imprisonment. The verdict and sentence in the Lubanga case were confirmed by the Appeals Chamber on December 1st, 2014, while on December 19th, 2015, the convict was transferred to a prison facility in the DRC to serve his jail term. The reparations proceedings kicked off on August 27th, 2012.

---

386   http://www.coalitionfortheicc.org/cases/bosco-ntaganda

387   https://www.icc-cpi.int/drc/katanga/Documents/KatangaEng.pdf

In Ntaganda's case, the trial opened on September 2nd, 2015. He was charged with thirteen counts of war crimes as well as five crimes against humanity.[388]

In Katanga's case, he was found guilty as an accessory to one count of crimes against humanity and four counts of war crimes committed in February 2003 during the attack on the village of Bogoro, in the DRC's Ituri district. The ruling is final, as both the Defence and Prosecution withdrew their appeals on June 25th, 2014. The ICC has sentenced him to twelve years' imprisonment.

The Ngudjolo Chui case[389] has been closed. Chui was acquitted in the case on December 18th, 2012 by Trial Chamber II. Chui was accused of war crimes and crimes against humanity; however, the court ordered his immediate release. The Prosecution appealed the verdict on December 20th, 2012. At last, the verdict was upheld by the Appeals Chamber on February 27th, 2015.

In Mbarushimana's case,[390] the charges were not confirmed, and as such the trial has been closed. Mbarushimana was accused of crimes against humanity and war crimes. PTC I refused to confirm the charges against him, and did not carry the case to trial. The Prosecution's appeal was rejected. Mbarushimana was released from ICC custody on December 23rd, 2011. At present, the case is considered closed, unless the Prosecutor submits new evidence.

The Mudacumura case[391] is presently in the pre-trial segment. The ICC issued a warrant of arrest against Mudacumura on July 13th, 2012. He is suspected of nine counts of war crimes purportedly executed between January 20th, 2009 and September 2010 during the conflict in the Kivus (DRC). As of now, Mudacumura is not in ICC custody.

Since July 1st, 2002, the ICC probes in the DRC have focused on alleged crimes against humanity and war crimes, mostly committed in eastern DRC, particularly in the regions of Ituri and the north and south Kivu provinces. Though the ICC's jurisdiction commenced on July 1st, 2002, the opening investigation was not until June 2004, when the ICC's Office of the Prosecutor released a press-note stating that alleged crimes had been reported since the 1990s. The ICC's press release stated that "states, international organisations and non-governmental organisations have reported thousands of deaths by mass murder and summary execution

---

[388] https://www.icc-cpi.int/drc/ntaganda https://www.ijmonitor.org/2019/11/defense-lawyer-says-ntaganda-not-surprised-by-30-year-sentence/

[389] https://www.icc-cpi.int/drc/ngudjolo

[390] https://www.icc-cpi.int/drc/mbarushimana/Documents/MbarushimanaEng.pdf

[391] https://www.icc-cpi.int/drc/mudacumura/Documents/MudacumuraEng.pdf

in the DRC since 2002. The reports allege a pattern of rape, torture, forced displacement, and the illegal use of child soldiers."[392]

In August 2018, *Voice of America* reported that "the allegations in the DRC are horrendous: mass rapes, mutilations and beheadings."[393] Bacre Waly Ndiaye, the leader of a UN team investigating violence in the DRC's Kasai province noted that, if proven, these atrocities would constitute war crimes and crimes against humanity. "But there will never be enough courts or resources to prosecute thousands of perpetrators," he said.[394]

Two years of fighting in Kasai between the army and the two opposing militias have left thousands of people dead, 1.4 million displaced, and many fleeing to nearby Angola. However, as reported by *VOA*, Ndiaye emphasized that "such horrific acts still fall short of genocide, which must include a proven intent to wipe out an entire ethnic, national, racial, or religious group."[395]

Ndiaye's remarks were in sharp contrast to the UN's special rapporteur on torture worldwide, Nils Melzer, who recently suggested that conditions in the DRC were dangerously similar to those which led to the Bosnian and Rwandan genocides. "My greatest concern is that what we are witnessing today may be only the prelude of what is still to come," he said.[396]

The international community is looking for ways to end the conflict. The UN high commissioner for human rights, Zeid Ra'ad Al Hussein, has noted the country's "deteriorating situation," and called for "much stronger efforts to hold the perpetrators of violations responsible. The perpetrators of conflict-related sexual violence must also be held to account even, and perhaps especially, when they are agents of the State."[397]

Ending the violence requires an end to impunity, and much more must be done to end the killings in the Democratic Republic of the Congo.

Yemen

The Yemeni Civil War is an ongoing conflict which began in 2015 and is being fought between two main groups: the Yemeni government, which is internationally recognized and headed by Abdrabbuh Mansur Hadi; and the Houthi armed movement, whose supporters and allies are also

---

[392]   https://www.icc-cpi.int/drc

[393]   https://www.voanews.com/africa/un-investigator-atrocities-drc-fall-short-genocide

[394]   https://www.voanews.com/africa/un-investigator-atrocities-drc-fall-short-genocide

[395]   https://www.voanews.com/africa/un-investigator-atrocities-drc-fall-short-genocide

[396]   https://www.voanews.com/africa/un-investigator-atrocities-drc-fall-short-genocide

[397]   https://www.voanews.com/africa/un-investigator-atrocities-drc-fall-short-genocide

contributing to the fight. The conflict is a proxy sectarian war fought between Sunni Saudi Arabia and Shiite Iran. As reported by In Depth News, "[a]ccording to the UN and other sources, from March 2015 to December 2017, 8,670–13,600 people were killed in Yemen, including more than 5,200 civilians, as well as estimates of more than 50,000 dead as a result of an ongoing famine due to the war."[398]

A political crisis in any nation has a devastating impact not only on those stationed at the pedestals of power, but for the nation at large. It can have devastating effects on a nation due to the plethora of problems it creates which affect all strata of civic life. Such a crisis can easily escalate into violence of various forms, which can ultimately result in genocide or war.

The Middle Eastern has attracted attention for being more or less the global centre of extremist ideological struggle. Be it a political power struggle in order to gain the authority to rule, or an ideological struggle to implement the superiority of a particular religious group, the ones who always suffer in the power tussle are the civilians of the country.

Trapped amidst crises, whether political or religious in nature, civilians have been paying a heavy price, especially in Yemen, where political unrest has generated strife for the Yemeni population by throwing at them various uncertainties. Amidst the political crisis in Yemen, the most important factor that should be kept in mind is that even in the progressive era of the twenty-first century, what the people of Yemen have been facing is no less than extermination. It is of the utmost importance to analyze the pattern of violence in Yemen and to study what impact it has on the politics of the region and the world in general.

According to *Deutsche Welle*:

Yemen's recent history is one of division and bloodshed. Until the early 1960s, the country was ruled by a monarchy in the north and the British in the south. Coups in both regions plunged the country into decades of violence, ending with reunification in 1990. ... Prior to the war, Yemen's population of more than 20 million was projected to double by 2035. Amid high unemployment and dissatisfaction with the ruling Saleh family, the country was ready for change when the Arab Spring swept across North Africa and the Middle East in 2011. ... Yemen's war unfolded over several years, beginning with the Arab Spring in 2011. Pro-democracy protesters took to the streets in a bid to force President Ali Abed Allah Saleh to end his 33-year rule. He responded with economic concessions, but refused to resign. By March, tensions on the streets of the capital city, Sanaa, saw protesters dying at the hands of the military. One of Yemen's

---

[398] https://www.indepthnews.net/index.php/sustainability/peace-justice/2916-un-forced-to-close-down-life-saving-aid-operations-in-yemen

most prominent commanders backed the opposition, paving the way for deadly clashes between government troops and tribal militias. Thanks to an internationally-brokered deal, Yemen finally saw a transfer of power in November to Vice President Abed Rabbo Mansour Hadi, paving the way for elections in February—in which he was the only candidate.[399]

The political transition was envisioned to bring stability and peace to Yemen, and was the result of the popular Arab Spring movement that was bringing about substantial stability and political transitions in other Middle Eastern and African nations. The "success" of the Arab Spring uprising in Yemen forced its long-time authoritarian president, Ali Abdullah Saleh, to hand over power to rule to his deputy, Abdrabbuh Mansour Hadi, back in 2011.

The political transition was an utter failure. The new leaders attempted to implement constitutional and budget reforms, which sparked a huge outcry by Houthi rebels from the north, initiating civil war in Yemen. President Hadi "struggled to deal with a variety of problems, including attacks by jihadists, a separatist movement in the south, the continuing loyalty of security personnel to Saleh, as well as corruption, unemployment, and food insecurity."[400]

According to *Deutsche Welle*:

[b]y September 2014, Houthi insurgents had taken the capital city, forcing Hadi to relocate his government to the southern port city of Aden. ... Multiple factions are entangled in Yemen's war. However, the conflict divides into two main categories: pro-government forces led by President Hadi and anti-government forces led by the Houthis, who are backed by former President Saleh. The Houthis hail from Yemen's north and belong to a small branch of Shiite Muslims known as Zaydis. Until summer 2015, the insurgents had infiltrated much of the country's south. They currently maintain control over key central provinces in the north. Hadi's government has accused Iran of smuggling them military arms, an accusation which Tehran has denied. President Hadi's government is headquartered in Aden and is the internationally-recognized government of Yemen. In 2015, Saudi Arabia launched an international coalition in a bid to reinstate Hadi.[401]

Yemen's Zaidi Shia Muslim minority fought a series of rebellions against Saleh, this Houthi movement:

---

399   https://www.dw.com/cda/en/yemens-war-explained-in-4-key-points/a-40056866

400   https://www.bbc.com/news/world-middle-east-29319423

401   https://www.dw.com/cda/en/yemens-war-explained-in-4-key-points/a-40056866

took advantage of the new president's weakness by taking control of their northern heartland of Saada province and neighbouring areas. Disillusioned with the transition, many ordinary Yemenis—including Sunnis—supported the Houthis, and in late 2014 and early 2015, the rebels took over Sanaa. The Houthis and security forces loyal to Saleh—who is thought to have backed his erstwhile enemies in a bid to regain power—then attempted to take control of the entire country, forcing Mr Hadi to flee abroad in March 2015. Alarmed by the rise of a group they believed to be backed militarily by regional Shia power Iran, Saudi Arabia and eight other mostly Sunni Arab states began an air campaign aimed at restoring Mr. Hadi's government. The coalition received logistical and intelligence support from the U.S., U.K., and France. At the start of the war, Saudi officials forecast that the war would last only a few weeks. But four years of military stalemate have followed.[402]

The situation in Yemen has witnessed no significant change to date, and Yemen's civilians have been at the receiving end of atrocities that know no bounds.

Being one of the poorest regions in the Middle Eastern nations, Yemen is in desperate need of help and international recognition of its distress. According to the BBC:

[t]he alliance between the Houthis and Mr. Saleh collapsed in November 2017 following clashes over control of Sanaa's biggest mosque that left dozens of people dead. Houthi fighters launched an operation to take full control of the capital and on December 4th, 2017 announced that Mr. Saleh had been killed. Only weeks later, infighting among pro-government forces erupted. Separatists seeking independence for south Yemen, which was a separate country before unification with the north in 1990, formed an uneasy alliance with troops loyal to Mr. Hadi in 2015 to stop the Houthis capturing Aden. But in January 2018, the separatist movement known as the Southern Transitional Council (STC) accused the Hadi government of corruption and mismanagement, and demanded the removal of the prime minister. Clashes erupted when separatist units attempted to seize government facilities and military bases in Aden by force. The situation was made more complex by divisions within the Saudi-led coalition. Saudi Arabia reportedly backs Mr. Hadi, who is based in Riyadh, while the United Arab Emirates is closely aligned with the separatists. Calm was restored in Aden after a few weeks, but tensions between the two groups remain. In September, there were protests after separatist officials called for a peaceful popular uprising in the South.[403]

---

402   https://www.bbc.com/news/world-middle-east-29319423

403   https://www.bbc.com/news/world-middle-east-29319423

According to *Deutsche Welle*:

> [a]long with Saudi Arabia, the United Arab Emirates has conducted airstrikes on Yemeni soil. Kuwait, Bahrain, Qatar, Morocco, Sudan, Jordan and Egypt have also contributed to the operations. The United States and the United Kingdom have both provided logistical support and intelligence to the Saudi-led coalition.[404]

The Yemen war has more or less left the world polarized, as global powers back forces they deem beneficial to them. Instead of fighting for the ideals of humanity, the powerful economies are taking advantage of the political crisis to suit their own respective purposes.

As reported by the Council on Foreign Relations:

> [s]eparate from the ongoing civil war, the United States continues counterterrorism operations in Yemen, relying mainly on airstrikes to target al-Qaeda in the Arabian Peninsula (AQAP) and militants associated with the self-proclaimed Islamic State. In 2016, the United States conducted an estimated 35 strikes in Yemen; in 2017, it conducted about 130. In April 2016, the United States deployed a small team of forces to advise and assist Saudi-led troops to retake territory from AQAP. In January 2017, a U.S. Special Operations Forces raid in central Yemen killed one U.S. service member, several suspected AQAP-affiliated fighters, and an unknown number of Yemeni civilians.[405]

Genocide Watch has issued a Genocide Emergency for Yemen, reporting that:

> [f]or the last three years, Yemen has been experiencing a bloody war between the Houthi rebels and supporters of Yemen's internationally recognized government, which the UN has described as 'the worst man-made humanitarian crisis of our time.'[406]

Genocide Watch also reports that:

> [a]s of March 26th, 2018, at least 10,000 Yemenis have been directly killed by the fighting, with more than 40,000 direct casualties overall. Getting accurate information on the overall death toll caused by food shortages and the collapse of the country's health system is difficult, but Save the Children estimates at least 50,000 children died in 2017,

---

404 https://www.dw.com/cda/en/yemens-war-explained-in-4-key-points/a-40056866

405 https://www.cfr.org/interactive/global-conflict-tracker/conflict/war-yemen

406 http://www.genocidewatch.com/copy-of-current-genocide-watch-aler

an average of 130 every day. The United Nations High Commissioner for Human Rights has estimated that Saudi-led coalition air attacks have caused almost two-thirds of the reported civilian deaths while the Houthis have been accused of causing mass civilian casualties due to their siege of Taiz, Yemen's third-largest city.[407]

The airstrikes or ground strikes in Yemen, be it by any faction, have been committed regardless of the age or gender of the civilians in the targeted areas. According to Genocide Watch:

> [i]n October, the UN Committee on the Rights of the Child reported that at least 1,248 children have been killed since the start of the war. To date, it is reported that approximately 85,000 children under five years old have starved to death since the outset of the war.
>
> Until very recently, the United States supported the Saudi aerial attacks by providing for mid-air refuelling of Saudi planes. Those aerial attacks are said to be responsible for 35,000 civilian casualties. It appears that the Saudi warplanes have deliberately targeted civilians in their homes and schools, on their farms and buses, and in their businesses. They have targeted petrol stations, killing scores of people with each air strike. Not only have farms been bombed and prices for food in markets soared as a result of the war, but the Saudis, with the complicity of the United States, have virtually blocked food from entering all but one of the main ports in Yemen. They have also systematically prevented movement between the ports and cities, towns and villages, thus preventing aid from reaching those in dire need. Both sides in this genocidal civil war have murdered humanitarian aid personnel and erected barricades along the roads, where they extort bribes from ordinary citizens who have gone to buy food.[408]

The United Nations figures have demonstrated that by the end of 2019, fighting in Yemen will have claimed about 102,000 lives. A UN-commissioned report has also revealed that more Yemenis are "dying of hunger, disease and the lack of health clinics and other infrastructure than from fighting."[409] Contributing to the crisis has been the ongoing Saudi-led coalition air strikes.[410] An international group tracking the civil war believes the death toll is far higher than other reported figures.

---

[407] http://www.genocidewatch.com/copy-of-current-genocide-watch-aler

[408] http://www.genocidewatch.com/single-post/2018/12/18/Abrar-of-Yemen-Appeal-to-Congress

[409] https://www.middleeasteye.net/news/yemen-death-toll-surpass-230000-end-2019-un-report

[410] https://www.middleeasteye.net/news/saudi-led-coalition-yemen-targets-houthi-drone-storage-near-presidential-palace-state-media

Approximately 80% of the population (24 million people) are in need of humanitarian assistance and protection. About 20 million need help gaining access to food, including almost 10 million whom the UN says are "just a step away from famine." Almost 240,000 are facing "catastrophic levels of hunger."[411] Over 3 million people—2 million of whom are children—are "acutely malnourished,"[412] which makes them more vulnerable to disease. According to the BBC:

> [w]ith only half of the country's 3,500 medical facilities fully functioning, almost 20 million people lack access to adequate healthcare. And almost 18 million do not have enough clean water or access to adequate sanitation. Consequently, medics have struggled to deal with the largest cholera outbreak ever recorded, which has resulted in more than 1.49 million suspected cases and 2,960 related deaths since April 2017. The war has also displaced more than 3.3 million from their homes, including 685,000 who have fled fighting along the west coast since June 2018.[413]

Al Jazeera reports:

> The Armed Conflict and Location Event Data Project (ACLED) said it has recorded 3,155 direct attacks that targeted civilians, resulting in more than 7,000 reported civilian deaths. The Saudi-led coalition was responsible for the highest number of civilian deaths—more than 4,800 since 2016, the group said. The Houthis, meanwhile, had killed 1,300 civilians in direct attacks, it added. The fighting and ensuing economic collapse have also unleashed the world's most urgent humanitarian crisis, with 14 million of the impoverished country's 29 million population on the brink of starvation. The UN said last month that 100 civilians were either killed or wounded every week in Yemen in 2018, with children accounting for a fifth of all casualties. According to the figures released by the UN's refugee agency, more than 4,800 civilian deaths and injuries were reported over the course of 2018. Children accounted for 410 deaths and 542 injuries.[414]

Despite these disturbing statistics, the conflict in Yemen has been referred to as "the forgotten war."[415] The situation calls for global attention, not

---

411 https://reliefweb.int/report/yemen/under-secretary-general-humanitarian-affairs-and-emergency-relief-coordinator-mark-15

412 https://reliefweb.int/report/yemen/under-secretary-general-humanitarian-affairs-and-emergency-relief-coordinator-mark-15

413 https://www.bbc.com/news/world-middle-east-29319423

414 https://www.aljazeera.com/news/2019/04/yemen-war-death-toll-reaches-70000-report-190419120508897.html

415 https://www.dw.com/cda/en/yemens-war-explained-in-4-key-points/a-40056866

only in military strikes to battle the seeds of extremism and radicalization in the Middle East, but in humanitarian assistance for the long-suffering civilians of Yemen. The contemporary situation in Yemen—a lack of basic food amenities, health facilities, and personal security—paints a picture of the area in red, against a backdrop of destruction.

Libyan Civil War

The ongoing conflict among rival factions seeking control of the territory and oil of Libya started soon after the toppling of Muammar Mohammed Abu Minyar Gaddafi, commonly known as Colonel Gaddafi, who was a Libyan revolutionary and authoritarian leader who governed Libya from 1977 to 2011.

The ICC came into force in 2002, and became a vital part of the international political relations as well as human rights system. Many states became parties to the Rome Statute by ratifying it at the time of the Court's establishment, and later became member states of the ICC. At present, at least 124 countries are party to the Rome Statute, and as a result of it members of the Court.[416] As of 2013, the International Criminal Court Prosecutor had taken up eight countries' situations, including the Democratic Republic of Congo, Uganda, Central African Republic, Mali, Sudan (Darfur), Libya, Kenya, and Côte d'Ivoire.

The UN Security Council (UNSC) adopted Resolution 1970[417] by a vote of 15–0 referring the situation in Libya to the ICC.[418] Under the Rome Statute, the ICC's founding treaty, the Security Council may refer a situation in any country to the ICC Prosecutor under its Chapter VII mandate if it determines that the situation threatens international peace and security. The situation in Libya is the ICC's sixth investigation.[419]

The UNSC passed another resolution in February 2011, this time unanimously referring to the ICC the situation in Libya with respect to its civil war in 2011. The ICC Prosecutor accordingly issued warrants in June 2011 for Muammar Mohammed Abu Minyar Gaddafi (head of state), Saif al-Islam Gaddafi (former *de facto* prime minister), and Abdullah al-Senussi

---

[416] https://asp.icc-cpi.int/en_menus/asp/states%20parties/pages/the%20states%20parties%20to%20the%20rome%20statute.aspx

[417] https://www.icc-cpi.int/NR/rdonlyres/2B57BBA2-07D9-4C35-B45E-EED275080E87/0/N1124558.pdf

[418] https://www.hrw.org/sites/default/files/related_material/QA_Libya_ICC_May_2013.pdf

[419] https://s3.amazonaws.com/documents.nycbar.org/files/ICC_Digest_Supplement_African_1.22.18.pdf

(former head of military intelligence) on the charges of crimes against humanity based on murder and persecution. The case against Muammar Gaddafi was terminated following his death in November 2011, while the other two suspects remain in the custody of Libyan authorities who wish to try them in domestic court rather than the ICC. Libya is not a state party to the Rome Statute. However, Pre-Trial Chamber (PTC) I declined Libya's challenge to the ICC's jurisdiction over the case of al-Islam Gaddafi.[420]

On March 3rd, 2011, the investigation into the situation in Libya was formally kicked off by the ICC Prosecutor, after the Court conducted a preliminary examination of available information. An official declaration was made by the ICC's Prosecutor after the UNSC adopted Resolution 1970 on February 26th, 2011, referring Libya's situation as a state not party to the Rome Statute or to the ICC. "This was the second time that a situation was referred to the Court by the UNSC under its Chapter VII authority, and the first time such a resolution was passed unanimously."[421] The ICC Presidency handed over the situation to PTC I, which at present includes Judge Hans-Peter Kaul (Germany), Judge Christine Van den Wyngaert (Belgium), and Judge Silvia Fernandez Gurmendi (Argentina).[422]

After the Prosecutor filed an application on June 27th, 2011, "PTC I issued arrest warrants for the Libyan leader Muammar Mohammed Abu Minyar Gaddafi, his son Saif al-Islam Gaddafi, who was the Libyan government spokesman, as well as Abdullah al-Senussi, Director of Military Intelligence."[423] All three were charged for alleged crimes against humanity, including murder and persecution, committed in the country from February 15th–28th, 2011. However, on November 20th, 2011, PTC I terminated the case against Muammar Gaddafi following his demise, while Saif Gaddafi was held by Libyan authorities on November 19th, 2011. Al-Senussi was arrested in Mauritania on March 17th, 2012. He was extradited to Libya on September 5th, 2012.[424]

Libya submitted some confidential observations on January 23rd, 2012, in regards to Safi Gaddafi's arrest and detention after a request from PTC I was made on December 6th, 2011. Following the objection, PTC I reiterated its order on April 4th, 2012 which stated that Libya must instantaneously surrender Saif Gaddafi to the ICC. The appeal by

420   http://www.lop.parl.gc.ca/Content/LOP/ResearchPublications/2002-11-e.pdf

421   http://iccnow.org/?mod=libya

422   http://iccnow.org/?mod=libya

423   http://iccnow.org/?mod=libya

424   https://trialinternational.org/latest-post/abdullah-al-senussi/

Libya against the order was declined on April 25th, 2012 by the Appeals Chamber.

Meanwhile, PTC I slammed the applications for leave to submit *amicus curiae* observations by Mishana Hosseinioun and Aisha Gaddafi on February 2nd, 2012, as well as their following requests for leave to plea. In addition, the applicants also appealed directly to the Appeals Chamber in regards to issues of admissibility and jurisdiction.

On May 1st, 2012, Libya put forward the admissibility of the cases before the ICC, and on June 1st, 2012, PTC I postponed the obligation to hold Saif Gaddafi pending the outcome of the admissibility challenge. This was the first time when things looked in Libya's favour. However, on October 8th–9th, 2012, PTC I conducted a public hearing to examine and discuss Libya's challenge of the admissibility in the Gaddafi cases.

PTC I stated on February 6th, 2013 that Libya was still under an obligation to surrender al-Senussi to the ICC. However, PTC I delayed the obligation to surrender Saif Gaddafi until it had decided on Libya's May 2012 challenge to the ICC's jurisdiction of the case.

On April 17th, 2013, the chamber approved a request by the Office of the Public Counsel for Defence (OPCD), "that it be relinquished from its court-appointed representation of Saif Gaddafi citing an imminent depletion in staffing."[425] Following this, John Jones QC was appointed, replacing the OPCD. However, on April 2nd, 2013, Libya submitted an appeal challenging the ICC case against al-Senussi, mentioning the ongoing domestic probes into alleged crimes by him in the country.[426]

In Saif Gaddafi's case, PTC I found that there were valid reasons to believe that after the happenings in Tunisia and Egypt during the early months of 2011, one of the policies of Libya, formulated at the utmost level of the Libyan state machinery, was intended to discourage and suppress the demonstrations of civilians against the regime of Muammar Gaddafi. This particular policy stated that people can be legally suppressed by any means, including by the use of lethal force.[427] From February 15th to at least February 28th, 2011, the security forces of Libya carried out actions against protests throughout Libya. The government used all forces, including units of the security and military systems, to neutralize the situation—especially in Tripoli, Misrata, and Benghazi, in addition to cities near Benghazi, such as Al-Bayda, Derna, Tobruk, and Ajdabiya.

---

[425] http://www.iccnow.org/?mod=libya

[426] Ibid.

[427] https://www.icc-cpi.int/libya/gaddafi/Documents/GaddafiEng.pdf

In this crackdown, security forces used force to attack the civilian population taking part in demonstrations. Many people were killed and injured, and hundreds of civilians were arrested and imprisoned.

On May 31st, 2013, PTC I "rejected Libya's challenge to the admissibility of the case against Saif Gaddafi before the ICC," and asked him to surrender.[428] The chamber concluded that Libya's domestic probe did not adequately cover the alleged crimes as mentioned in the case by the ICC. Judges recognized the state's efforts to reinstate the rule of law, but stressed that it "continue[d] to face problems in exercising its judicial powers, including the ability to secure Gaddafi into state custody."[429]

Libya has since appealed the decision, but during the appeal of the admissibility judgment, the obligation to surrender Gaddafi will remain in place. The Appeals Chamber on July 18th, 2013 dismissed Libya's appeal to suspend Saif Gaddafi's surrender to the ICC, while a final decision is pending on its challenge to the admissibility of the case. In May, the chamber had finalized that Gaddafi must be transferred as well as tried at the ICC. On July 23rd, 2013, Gaddafi's defence appealed to PTC I to find that Libya had failed to cooperate by refusing to surrender him to the ICC and to refer the matter to the UNSC.[430]

On October 11th, 2013, PTC I ruled that the case against al-Senussi was inadmissible before the ICC, as the Libyan authorities were willing and able to effectively prosecute him. It was the first incidence of judges having ruled in favour of a government challenge to the ICC's jurisdiction over a case. The Appeals Chamber unanimously confirmed PTC I's decision on July 24th, 2014, putting an end to the proceedings against al-Senussi before the Court.[431]

The Appeals Chamber on May 21st, 2014 authorized the admissibility of the Saif Gaddafi case before the International Criminal Court. The Chamber confirmed that the PTC I judges had not been mistaken in finding that Libya had not adequately proven that its investigation at the national level covered the same case as the one put before the ICC.[432]

The population of Libya faced inhumane atrocities during the reign of Muammar Gaddafi, who suppressed the civilians for standing against his rule. The ICC has taken up cases of national and international importance, and the case of Libya is one of them. The trials of the ICC are

---

[428] http://iccnow.org/?mod=libya&idudctp=14&show=all&order=authorasc&lang=en

[429] http://iccnow.org/?mod=libya&idudctp=14&show=all&order=authorasc&lang=en

[430] http://iccnow.org/?mod=libya&idudctp=14&show=all&order=authorasc&lang=en

[431] http://iccnow.org/?mod=libya&idudctp=14&show=all&order=authorasc&lang=en

[432] http://iccnow.org/?mod=libya&idudctp=14&show=all&order=authorasc&lang=en

somewhat slow and expensive, but its decisions act like milestones in the global political situation. Saif Gaddafi, the forty-two-year-old successor of Muammar Gaddafi, is "the subject of a legal tug-of-war between Libya and the ICC over charges related to the repression of the 2011 uprising that toppled and killed his father."[433]

South Sudan

South Sudan is the youngest nation on earth, the product of civil war.

Since the twentieth century, Sudan has faced a serious humanitarian crisis, with the so-called modern and progressive era of the twenty-first century providing the nation with no relief. Sudan has always been plagued by violence, and the civil wars in the country created a substantial rift between the geographical north and south, ultimately leading to the formation of South Sudan in 2011. The formation of the new country was no end to the destructive attitude of those occupying the top positions in the hierarchy of power and authority. Though political and economic factors have played a major role, the conflict in South Sudan could be deemed to be largely about ethnicity.

The ethnic conflict was triggered due to a leadership conflict in South Sudan that has to date engaged the involvement of civilians supporting their respective leaders and their ethnic tribes. Though the founding stone of the world's newest country was laid with the hope of establishing democratic order in the nation, the deep-rooted biases within the sociopolitical sphere of South Sudan have continued to fuel the fire of rebellion and violence. According to Michal Kranz, "South Sudan's President Salva Kiir, a member of the Dinka ethnic group, has been using his army to wage a campaign of genocide and ethnic cleansing against the Dinkas' main rival ethnic group, the Nuer, as well as other smaller local groups."[434] This has raised a rebellious zeal in the groups at the receiving end of persecution by the so-called protector of the country.

The conflict in South Sudan is not at all unidimensional in nature. It is a complex, cyclic process of violence, wherein the Dinkas' actions of ethnic cleansing are being repeated with the same magnitude in reverse by the Nuers. The targeted mass killing in South Sudan qualifies internationally as a genocide, as the intent behind the massacre is no less than deliberate extermination. The struggle in South Sudan is not limited to

---

[433] https://www.aljazeera.com/news/middleeast/2014/12/icc-refers-libya-un-over-gaddafi-son-2014121018401696198.html

[434] https://www.businessinsider.com/genocides-still-going-on-today-bosnia-2017-11#the-nuer-and-other-ethnic-groups-in-south-sudan-2

the Dinka-Nuer conflict: it has extended its venomous fangs to other small tribes in the country as well. The fight for identity, recognition, and resources has implicated all the ethnic tribes in South Sudan, resulting in a dizzying array of violent acts across the country.[435]

Since civil war erupted in the region in December 2013, some 50,000 people have lost their lives. Over 2.3 million people have fled their homes, around 6 million are at risk of starvation, and 70% of schools have been closed due to the conflict.[436] In South Sudan, widespread violence is now commonplace. The massacre of people due to their tribal affinity, the burning of entire villages for the same purpose, as well as gang rapes, starvation, and violence against children and the elderly, have all become day-to-day realities.

As a new country comes into existence, many complexities arise. As power shifts its course, it should be assured that this shift of power is occurring for the betterment of the country—that it is watering the seeds of equality and justice for the people. But as the split of the geographical south from the north of Sudan was negotiated, creating the independent nation of South Sudan, due attention was not paid to the simmering ethnic tensions which then sprung up like a violent volcanic eruption across the country, engulfing thousands in the lava of hatred.

South Sudan itself comprises about sixty different ethnic groups that have been engaged in conflict with each other over the meagre availability of resources. These ethnic tensions were masked by the façade of unity in the mission for national independence from the north. Since the resolving of the differences between the groups was overlooked during the independence process, the tensions bubbled up into genocidal ideology.

The ongoing genocide in South Sudan has known no bounds in terms of human rights violations, especially in the past few years as the conflict has taken a particularly dangerous turn. Kiir, the South Sudanese President at the time of the nation's formation, attempted to convey a message of inclusion, but with time, his real intent of establishing an authoritarian regime came to the fore. He failed miserably to maintain the integrity of South Sudan as he has promised to do in his maiden speech after becoming President. In his speech marking South Sudan's official independence on July 9th, 2011, Kiir proclaimed:

---

[435] Silva, Mario, "After Partition: The Perils of South Sudan," University of Baltimore Journal of International Law, Journal of International Law, Vol. 3, Iss. 1, 2014-2015.

[436] https://www.vox.com/world/2016/12/8/13817072/south-sudan-crisis-explained-ethnic-cleansing-genocide

May this day mark a new beginning of tolerance, unity and love for one another. Let our cultural and ethnic diversity be a source of pride and strength, not parochialism and conflict. ... We are all South Sudanese. We may be Zande, Kakwa, Nuer, Toposa, Dinka, Lotuko, Anyuak, Bari, and Shiluk, but remember you are South Sudanese first![437]

In an attempt to appeal to the entire nation and to put a rest to the internal conflict, President Kiir of the Dinka tribe appointed Riek Machar of the Nuer—the arch-enemy of the Dinka—to the post of Vice President, in order to set an example of ethnic integration. With the President of South Sudan belonging to the largest ethnic tribe and the Vice President to the second-largest, it was predictable that the rivalry between the tribes would escalate into violence whenever the pressure went above the watermark. The Nuer and the Dinka share a violent past: the brutal massacre in 1991, chiefly led by Riek Machar, claimed the life of about 2,000 civilians in the town of Bor, and the political after-effects of the fight eventually morphed into all-out ethnic conflict in South Sudan.[438] The two ethnic rivals occupying two hierarchical positions of power were destined to clash. According to *Vox*:

> [i]n early 2013, Machar began vocally criticizing Kiir's leadership of the country and his handling of the economy, and announced his intention to challenge Kiir for the presidency in 2015. Kiir, not surprisingly, didn't particularly appreciate that, and responded in July by firing Machar—as well as all 28 of Kiir's cabinet ministers and their deputies, leaving government ministries in the hands of civil servants. Then, in December 2013, all hell broke loose. Forces loyal to Machar clashed with forces loyal to Kiir.[439]

Within a week of its outbreak, the brutal violence brought death to about 1,000 people and caused the displacement of some 100,000. The trumpet of war blown by the leaders of the nation has resounded to date in the helplessness of the civilians who have been brought to the verge of starvation by the ongoing conflict. The violence in South Sudan since 2013 has been so gruesome that Machar has fled the country's capital Juba twice to save himself and his tribe, both in 2013 and in 2016 when the violence took an ugly turn.

---

437   https://www.vox.com/world/2018/6/20/17483232/south-sudan-civil-war-meeting-ethiopia-riek-machar-salva-kiir-peace-talks

438   https://www.vox.com/world/2018/6/20/17483232/south-sudan-civil-war-meeting-ethiopia-riek-machar-salva-kiir-peace-talks

439   https://www.vox.com/world/2018/6/20/17483232/south-sudan-civil-war-meeting-ethiopia-riek-machar-salva-kiir-peace-talks

South Sudan has turned into a hotbed of ethnic genocide. The conditions of its civilians are abhorrent and inhuman. Despite international pressure, South Sudan has been continuing the genocide, and restraining the liberal elements of the country. Several global powers have a vested interest in South Sudan because of its natural resources—especially oil—which could benefit the global powers in several ways. South Sudan has recently seen an increase in hate speech and a crackdown on the media and civil society that has had the effect of strengthening the divisions between South Sudan's sixty-four ethnic groups. All the parties involved in the genocide of South Sudan have committed grave wrongdoings, including indiscriminate attacks on civilians such as aid workers, people with disabilities, and the elderly (those who lacked resources and the ability to safeguard themselves); unlawful killings; beatings; arbitrary detentions; torture; sexual violence; recruitment and use of child soldiers; and looting and destruction of civilian property. Most of the abuses committed within the region of South Sudan qualify as war crimes or crimes against humanity as per international measures.

Human Rights Watch reported that:

[s]ince the conflict started in December 2013, more than 4 million people have fled their homes, with 2.47 million taking refuge in neighbouring countries. Close to 200,000 people are living in six UN 'protection of civilians' sites across the country. Seven million people need humanitarian assistance, most of whom faced acute food shortages.[440]

Food has been used a weapon of war in South Sudan, as reported by UN monitors, who stated that "[t]he government has during much of 2017 deliberately prevented life-saving food assistance from reaching some citizens."[441]

Rape has also been used as a weapon of war in the conflict. Women have been brutally raped, abducted, and even sold. According to Human Rights Watch:

The UN mission in South Sudan (UNMISS) documented how, in April and May, government and aligned fighters attacked 40 villages in opposition-controlled parts of southern Unity, killing at least 232 civilians and injuring many more, looted and burned homes, and used rape 'as a

440   https://www.hrw.org/world-report/2019/country-chapters/south-sudan

441   https://www.reuters.com/article/us-southsudan-security-un-exclusive/exclusive-south-sudans-government-using-food-as-weapon-of-war-u-n-report-idUSKB-N1DA2OX

weapon of war,' against at least 120 women and girls, and ordered civilians to leave their villages. Thousands fled their homes or hiding places.[442]

It is not only the women of South Sudan who are vulnerable. Small children are frequently targeted and abducted, forced to serve in armed groups. A UN report notes that 6,500 children were recruited between October 2014 and June 2018, and were victims of other abuses such as abductions, killing, maiming, and sexual abuse.[443] Despite the world taking note of the atrocities in South Sudan, the condition of the nation is deteriorating day by day as several international aid agencies face the heat of the authoritarian regime of South Sudan. All parties involved in the conflict restricted access for the UN mission which has been providing humanitarian assistance and ceasefire monitors with the capacity to challenge the authority of South Sudan.

Human Rights Watch reports:

> At least 12 aid workers were killed in 2018, bringing the toll to over 100 since December 2013. In February [2018], rebel forces detained 29 aid workers in greater Baggari area and released them after one day. In April [2018], 10 aid workers were abducted for five days in Yei, in the former Central Equatoria state. In July [2018], armed youth in Maban county, in Upper Nile, looted and burned UN and humanitarian facilities to protest lack of job opportunities, forcing aid groups to suspend operations. Armed groups and government soldiers continued to attack UNMISS compounds, including in Juba Bor, Bentiu, Malakal, Wau, Akobo and Melut. Government security forces, especially the National Security Service (NSS), detained perceived government opponents and critics, including human rights activists and academics.[444]

A UN report identified sixty incidents, including killings, arbitrary arrests and detentions of journalists and editors, closure, suspension or censorship of newspapers, and blocking of websites, from the period of July 2016 to Dec 2017.[445]

The violence in South Sudan began in 2013, and has continued to date, affecting the overall health of the country in the adverse. In a clash

---

[442] https://www.hrw.org/world-report/2019/country-chapters/south-sudan

[443] Report of the Commission on Human Rights in South Sudan, Human Rights Council, Fortieth session, 25 February – 22 March 2019.

[444] Report of the Commission on Human Rights in South Sudan, Human Rights Council, Fortieth session, 25 February – 22 March 2019.

[445] Report of the Commission on Human Rights in South Sudan, Human Rights Council, Fortieth session, 25 February – 22 March 2019.

that began on January 19th, 2019 between the army and the rebel group under the banner of the National Salvation Front, all humanitarian aid was blocked for South Sudan's Equatoria state. The outbreak led several thousands of civilians to flee the area and seek safety in the neighbouring Democratic Republic of the Congo. The UNHCR has noted that some 5,000 refugees from South Sudan have settled in various villages along the border near the town of Ingbokolo in Ituri province in northeastern DRC. Many of these people are suffering from malaria or other illnesses and are in a state of trauma, as they have "witnessed violent incidents, including armed men reportedly murdering and raping civilians and looting villages."[446]

There may be no near end to the violence in South Sudan, but the situation urgently requires international attention. Humanitarian concern and assistance could aid the country in dealing with its horrific past and intimidating present, and bring hope for the future.

Central African Republic

The African continent is at the centre stage of conflicts of varying degrees. The conflicts encompassing the continent may have similarities when the politics and pattern of genocidal tendencies are examined, but the distinctive characteristics and intricacies of each situation cannot be ignored. Like several African nations fighting their battles of retaining humanitarian ideology within their national boundaries, the Central African Republic (CAR) is undergoing a war of an altogether different dimension.

Most of the world finds it difficult to locate the Central African Republic on the world map, and are unaware of the events that are bringing the country to the verge of genocide. The nation—once colonized by France although bigger in area than its colonizer—has long been a blind spot for the world at large.[447]

The CAR has been largely unstable since gaining independence from France in 1960. Violence is nothing new for the country's people. The Christian-dominated nation has been engaged in a kind of religious war with other religious minorities of the country, especially the Muslims. Though the conflict in the CAR has not been overtly termed a genocide by the international community, there is no denying that the rate at which the country's violence is growing is significant enough that it will soon merit the category of genocide.

---

[446] https://news.un.org/en/story/2019/02/1032541

[447] https://www.theguardian.com/world/2013/nov/22/central-african-republic-verge-of-genocide

Violence in any form is destructive, and when the scale of violence reaches a national level, the dangers to the country become unmanageable. The CAR has been dealing with the worst form of humanitarian crisis since 2012, though the country has a violent past stretching back far further. The events that unfolded on December 5th, 2013 brought the crisis of the Central African Republic to the fore, attracting international concern. The transformation of a religious conflict into a political one has affected the overall integrity of the country in the adverse.

The UN has raised serious concerns about the "early warning signs of genocide" in the CAR.[448] The country's situation is worsening day by day, and the region has now turned into a battlefield between the majority Christians and minority Muslims. Religious supremacy has always played a crucial role across the globe as a justification for violence. But the situation in the Central African Republic is not only explained by religion. Unlike other countries where genocide has left its mark, the crisis of the CAR has not been unidimensional where violence is perpetrated by a single group against another. In fact, what has plagued this African nation is the perpetration of violence from both sides, depending on who has held, or who is attempting to hold, power.

In order to understand the present-day crisis, it is important to unravel the history of the region's violence. As *The Washington Post* explains:

> The violence began when a predominantly Muslim coalition of rebels called the Seleka swept to power in 2013 after killing and burning their way through this majority Christian country. Mostly Christian groups known as the anti-balaka formed to fight back. Many of the armed groups subsequently splintered. The Seleka rulers were eventually replaced by an interim government, and a former prime minister, Faustin-Archange Touadéra, became president ... in what many saw as a sign of progress.[449]

Christians in the CAR account for 80% of the population, and their rebel-group under the name "Anti-balaka" is a reference to the machetes used by the Muslim rebels.[450] The rebellion launched by the Seleka rebels in December 2012 began in the geographical north of the country, where most of the Muslims (who, as a religious minority, account for

---

448 https://www.aljazeera.com/news/2017/08/sees-early-warning-signs-genocide-car-170807215828039.html

449 https://www.washingtonpost.com/world/africa/the-central-african-republic-could-be-on-the-brink-of-a-bloodbath/2017/10/09/b26e59d0-a7bf-11e7-9a98-07140d2eed02_story.html?utm_term=.0ec2fe6df272

450 https://www.aljazeera.com/news/2017/08/sees-early-warning-signs-genocide-car-170807215828039.html

about 15% of the CAR's 5 million inhabitants) were based. The ongoing conflict has changed the demography of the country drastically, as both groups are engaged in the game of slaughter. As reported by Stop Genocide Now:

> [i]n 2013, a Muslim-majority rebel group Seleka ('alliance') ousted then-president François Bozizé after accusing him of breaking the cease-fire agreements from both 2007 and 2011. These cease-fire agreements had ended the CAR Bush War, a civil war that spanned the years between 2004 and 2011, and not only ended the violence but pledged to integrate the rebel groups into CAR society as well as into the political process. Seleka accused President Bozizé of not adhering to the power-sharing agreements with the rebel groups while the government blamed Seleka for attacking government garrisons unprovoked. ... In an attempt to restore order to the CAR, President Djotodia stepped down in 2014 and Catherine Samba-Panza, a Christian, took power. Despite the political transition, violence has continued, with both religious communities facing daily attacks. While the conflict has not yet been labelled a genocide, growing sectarian violence in the region may turn the CAR into the world's next Rwanda or Darfur.[451]

Most of the Seleka are Muslim, "including mercenaries from neighbouring Chad and the notorious Janjaweed from Sudan's Darfur region. An 'us and them' mentality of mutual distrust and paranoia has taken its roots in the country."[452]

Diplomats and relief workers have warned that the situation in the CAR is at risk of becoming "an all-out civil war, which would compound the humanitarian crisis and create new security problems in a region already grappling with extremist groups such as Boko Haram."[453] Gruesome reports of massacres, mass rapes, torture, and even forced cannibalism against the civilian populations flood the information channels. How political dissatisfaction can lead to political crisis is clearly illustrated by the example of the Central African Republic.

In order to stabilize any region, it is of the utmost importance to adopt the ideals of integration and unity. When the principle of exclusivity is a

---

451 https://stopgenocidenow.org/conflicts/central-african-republic/

452 https://www.theguardian.com/world/2013/nov/22/central-african-republic-verge-of-genocide

453 https://www.washingtonpost.com/world/africa/the-central-african-republic-could-be-on-the-brink-of-a-bloodbath/2017/10/09/b26e59d0-a7bf-11e7-9a98-07140d2eed02_story.html?utm_term=.0ec2fe6df272

religion's dominant ideology, it becomes next to impossible for humanitarian goals to prosper in the region. The same has been true of the CAR, as those positioned at the helm of power have failed to satisfy the armed groups' demands for political representation and amnesty, thus paving the way for a war-like scenario in the country. For rebel groups to have such a powerful and devastating impact, the meagre power exercised by the central government outside the capital region of Bangui played a vital role. The army being ill-equipped as well as ineffective has added to the misery of the civilians, whose lives and property are seriously threatened.

David Brownstein, the senior U.S. diplomat in the region, has explained that because of the CAR's geographical position, it "plays a fundamental role in either enhancing and promoting regional stability, or, conversely, if it's weakened or failed, it could have a fundamentally negative impact on regional stability."[454]

Apart from dealing with the menace of violence, the CAR is also facing other barriers in terms of the country's infrastructural development, employment opportunities, political instability, corruption, and economic disparities: the country has been listed as one of the poorest in the world. The nation is rich in gold, diamonds, timber, and uranium, but instead of utilizing its strength and finances toward economic development, the CAR has only used them to fuel its sectarian conflicts, thus paving the way for external interests like extremist groups and warlords to take advantage of the drift for their personal motives. The CAR has proved irresistible to warlords such as Joseph Kony, the leader of a cult-like militia known as the Lord's Resistance Army, a guerrilla group that formerly operated in Uganda. The search for Kony has engaged both U.S. and Ugandan forces in the CAR.

Despite international efforts like the peacekeeping missions of the United Nations, humanitarian groups, and even Pope Francis, several thousands have died in the CAR due to the religious violence, and several thousands more have been displaced with no means of living at hand. Women, children, and elderly are literally starving, facing a severe food and water shortage in the country. At a UN meeting in 2017, UN Humanitarian Affairs chief Stephen O'Brien said that half of the country's population, or 2.4 million people, were in need of food aid to survive—the largest population in need per capita.[455]

---

[454] https://www.washingtonpost.com/world/africa/the-central-african-republic-could-be-on-the-brink-of-a-bloodbath/2017/10/09/b26e59d0-a7bf-11e7-9a98-07140d2eed02_story.html?utm_term=.0ec2fe6df272

[455] https://www.aljazeera.com/news/2017/08/sees-early-warning-signs-genocide-car-170807215828039.html

The escalating violence among dozens of armed factions in the CAR has adopted an overtly sectarian overtone. According to *The Washington Post*:

> [t]he capital city of Bangui, guarded by UN peacekeepers, remains calm, but taxicab radios blare the growing list of hot spots across the country: Zemio, Batangafo, Obo. In addition to the internally displaced—who now number 600,000—about 500,000 people have fled to neighbouring countries since 2013, according to the United Nations.[456]

Some 180,000 people had been driven from their homes in 2017, bringing the total number of displaced in the CAR to well over half a million.[457]

The crisis has exacerbated the problems of food shortage and disease. Several civilians in the CAR are succumbing to deathly diseases such as malaria. As *The Guardian* reports, "[t]he US estimates that nearly 400,000 people have been displaced—many hiding in the jungle without access to malaria or HIV treatment—and 68,000 have gone to neighbouring countries."[458] The spiral of violence has resulted in the recruiting of thousands of child soldiers. Not only are children being recruited irrespective of age and gender by Christian and Muslim rebel groups, but the country is also witnessing public executions and violent deaths in the form of beheading. The ghost villages of the CAR paint a disturbing picture. Several reports note that many of the rebels have veered completely out of control—killing, looting, and burning villages. They have also systematically stripped administrative offices down to the light fixtures and destroyed public records.

The Seleka and the anti-balaka are engaged in a competitive battle, both continuing the cycle of violence. International reports are inundated with accounts of violence perpetrated by both groups along with dozens of other sectarian groups. Most of the Muslims in the CAR have fled their villages to find refuge in Bossangoa, "where about 34,000 people have sought refuge at the St. Antoine de Padoue Cathedral."[459] Some 2,000 Muslims took refuge in Bangassou Catholic church in 2017,

---

[456] https://www.washingtonpost.com/world/africa/the-central-african-republic-could-be-on-the-brink-of-a-bloodbath/2017/10/09/b26e59d0-a7bf-11e7-9a98-07140d2eed02_story.html?utm_term=.0ec2fe6df272

[457] https://www.aljazeera.com/news/2017/08/sees-early-warning-signs-genocide-car-170807215828039.html

[458] https://www.theguardian.com/world/2013/nov/22/central-african-republic-verge-of-genocide

[459] https://www.theguardian.com/world/2013/nov/22/central-african-republic-verge-of-genocide

"surrounded by anti-balaka Christian fighters who were threatening to kill them."[460]

As *Forbes* reports:

On May 2nd, 2018, gunmen with grenades attacked the Notre-Dame de Fatima church, a Roman Catholic church, in Bangui. 15 people were killed, and dozens injured. The attack [came] a few weeks after 28 people were killed in violent clashes after an operation launched by UN peace-keepers and local security forces in the neighbouring Bangui district of PK5. This sectarian violence has been escalating since February 2018. The recent attacks are nothing new as religious (and ethnic) conflicts have haunted the country for several years, reaching a peak at the end of 2012. In December 2014, the International Commission of Inquiry on the Central African Republic released a report confirming that there had been a 'pattern of ethnic cleansing committed by the anti-balaka in the areas in which Muslims had been living.' This finding followed the January 2014 violence unleashed by anti-balaka fighters who had begun to kill Muslims based on their religious identity. This violence led to the forcible displacement of 99% of the Muslim population of Bangui. Furthermore, 80% of the Muslim population of CAR has since fled to Cameroon and Chad. Reports suggested that out of 436 mosques in the country, 417 were destroyed.[461]

Facing the brunt of the violence, the women and children of the CAR have not only fallen victim to the rebel groups of their own country, but also to the forces of terror trying to fill the power vacuum in the region. There have been reports of mass rapes and infiltration by Islamist militant groups such as Boko Haram from Nigeria or al-Shabaab from Somalia.

Those providing the country with a helping hand are also falling victim to the humanitarian crisis in the CAR. According to *The Washington Post*:

[c]ivilian animosity toward peacekeepers has grown, exacerbated by a sexual abuse scandal and allegations of inaction in the face of attacks. ... Eleven aid workers have been killed since the start of the year 2017—making it one of the most dangerous places in the world for humanitarian work. Aid compounds have been looted and attacked, prompting many organizations to pull back or limit their activities.[462]

---

[460] https://www.france24.com/en/20170815-central-african-republic-car-fighting-militia-conflict

[461] https://www.forbes.com/sites/ewelinaochab/2018/05/09/the-religious-war-in-central-african-republic-continues/

[462] https://www.washingtonpost.com/world/africa/the-central-african-republic-could-be-on-the-brink-of-a-bloodbath/2017/10/09/b26e59d0-a7bf-11e7-9a98-07140d2eed02_story.html

In 2017, nine MINUSCA peacekeepers were killed, "raising alarm that the country [was] sliding back to the bloodletting that exploded in 2013 following the overthrow of Bozizé."[463]

This twenty-first century conflict, which brings the evils of genocide in this progressive era, raises several important questions about the past, present, and future of violence. Is there no end to this madness? Will the international political system of this modern era continue to fall victim to power politics? Will the world remain indifferent at worst, and power-less at best, to the progenies of this modern conflict? All these questions urgently need an answer.

Uganda – Lord's Resistance Army

Uganda gained independence from the United Kingdom on October 9th, 1962, becoming a republic the following year. In the years immediately following independence, the relationship between the Ugandan central government and Buganda, the largest regional kingdom, was the most salient issue for the new nation. The power struggle between the kingdom and the state eventually led to a military coup on January 25th, 1971 by General Idi Amin, who seized control of the country. For the following eight years, Amin ruled Uganda as dictator with the support of the military, carrying out mass killings throughout the country to maintain his rule. It has been reported that up to 500,000 Ugandans perished during his regime.[464] Amin carried out a campaign of ethnic cleansing and forcibly removed the entrepreneurial Indian minority from Uganda.

Formulated in 1987, the Lord's Resistance Army (LRA), also known as the Lord's Resistance Movement, is a rebel group operating in northern Uganda, South Sudan, the Central African Republic, and the Democratic Republic of the Congo. The group has been accused of widespread human rights violations, including murder, mutilation, abduction, and slavery (including child sex-slavery and forcing children to become soldiers).[465]

According to the UN Office for the Coordination of Humanitarian Affairs in 2006, the Lord's Resistance Army had by that point resulted in the displacement of nearly 95% of the Acholi population in three districts of northern Uganda. At that time, 1.7 million people were living in more

---

[463] https://www.aljazeera.com/news/2017/08/sees-early-warning-signs-genocide-car-170807215828039.html

[464] Keatley, Patrick, "Obituary: Idi Amin." The Guardian. Retrieved 18 March 2008.

[465] International Criminal Court, Warrant of Arrest unsealed against five LRA Commanders, 14 October 2005.

than 200 internally displaced persons (IDP) camps.[466] These camps had some of the highest mortality rates in the world.

In 2005, the Ugandan Ministry of Health conducted a report in partnership with the UN World Health Organization, the UN Children's Fund, the UN World Food Programme, the UN Population Fund, the International Rescue Committee, and the UK Department for International Development. Their findings estimated that between January and July 2005, approximately 1,000 people were dying every week, mainly from malaria and AIDS. Some 40% of these deaths were children under five.[467]

According to *The New Humanitarian*:

> Northern Uganda has been the scene of one of the world's most bizarre and brutal conflicts: a war that pits the government against the rebel [LRA], a group that mainly targets civilians. The conflict has displaced some 1.6 million people, 1.3 million of whom are in the Acholi subregion. The report ... said the situation presented 'a very serious humanitarian emergency.'[468]

In early 2005, the LRA abducted over 1,286 persons, almost half of whom were children under fifteen years of age.[469]

In 2006, the Ugandan government and the LRA signed a truce. Under the terms of the agreement, LRA forces had to leave Uganda for two assembly areas in the Garamba National Park area of the northern DRC. The Ugandan government agreed not to attack them there.[470]

This did not stop the LRA from massacring hundreds of villagers during the Christmas of 2008. At least 143 people were killed, and 180 were abducted in the Democratic Republic of Congo.[471] In August 2009, the LRA attacked civilians in South Sudan, crucifying seven Christians during a series of raids, and storming a Catholic church in Ezo on the Feast

---

[466] "Uganda Complex emergency Situation Report #3 09/13/2006" (PDF). Archived from the original (PDF) on 30 October 2011. Available at: https://web.archive.org/web/20080409210756/https://www.usaid.gov/our_work/humanitarian_assistance/disaster_assistance/countries/uganda/fy2006/uganda_ce_sr03_09-15-2006.pdf

[467] http://www.thenewhumanitarian.org/news/2005/08/29/1000-displaced-die-every-week-war-torn-north-report

[468] http://www.thenewhumanitarian.org/news/2005/08/29/1000-displaced-die-every-week-war-torn-north-report

[469] http://www.thenewhumanitarian.org/news/2005/08/29/1000-displaced-die-every-week-war-torn-north-report

[470] "Uganda to continue Congo LRA hunt." BBC. 5 March 2009.

[471] Human Rights Watch (January 17th, 2009). DR Congo: LRA Slaughters 620 in 'Christmas Massacres' Archived 28 December 2014 at the Wayback Machine.

of the Assumption. Villagers who found their bodies reported that it was like a "grotesque crucifixion scene."[472] Bishop Eduardo Hiiboro Kussala urged the international community for help in stopping the LRA attacks, declaring that his government seemed powerless to prevent them.[473] In the same year, LRA forces killed at least 321 civilians and abducted 250 others during a "four-day rampage" in the Makombo region of the DRC.[474]

Between September 2008 and July 2011, the LRA "killed more than 2,300 people, abducted more than 3,000, and displaced over 400,000" across the DRC, South Sudan, and the Central African Republic."[475]

The ICC prosecutes those who commit major political crimes, including genocide, crimes against humanity, and war crimes. Since the Rome Statute was adopted in 1998 and the required number of sixty states parties was reached in April of 2002, the ICC has taken on many cases, with those of Uganda, the DRC, and the CAR being the first few. These countries were the first to make self-referrals to the ICC—when a country calls an investigation on its own people.

In 2003, the havoc caused by the rebellion in the north of Uganda prompted the government of Uganda to register the cases with the ICC. The civil war between July 2002 and June 2004 in Uganda was the central point of chaos, resulting in multiple killings, abductions, and forced recruitment of civilians by the LRA.[476]

The LRA has been waging war in the north of Uganda and violating various human rights since 1989. Uganda's support for the Sudan People's Liberation Army[477] is the main reason that the LRA is able to commit such crimes. It is a form of retaliation for which many officers are under scrutiny by the ICC. The LRA does not have a set political agenda apart from an articulated vision of a community that follows the Ten Commandments.[478] The cruel army commits violence towards civilians and forces them to be slaves and soldiers, among other things. They attempt to maintain control over the population through brutality and war. Many LRA commanders

---

[472]   https://web.archive.org/web/20111019111850/http://www.catholic.org/international/international_story.php?id=34496

[473]   https://web.archive.org/web/20111019111850/http://www.catholic.org/international/international_story.php?id=34496

[474]   https://www.hrw.org/news/2010/03/28/dr-congo-lords-resistance-army-rampage-kills-321

[475]   "90 per cent of people in LRA areas of Congo still live in fear of their safety, new Oxfam survey reveals | Oxfam International." Oxfam.org. 28 July 2011.

[476]   http://www.haguejusticeportal.net/index.php?id=6175

[477]   http://www.globalsecurity.org/military/world/para/lra.htm

[478]   http://www.enoughproject.org/files/pdf/lra_leaders.pdf

have never been convicted for their crimes, but steps are being taken to bring them to justice.

The cases referred to the Prosecutor of the ICC include that of Joseph Kony, the commander of the LRA, as well as those of the high-ranking LRA officials Vincent Otti, Okot Odhiambo, Dominic Ongwen, and Raska Lukwiya. The Prosecutor declared that ICC would study all the cases and crimes for which the LRA and the government of Uganda are responsible.[479] The ICC called for the trials of the five LRA officers; however, Otti was assassinated on Kony's command in 2007, and Lukwiya was killed during a fight with the army of Uganda. The other three—Kony, Odhiambo, and Ongwen—remained at large for some years.[480]

Joseph Kony, one of the accused commanders of the LRA was the former head of the Sinia brigade and a member of the LRA's "Control Altar," who is under investigation for twelve crimes against humanity and twenty-one war crimes, including "rape, murder, sexual enslavement, and forced enlistment of children."[481] Under his supervision, cult extremism was cultivated with cruel military efficiency; he called for many senior commanders to be executed, and around 38,000 children and 37,000 adults were captured and forced to be soldiers, porters, and sex slaves. Many of these people died, but some managed to escape. As has been expressed by many, no children are more abused, traumatized, or robbed of their childhoods than those in the LRA.

Kony also abducted many girls and enslaved them in his household. He distributed them among the LRA commanders, and they were frequently married off to much older men as rewards to the officers in the army. Among other crimes, Kony has also declined to participate in peace proposals, refusing to sign peace deals such as the one in November of 2008.

Recently, the Ugandan, Congolese, and Southern Sudanese militaries attempted to apprehend Kony and his commanders, but to their dismay, their mission failed. The LRA retaliated by killing 1,000 people and capturing many others, before being pushed out of Uganda and ending up somewhere around the border areas of the DRC and southern Sudan (now South Sudan).[482] Kony remained at large, and in 2017 the U.S. and Ugandan armies abandoned their mission to find him, arguing that his power had degraded to the point that he no longer posed a serious threat.[483]

---

[479] http://www.haguejusticeportal.net/index.php?id=6175

[481] http://www.enoughproject.org/files/pdf/lra_leaders.pdf

[482] https://www.bbc.com/news/world-africa-17299084

[483] https://www.bbc.com/news/world-africa-17299084

Okot Odhiambo, Deputy Army Commander of the LRA and an active member of the "Control Altar," controlled the planning and execution of LRA army tactics, including the dehumanizing attacks on civilians. He was also believed to be responsible for the massacre at the Barlonyo internally displaced persons camp in the Lira district in 2004, where at least 300 people were shot, burned, and slain with knives. Another attack against a camp in northern Uganda on Kony's orders was implemented by Odhiambo, resulting in more killings and abductions than the previous attack.

After the assassination of Vincent Otti, Kony's right-hand Odhiambo—due to his staggering record of mass killings—was appointed the LRA's deputy chairman. According to the ICC, former members of the Lord's Resistance Army have described Odhiambo as a "ruthless killer," as "one who killed the most," and as a "bitter man who would kill anyone."[484]

Another attack occurred in Uganda on the orders of Odhiambo, reported in February, 2008, when he led a rebel group from the CAR into southern Sudan and targeted the town of Yubu. The attack resulted in the deaths of about eleven people and the abduction of more than twenty-five. After the ICC began proceedings against him, Odhiambo was believed to be living as a fugitive somewhere in the Dungu area of north-eastern Congo.[485] In October 2013, it was reported that Odhiambo had been critically injured in an ambush by the soldiers of the Ugandan army.[486] In 2015, his body was found and identified, confirmating that his death had occurred in October 2013. Upon confirmation of his death, the ICC dropped its proceedings against him.[487]

Dominic Ongwen is the former head of the Sinia Brigade, one of the four LRA brigades. He held the third highest position in the LRA as Director of Operations. He is the youngest person to be charged with war crimes and crimes against humanity by an international court.[488] He was charged with a total of seventy crimes by the ICC, including attacks on the civilian population, cruel treatment, homicide, rape, sexual slavery, forced marriage, torture, pillaging, destruction of property, outrages on personal

[484]   http://www.enoughproject.org/files/pdf/lra_leaders.pdf

[485]   http://www.enoughproject.org/files/pdf/lra_leaders.pdf

[486]   https://www.nytimes.com/2015/04/07/world/africa/body-of-a-lords-resistance-army-leader-is-identified-in-uganda.html?_r=0

[487]   https://www.icc-cpi.int/pages/item.aspx?name=PR1147

[488]   https://mediadiversified.org/2017/05/23/dominic-ongwen-the-abducted-child-soldier-tried-for-crimes-against-humanity/

dignity, the recruitment of child soldiers, persecution, and other inhumane acts.[489]

Reports suggested that the incursions into the Lira and Teso districts in northern Uganda were executed by Ongwen on the orders of Kony. During these attacks, the LRA battled with the Ugandan military several times, and an estimated 2,200 people were killed and 3,000 captured. The dead included several members of the LRA, but Ongwen and his men nevertheless gained the reputation of being able to arise from the deadliest of wars with limited casualties.[490] In January 2015, Ongwen surrendered himself to a joint military task force of the U.S. and the African Union.[491] He was the first of the IRA leaders to appear before the ICC.[492]

Ongwen was abducted and recruited as a child solider when he was a boy,[493] and defence lawyers have argued that this irreparably traumatized him. "He was tortured ... forced to watch people being killed, used for fighting as a child soldier," said lawyer Thomas Obhof, part of Ongwen's defence team. "Even the prosecution have said that what he went through is a serious mitigating factor."[494]

In all, the LRA has captured around 3,000 children to recruit them as soldiers. It is believed that the group currently consists of 100 fighters and is considered an inspiration for other military groups who want to destroy various other communities. Of the five LRA leaders charged by the ICC, Ongwen and Kony are the only two still alive.

The Lord's Resistance Army has slain many civilians and traumatized countless others with its inhumane actions. The missions of groups like these and the people associated with them are always charged by a political agenda that dismisses the rights of human beings. The human rights violations and crimes committed in this region have now become everyday news, with numerous cases being highlighted.

In Uganda, crimes against humanity have become a part of the country's natural existence. Initially, the perpetrators of such crimes were not

---

489   https://web.archive.org/web/20170110033637/https://www.icc-cpi.int/uganda/ongwen/Documents/OngwenEng.pdf

490   http://www.enoughproject.org/files/pdf/lra_leaders.pdf

491   https://web.archive.org/web/20150410081854/https://www.nytimes.com/2015/04/07/world/africa/body-of-a-lords-resistance-army-leader-is-identified-in-uganda.html, and https://enoughproject.org/blog/moment-momentum-surrender-dominic-ongwen

492   https://www.refworld.org/pdfid/58b0587e4.pdf

493   http://www.coalitionfortheicc.org/cases/dominic-ongwen

494   https://www.theguardian.com/law/2016/dec/06/dominic-ongwen-trial-begins-international-criminal-court-lords-resistance-army-uganda

punished, but due to the growing brutality, the government of Uganda has stood up to its criminals and asked the ICC to register and investigate these cases. The government is now refusing to tolerate the violence and torture being committed against its civilians, and is attempting to bring the perpetrators of these heinous crimes to justice. The ICC is the instrument through which this justice can be achieved.

Nigeria – Boko Haram

The Islamic State in West Africa (or the Islamic State's West Africa Province), commonly known as Boko Haram, is a jihadist terrorist organization. Based in northeastern Nigeria, it is also active in Niger, Chad, and northern Cameroon. The group has been led by Abubakar Shekau since 2009, and was founded in 2002 by Mohammed Yusuf. In March 2015, the group pledged allegiance to ISIS/ISIL, and has been aligned with them since.[495] Boko Haram has killed tens of thousands of people and displaced over 2 million, and in 2015 was recognized as the world's deadliest terror group.[496]

The conflict in Nigeria, which was once limited to occupational fights between tribes with different livelihoods, has taken on a genocidal speed and aggression. The nation, apart from dealing with political crisis, economic disparity, and social unrest, has become the centre of the perpetration of an extremist mentality that threatens the day-to-day existence of Nigerian civilians.

Nigeria is diverse in all forms of civic existence, and its population is composed of a wide array of tribes and ethnic groups, each with its own unique characteristics. Since its independence from the United Kingdom in 1960, Nigeria has experienced many periods of ethnic tension due to its colonial borders. The north of the country is predominantly Hausa and Fulani Muslim, while the southern states are dominated by Yoruba Muslims and Christians, and Igbo Christians. The Fulani are mainly nomadic herders, while the Christians living in the south have long survived on agriculture. The jihadist group Boko Haram's terrorist activities, added to changing climate conditions in the north, have caused the large-scale migration of the Fulani to the south. Cattle belonging to the Fulani have destroyed crops and cultivable lands in the south, angering the Christians who farm there.[497] The "Middle Belt" of Nigeria, the Christians' prime

---

495 https://fas.org/sgp/crs/row/IF10173.pdf

496 http://economicsandpeace.org/wp-content/uploads/2015/11/Global-Terrorism-Index-2015.pdf

497 https://www.crisisgroup.org/africa/west-africa/nigeria/252-herders-against-farmers-nigerias-expanding-deadly-conflict

farmland, is at the centre of the conflict zone.[498] The area that was once called the "food basket of Nigeria" has now been transformed into a "blood basket."

The traditional conflict between the Muslims and Christians in Nigeria has paved way for extremism and terrorism to propagate in the region. As the Global Terrorism Index from 2018 notes, Fulani extremists killed about 2,827 people between the years of 2010 and 2016 in 450 separate incidences in Nigeria.[499] According to the *Christian Post*, "Human Rights Watch estimates through monitoring of credible media that at least 1,600 were killed on both sides of the conflict in 2018."[500] The *Christian Post* also explains that:

> [t]he Nigeria-based advocacy and research NGO International Society for Civil Liberties & the Rule of Law (Intersociety) estimates that no less than 2,400 Christian farming community members were killed by Fulani extremists in 2018. ... According to Amnesty International, a November 2017 attack on a Fulani community in the town of Numan in Adamawa state took the lives of 80 people, the majority of whom were women and children because most of the men were at a meeting or out grazing at the time. The attack, which also saw the killing of a 3-year-old child, was suspected to have been carried out by dozens of youth from the predominantly-Christian Bachama tribe.[501]

The ethnic conflict between the tribal groups is more or less a fight for livelihood, but the tribal fighting has recently taken a violent turn, engulfing the region in the flames of religious extremism, with each narrative fighting for validation.

The Fula or Fulani people, are regarded as "the world's largest nomadic group: about 20 million people dispersed across Western Africa. They reside mostly in Nigeria, Mali, Guinea, Cameroon, Senegal, and Niger. They also can be found in Central African Republic and Egypt."[502] In Nigeria, the Fulani comprise "the most populous and politically influential" of more than 250 ethnic groups in the country.[503] They have been engaged in

---

498 https://www.christianpost.com/news/christian-genocide-in-nigeria-5-facts-you-need-to-know.html

499 http://visionofhumanity.org/app/uploads/2018/12/Global-Terrorism-Index-2018-1.pdf

500 https://www.hrw.org/world-report/2019/country-chapters/nigeria

501 https://www.christianpost.com/news/christian-genocide-in-nigeria-5-facts-you-need-to-know.html

502 https://www.worldwatchmonitor.org/who-are-the-fulani/

503 https://www.pbs.org/frontlineworld/stories/nigeria/facts.html

attacks on the Christians either to impose religious dominance or to take over their agricultural lands. According to the Global Terror Index, only a small subset of Fulani herders engage in these extremist attacks, but this small group is nonetheless powerful: between 2012 and 2016 they were responsible for the deaths of over 2,500 people in Nigeria.[504]

The situation in the Middle Belt of Nigeria has generated much chaos across the world, and demands urgent intervention. The presence of competing narratives in the conflict makes it difficult to ascertain the complex origins of the violence.

One narrative describes the Fulani attacks as a genocide perpetrated by "radicalized Islamic herders looking to drive out Christians from their homes," while another narrative characterizes the killings as "part of a years-old conflict exacerbated by several factors, including increased Fulani herdsmen migration due to the Boko Haram insurgency and the desertification in the north."[505] What is important to note is that regardless of the motivation for the violence, the actions of the fundamentalist Boko Haram are marked by clear genocidal intent, and have detrimentally impacted the peace, order, and stability of the region.

The rising tensions surrounding land disputes between the geographical north and south led to several legal reforms in the country. But to the disappointment of many, these reforms only served to further escalate the tensions. In November 2017, Nigeria's government passed a law forbidding the Fulani to let their cattle graze freely, which led to an intensification of the violence.[506]

According to Genocide Watch:

> Motivated by violently anti-Western jihadist theology, since 2009 Boko Haram has killed anyone they perceive to be promoting Western or Christian education, including government officials who prevent Nigeria from becoming a homologous sharia-abiding Muslim state. Trained by members of al-Qaeda, Boko Haram has carried out many mass casualty terrorist attacks.[507]

Boko Haram's violence peaked in 2014, when over 270 schoolgirls were abducted in Borno State. Since then, 2.2 over 2 million Nigerians have

---

[504] http://visionofhumanity.org/app/uploads/2017/11/Global-Terrorism-Index-2017.pdf

[505] https://www.christianpost.com/news/christian-genocide-in-nigeria-5-facts-you-need-to-know.html

[506] https://advancingnativemissions.com/nigerias-ongoing-conflict-christian-genocide/

[507] http://docs.wixstatic.com/ugd/e5b74f_cff3098f3c3a4ae8ad24f60799142d1e.pdf

become internally displaced, and over 1.3 million children have become refugees in Niger, Chad, and Cameroon.[508]

Boko Haram's terrorism can be witnessed in:

> two main forms, both primed for maximum devastation. The first is armed assault. The group has been known to torch entire villages, hacking men to death, raping women and forcibly marrying them to jihadis, and kidnapping children. The other is suicide attacks. It is not uncommon for children—usually from among those that have been kidnapped to be used to carry out these suicide attacks.[509]

According to Genocide Watch, Boko Haram (which translates to "Western education is a sin") is a terrorist movement "led by Islamist extremists Abubakar Shekau and Abu Musab al-Barnawi, who control different and often antagonistic groups within the larger umbrella organization."[510] The extremist group has "vowed to destroy every Christian school in Nigeria, and to carry out terrorist attacks on Nigerian government police and government officials."[511] Genocide Watch also reports that:

> [i]n 2015 Shekau pledged the allegiance of Boko Haram to the Islamic State of Iraq and Syria (ISIS). Since then the group is also known as the Islamic State in West Africa (ISWA), though since ISIS's military defeat in Iraq in 2017, the ties between the two groups appear to have weakened considerably.[512]

The violence of Boko Haram is predominantly targeting the marginal and vulnerable sections of the population. The most obvious targets have been children, irrespective of age and gender. Young boys are trained as soldiers to carry out fundamentalist violence, and young girls are used as weapons of war. They are mutilated, raped, and sold in slave markets or given to other jihadists as rewards or compensation. The ugly picture of brutality in Nigeria has attracted the sympathy and concerns of those fighting for humanitarian goals. Much research has been done in recent years on the subject of genocide in the region, demonstrating the necessity of bringing it to the attention of the international community. The most important aspect of these studies has been the focus on children being used as instruments of war. Boko Haram is particularly notorious for:

---

[508]   http://docs.wixstatic.com/ugd/e5b74f_cff3098f3c3a4ae8ad24f60799142d1e.pdf

[509]   https://reliefweb.int/report/nigeria/boko-haram-s-war-children

[510]   https://www.genocidewatch.com/copy-of-current-genocide-watch-aler

[511]   http://genocidewatch.net/2015/02/24/the-historical-background-of-boko-haram/

[512]   http://www.genocidewatch.com/countries-at-risk

having kidnapped 276 girls from a Christian school in Chibok in April 2014. However, Boko Haram has preyed on children since 2013, when it launched a series of attacks against schoolchildren that killed dozens of boys. UNICEF estimates that Boko Haram has kidnapped more than 1,000 children in north-eastern Nigeria since 2013. Through the efforts of the Nigerian government and international pressure, many of the captives have been returned, including dozens of the Chibok girls as well as 104 of the 110 girls abducted from the government secondary school in Dapchi in February 2018.[513]

According to Human Rights Watch, "[f]ive of the remaining girls reportedly died in captivity and one girl, Leah Sharibu, continues to be held hostage allegedly for refusing to deny her Christian faith. About 100 of the Chibok schoolgirls remain unaccounted for."[514] Genocide Watch reports that "[i]n May 2018 the Nigerian government claimed to have rescued 1,000 Boko Haram prisoners, mostly women and children, as part of a regional anti-Boko Haram task force involving forces from Nigeria, Chad, Cameroon, Benin and Niger."[515]

According to a report by *Mail & Guardian*:

[i]n one especially brutal incident, on the night of February 24th, 2014, 58 school boys were murdered in Buni Yadi, Yobe State, while they slept in their beds. In 2017 alone, 881 children were killed or maimed in Boko Haram-related violence, although not always at the hands of the militant group. The Nigerian military killed more than 200 minors in a miscalculated military attack on a displaced persons camp. About 1.4 million children have so far been displaced, 1,400 schools have been destroyed, and 2,295 teachers killed, according to the UN. The barbarity with which Boko Haram operates and its disregard for children's rights has brought it global notoriety.[516]

The abducted children have faced the worst forms of violence, ranging from psychological, to physical, to sexual. This barbarity demands urgent intervention.

In 2018, following strong advocacy by rights groups, children aged under 18 were released from military custody into rehabilitation programmes, with the goal of reuniting them with their families. ... All of the children

---

[513]   https://www.genocidewatch.com/countries-at-risk

[514]   https://www.hrw.org/world-report/2019/country-chapters/nigeria

[515]   http://www.genocidewatch.com/countries-at-risk

[516]   https://reliefweb.int/report/nigeria/boko-haram-s-war-children

who arrived at the Unicef centre needed medical and psychological care. ... At the centre, trained counsellors give the children trauma care; social workers prepare to reunite them with their families.[517]

In 2014 alone, Boko Haram killed over 6,600 people[518] in its jihadist mission to expand its "self-declared Islamic caliphate" in northern Nigeria. In 2015, it killed over 4,000, "including 2,000 of the residents of the town of Baga in the northeastern state of Borno on January 7th."[519] The number of casualties has decreased since then, with some 900 people murdered by Boko Haram in 2017. Genocide Watch reports that the conflict between Boko Haram and the Nigerian government is estimated to have resulted in the deaths of 20,000 to 40,000 people since 2009. Approximately 2.3 million people have been displaced by the fighting, and at least 250,000 have fled to Cameroon, Chad, and Niger.[520]

Despite political and military interventions both on the national and international front, violence and extremism in Nigeria has led to genocide for the civilians of the nation. To date, violent attacks on civilians persist in the form of mass-scale abductions, arbitrary detentions, suicide bombings, and massacre. Human Rights Watch suggested that the hope for humanitarian ideals in Nigeria is fading day by day.[521] The figures presented by the organization force the world to consider the deteriorating conditions in Nigeria.

According to Human Rights Watch:

at least 1,200 people died and nearly 200,000 were displaced in the northeast in 2018. In June, at least 84 people were killed in double suicide bomb attacks attributed to Boko Haram at a mosque in Mubi, Adamawa State. ... In September and October [2018], Boko Haram insurgents executed Saifura Ahmed and Hauwa Liman, both aid workers with the International Committee of the Red Cross (ICRC). The group kidnapped them in March. In June, twin suicide bomb attacks and grenade explosions by suspected Boko Haram fighters killed 31 people and injured 48 others during Muslim religious celebrations in Damboa, Borno State. The attack occurred in the wake of Chief of Army Staff Tukur Buratai's speech encouraging displaced people to

---

517 https://reliefweb.int/report/nigeria/boko-haram-s-war-children

518 "Nigerian troops were denied guns to fight Boko Haram – Buhari." Vanguard. 18 November 2015. Retrieved 18 November 2015.

519 https://www.genocidewatch.com/countries-at-risk

520 https://www.hrw.org/world-report/2019/country-chapters/nigeria https://www.hrw.org/world-report/2019/country-chapters/nigeria

521 https://www.hrw.org/world-report/2019/country-chapters/nigeria

return to their communities. Over 35,000 internally displaced people returned to northeast communities despite security concerns and lack of basic necessities, including food and shelter. ... In May, at least 45 people were killed in an attack by bandits in Gwaska village, Kaduna State. Zamfara state was perhaps the worst affected by frequent bandit attacks, who killed at least 400 people and displaced over 38,000 in 2018.[522]

Nigeria is now one of the most dangerous places in the world to be a Christian. Local leaders have referred to the crisis as "pure genocide," alleging that over 6,000 Christians—mostly women, children, and the elderly—have been "killed or maimed" by Muslim Fulanis.[523] On New Year's Day 2018, cattle herders massacred seventy-two Christians with machetes. In April of the same year, a Fulani group attacked Christians during an early morning church service, murdering seventeen parishioners and two priests. They then lit fifty homes on fire, causing the community to flee for their survival.[524]

The attacks of Boko Haram on the Christian community threaten the very existence of the community. With an intention to bring Nigeria under the control of Islamic fundamentalism, Boko Haram's militants continue to carry out violence with the genocidal intention of clearing Nigeria of all Christians. With the fall of the Islamic State in its strongholds, the role played by militant groups independently aligning themselves with ISIS becomes the centre of concern for the world at large. The Trump administration can claim the defeat of ISIS, but the world must not overlook the ideological threats posed by ISIS' affiliates such as Boko Haram. It is a very difficult task to eradicate the roots of extremist ideology, which tend to multiply and regenerate like cancer cells.

In the lead-up to the 2019 elections wherein President Muhammadu Buhari was seeking re-election, rising political tensions "defined Nigeria's rights landscape."[525] Despite significant military advances and proclamations of the government's supposed defeat of Boko Haram, "the group remained a threat to security in the northeast region."[526]

It is of the utmost importance that the international community make concrete efforts to counter extremism, to help not only Nigeria but all the regions affected by the evils of genocide. With their sustained efforts

---

[522] https://www.hrw.org/world-report/2019/country-chapters/nigeria

[523] https://advancingnativemissions.com/nigerias-ongoing-conflict-christian-genocide/

[524] https://advancingnativemissions.com/nigerias-ongoing-conflict-christian-genocide/

[525] https://www.hrw.org/world-report/2019/country-chapters/nigeria

[526] https://www.hrw.org/world-report/2019/country-chapters/nigeria

and determination to eradicate extremism, the contribution made by international organizations such as the United Nations is praiseworthy. The UN's global contribution requires detailed explanation, which the next chapter will provide.

Part III

Terrorism, Failed States, and UN Action to End Violations of Human Rights

Fifty years after the International Covenant on Civil and Political Rights and the International Covenant on Economic, Social and Cultural Rights, both adopted in 1966, mass human rights violations continue. The crisis in Syria calls into question the Security Council's willingness and capacity to halt mass atrocities and also prevent them. The failure to act by the Security Council suggests it may be advisable to outlaw of the use of veto in cases of mass atrocities, but this would require the five permanent members to agree to such a measure. This would no doubt redeem, to the limited extent possible, the UNSC's credibility and effectiveness in mass atrocity prevention.

These exceptional circumstances have continued to erode the universal nature of human rights, a trend that has led to greater inequality, injustice, violence, and mortality across the globe. We are witnessing an escalation of human rights violations, with huge numbers of people crossing borders to flee conflict zones and many states continuously failing to protect human rights. International human rights instruments are dependent on action by member states to both mobilize and fund efforts to combat terrorism and other forms of mass atrocities. Excessive and disproportionate attacks on civilians, humanitarian and health care personnel, and infrastructure must be brought to justice. Mass killings and other atrocities targeting individuals for their ethnicity or religion are being committed by terrorist groups such as the Islamic State. The Yazidi and Christian communities of the Middle East have faced genocidal acts. Christianity now faces the

159

possibility of disappearing from many parts of the Middle East where its roots go back 2,000 years.

It is also of urgent importance to address the issue of failed states, which according to John Yoo poses one of the deepest challenges to international peace and stability.[527] Finding a "comprehensive and effective solution to the challenges of terrorism [and] human rights violations" requires some understanding of how to prevent and restore failed states.[528] Mechanisms must be developed including allowing major states to assist in power-sharing agreements, such a trusteeship to deal with failed states' problems, and wherever possible under the architecture of the United Nations or NATO to deploy forces under the direction of the Responsibility to Protect doctrine to save and protect lives. It is also imperative to bring an end to impunity by punishing those responsible for mass murder and genocide by applying universal jurisdiction and the use of the ICC.

The primary reason why genocide is still being committed is largely due to a lack of political will and awareness as well as the need to develop the international institutions needed to predict and prevent it from occurring. Acknowledging early warning signs and working to prevent the failure of states is necessary to stop these atrocities. The Responsibility to Protect doctrine empowers individual states and the international community to protect civilian populations from acts of genocide, ethnic cleansing, war crimes, and crimes against humanity.

The doctrine allows states to consider all coercive and non-coercive measures under Chapter VI of the United Nations Charter, and to protect vulnerable populations from the four crimes as listed above. It is a political, moral, and to an extent legal commitment formed from pre-existing international legal agreements.

The power vacuum created by failing states and the rise of terrorist groups have further compounded the need for quick humanitarian intervention. There is a universal norm against the use of terrorism, but coordinated efforts to combat acts of terror have been protracted. A more robust form of action will be needed if these acts of violence are to end.

Terrorism

Many researchers maintain that while not all weak or failed states are afflicted with terrorism, be it national or transnational, it is still a sound assertion that weak or failed states represent a national and international security concern.

---

[527] John Yoo, "Fixing Failed States," California Law Review 99, no. 1 (2011): 95–150.

[528] Yoo, "Fixing Failed States."

Threats of terrorism emanate from these states as they provide safe havens for terrorists and create regional instability, threatening the rule of law, good governance and stability.[529] Furthermore, terrorism can prolong state weakness and failure, making it more difficult for countries to recover. Francis Fukuyama has noted that "[s]ince the end of the Cold War, weak and failing states have arguably become the single-most important problem for international order."[530] Terrorist groups, according to several analyses, base their operations in weak and failing states, where they can benefit from an absence of law which allows for the use of illicit economic activities to finance their operations and facilitates their access to weapons and territory for training purposes.[531] In 2002, following the September 11th, 2001 terrorist attacks on the United States, The White House National Security Strategy declared that:

> weak states, like Afghanistan, can pose as great a danger to our national interests as strong states...poverty may not turn people into terrorists, but poverty, weak institutions and corruption can make weak states vulnerable to terrorist networks and drug cartels.[532]

The reconstruction of rule of law, security and development in states such as Afghanistan has been complicated by the various terrorist activities still taking place after the fall of the Taliban.[533] Transnational terrorist organizations, such as al-Qaeda, for example, benefit from state failure in Afghanistan and Sudan which enables them to recruit members and build training camps for their terrorist activities as well as provides them with a safe haven.[534] A United States Congressional report notes that there is a link between transnational crime and terrorist groups:

> [T]he international community has seen a surge in the number of transnational crime groups emerging in safe havens of weak, conflict prone states. ... Criminal groups can thrive off the illicit needs of failing states. ... Rebel groups have been known to solicit the services of vast illicit arms

---

[529] Liana Sun Wyler, "Weak and Failing States: Evolving Security Threats and U.S. Policy," CRS Report for Congress (2008) at 6

[530] Francis Fukuyama, *State-Building: Governance and World Order in the 21st Century*, Ithaca: Cornell University Press (2004) at 92

[531] L. S. Wyle at 6

[532] The White House, *The National Security Strategy of the United States*, Washington D.C. (September 2002) at 4

[533] Stewart Patrick, "Weak States and Global Threats: Fact or Fiction?," *The Washington Quarterly*, Vol. 29, No. 2 (Spring 2006) at 37

[534] Ibid.

trafficking networks to fuel deadly conflicts embers of the international community.[535]

According to a World Bank report, the number of states that could provide a breeding ground for terrorism jumped from seventeen in 2003 to twenty-six in 2006.[536] It is clear that when states do not provide for the basic social needs of their populations, they present a ripe breeding ground for terrorist organizations to recruit and radicalize disadvantaged youth.[537]

With renewed focus on terrorism after 9/11, failed states such as Afghanistan, Somalia, and Sudan—to name but a few—have gained international attention. In Sudan, the United States "strongly pressured the government to co-operate against terrorism and, at the same time, became more involved in the peace process."[538]

A prevailing fear within the world community is the failure of a state which possesses nuclear weapons.[539] Several U.S. national security advisors worry that global terrorists are aggressively on the lookout for nuclear weapons.[540] Pakistan's porous borders, as well as the terrorist bombings in several major centres, have left many to question the safety guarantees of the country regarding nuclear weapons.[541] Adding to the problem is constant political instability and Taliban advancement in Pakistan and near the Pakistan–Afghan border. The militant group known as the Pakistan Taliban have links to al-Qaeda and have attacked several military installations.[542]

In her address to the UN General Assembly on September 27th, 2011, Pakistan Foreign Minister Hina Rabbani Khar expressed her country's anxiety concerning terrorism:

---

[535]   Liana Sun Wyler, "Weak and Failing States: Evolving Security Threats and U.S. Policy," CRS Report for Congress (28 August 2008) at 7

[536]   Karen DeYoung, "World Bank Lists Failing Nations That Can Breed Global Terrorism," *Washington Post* (15 September 2002) at 13

[537]   Stewart Patrick, "Weak States and Global Threats: Fact or Fiction?," *The Washington Quarterly*, Vol. 29, No. 2 (Spring 2006) at 36

[538]   Gérard Prunier and Rachel M. Gisselquist, "The Sudan: A Successfully Failed States," in Robert I. Rotberg (ed.), *State Failure and State Weakness in a Time of Terror*, Washington D.C.: Brookings Institution Press (2003) at 107

[539]   Kapil Komireddik, "Take Pakistan's Nuke, Please," *Foreign Policy* (24 May 2011)

[540]   Rolf Mowatt-Larssen, *Nuclear Security in Pakistan: Reducing the Risks of Nuclear Terrorism*, Arms Control Today (July/August 2009)

[541]   Liana Sun Wyler, "Weak and Failing States: Evolving Security Threats and U.S. Policy," CRS Report for Congress (28 August 2008) at 8

[542]   Robert Birsel, " Pakistan's Taliban: who are they what can they do?," *Reuters* (13 May 2011)

Our streets are filled with armed police posts. We cannot enter our parks or shopping centres or churches or mosques without being searched and frisked. Terrorists have attacked our military installations, attacked the gravesites of our spiritual leaders, attacked our minorities, and attacked the very idea of Pakistan.[543]

In Pakistan, the ever-increasing militant insurgency of the tribal rebellion in the Swat Valley, predominantly characterized in western media as actions of the Taliban occurring in the post-President Pervez Musharraf era, has undermined the initial sense of optimism that briefly emerged following the election of Asif Ali Zardari in September 2008. Since coming to power, the Zardari presidency has been marked with increased instability both domestically and regionally.[544] This has occurred in the context of the erosion of human rights, rampant corruption, tribal unrest, loss of control over many parts of its territory, and its land being used by terrorists to launch attacks against its civilians as well as neighbouring nations such as Afghanistan and India.[545] Much of these fights take place in tribal areas and reflect the fact that most of their allegiances cross seemingly invisible international boundaries, particularly between Pakistan and Afghanistan.

It appears that Pakistan's greatest internal threats stem from the dangerously autonomous regions of the Swat Valley and Southern Waziristan, where terrorist groups exploit instability and porous borders. Pakistan's failure to effectively control its territory provides a safe haven for insurgency groups from both Afghanistan and Pakistan.[546] According to Anita Demkiv:

There are a myriad of political and military calamities throughout the country that contribute to its near failed state status. Currently, Pakistan is one of the least stable countries possessing nuclear weapons; the economy is crippled; Kashmir remains contentious; the northwest region, known as the Federally Administered Tribal Areas (FATA) harbours exiled Taliban leaders and al Qaeda's leadership; and there is an ongoing radicalization throughout the country—not limited to the FATA.

---

[543] Speech by Pakistan Foreign Minister Hina Rabbani Khar at UN General Assembly (27 September 2011)

[544] Anita Demkiv, "Pakista's FATA, Transnational Terrorism and the Global Development Mode," *Journal of Global Change and Governance*, Vol. II, No. 1 (Winter/Spring 2009) at 2

[545] Hilary Synnott, "What is Happening in Pakistan?," *Survival: Global Politics and Strategy, 1468-2699*, Vol. 51, No. 1 (2009) at 65

[546] Liana Sun Wyler, "Weak and Failing States: Evolving Security Threats and U.S. Policy," CRS Report for Congress (28 August 2008) at 4

As seen in the December 2008 attacks on Mumbai, the security of countries near and far could be gravely affected by Pakistan's inability to reign in terrorist elements.[547]

Despite numerous denials by Pakistani government officials that Osama bin Laden was in Pakistan, the government of the country was profoundly embarrassed when on May 2nd, 2011 the terrorist leader was shot and killed inside a private residential compound in Abbottabad, Pakistan. Some officials have accused Pakistan's security establishment of protecting bin Laden.[548] The actions seriously undermine the Pakistani government's claim that it is serious in its efforts to tackle the Taliban. Doubts also remain over the army's willingness to fight those Taliban members involved in cross-border attacks in Afghanistan.[549] Pakistan ranks high in *Foreign Policy*'s Failed States Index due to its security concerns and loss of territorial sovereignty.[550]

In September 2011, United States Chairman of the Joint Chiefs of Staff, Admiral Mike Mullen, blamed the Inter-Services Intelligence of Pakistan for their support of the insurgents that attacked the American Embassy in Kabul and for supporting the Quetta Shura and the Haqqani Network based in tribal areas of Pakistan. According to Mullen, these networks:

> operate from Pakistan with impunity. Extremist organizations serving as proxies of the government of Pakistan are attacking Afghan troops and civilians as well as U.S. soldiers. For example, we believe the Haqqani Network—which has long enjoyed the support and protection of the Pakistani government and is, in many ways, a strategic arm of Pakistan's Inter-Services Intelligence Agency—is responsible for the September 13th attacks against the U.S. Embassy in Kabul. There is ample evidence confirming that the Haqqanis were behind the June 28th attack against the Inter-Continental Hotel in Kabul and the September 10th truck bomb attack that killed five Afghans and injured another 96 individuals, 77 of whom were U.S. soldiers.[551]

---

[547] Anita Demkiv, "Pakista's FATA, Transnational Terrorism and the Global Development Mode," *Journal of Global Change and Governance*, Vol. II, No. 1 (Winter/Spring 2009) at 2

[548] Nahal Toose and Zarar Khan, "Bin Laden Was Living in Pakistani Compound Built in 2005," Associated Press (2 May 2011)

[549] Afsir Karim, *Counter Terrorism: The Pakistan Factor*, New Delhi: South Asian Books (1992) at 34

[550] The Fund for Peace, "The Failed States Index," *Foreign Policy* (2011)

[551] Statement of Admiral Michael Mullen, U.S. Navy Chairman Joint Chiefs of Staff before the Senate Armed Services Committee on Afghanistan and Iraq (22 September 2011)

Terrorism is both a regional and international threat, with terrorist net-works operat   ing in several failed states. In January 2009, AQAP was formed by a merger between two regional Islamist militants operating in Yemen and Saudi Arabia.[552] AQAP has taken advantage of the state failure in Yemen which was a result of the 2011 uprising against the government.[553]

In Mali, the Tuareg tribal rebels (MNLA, Liberation Army of Azawad) that took control of the predominantly desert northern part of this African nation was defeated in 2012 by an Islamist group the Ansar Dine (Defenders of the Faith) linked to al-Qaeda members.[554] Terrorist groups from other parts of Africa including Nigeria are coming to assist Ansar Dine. Their leader Iyad Ag Ghali supports an independent Tuareg state based on the same principles that governed Afghanistan during the reign of the Taliban. Some of the cultural sites in Mali have already been damaged. In June 2012, Ansar Dine destroyed several ancient Sufi tombs which according to them should be destroyed as they view Sufis Mus-lims as heretics. The destruction of the tombs was condemned by many Moslem leaders worldwide and by UNESCO. The African Union had asked in June 2012 for the UN Security Council resolution to authorize a military intervention in northern Mali. Mali collapsed into chaos after soldiers toppled the president in March 2012, leaving a power vacuum which still exists. A ceasefire followed in 2018; however, the conflict con-tinues to this day.

UN Special Adviser Adama Dieng has warned of rising conflicts among different ethnic groups. The UN report noted that:

> the number of children killed in the conflict in the first six months of 2019 was twice as many for the entire year of 2018. Many of the children have been killed in inter communal attacks attributed to ethnic militias, with the majority of attacks occurring around Mopti. It is reported that around 900 schools have closed down and that armed militias are recruit-ing children.[555]

In Nigeria, the terrorist group Boko Haram which also has links to al-Qaeda has attacked several Christian churches killing hundreds of people. As noted above, since 9/11, the discourse regarding state fail-ure has focused on the security threats that it poses to the regional and

---

[552]   "Al-Qaeda in the Arabian Peninsula," BBC online profile, updated 14 June 2011

[553]   Aaron Ng, "Al Qaeda in the Arabian Peninsula (AQAP) and the Yemen Uprisings," *CTTA: Terrorist Trends and Analysis*, Vol. 3, No. 6 (June 2011) at 1

[554]   "The Causes of the Uprising in Northern Mali," *Think Africa Press* (6 February 2012)

[555]   "Sharp rise in number of children killed in Mali's deadly attacks," The Guardian, August 13, 2019

international community, and it is against this backdrop that terrorism has garnered considerable interest. How state failure is evaluated and measured is also important to such discourse, as will be enunciated in the following section.

Preventing Atrocities – Humanitarian Intervention

The use of military force against another state with the aim of ending grave human rights violations is the subject of many discussions in the public international law realm. Although there is no one standard legal definition of humanitarian intervention, the doctrine of non-intervention is enshrined in Article 2.7 of the UN Charter. This discussion centres on recent actions taken during the Kosovo War and some of the limited humanitarian intervention taken then by the Security Council. Most legal scholars would prefer that the Security Council take action under Chapter VII of the Charter and respond during humanitarian emergencies that constitute a threat to peace. The Security Council has broadened its interpretation of the Charter to include use of force in situations that are actually internal conflicts. Several arguments have surfaced justifying the new rules governing the use of force, however to date there is no consensus on an emergence of a new norm customary law.

As noted previously, the *Vienna Declaration*, proclaiming the universal, indivisible, interdependent and interrelated character of human rights, was unanimously adopted by all United Nations member states that were present, along with the recognition that the gap between rhetoric and reality needs to be bridged. This challenge is complicated by the daily litany of violations of human rights by several states. The predicament has led policymakers and legal scholars to advocate for humanitarian intervention in order to prevent gross and systematic violations of human rights. The use of force in international law in order to stop a humanitarian catastrophe is multifaceted in its characterization and implementation and is highly controversial when carried out without Security Council Chapter VII approval.

Most legal scholars argue that some of the essential characteristics of humanitarian intervention include: (a) the use of military force, (b) the absence of target state's permission, (c) the aim to help non-nationals and (d) acting either with or without United Nations authorization.[556] The classical definition is shared by a number of scholars, including Jeff Holzgrefe who defines it as the:

---

[556] Şaban Karda, "Humanitarian Intervention: The Evolution of the Idea and Practice," *Journal of International Affairs*, Vol. VI (2) (June-July 2001)

threat or use of force across state borders by a state (or group of states) aimed at preventing or ending widespread and grave violations of the fundamental human rights of individuals other than its own citizens, without the permission of the state within whose territory force is applied.[557673]

His criticism of humanitarian intervention is shared by many other legal scholars. In a legal sense, according to Wil D. Verwey, humanitarian intervention refers:

> only to coercive action taken by states, at their initiative, and involving the use of armed force, for the purpose of preventing or putting a halt to serious and wide-scale violations of fundamental human rights, in particular the right to life, inside the territory of another state[558]

However, others note that performing the duty of humanitarian intervention is just, especially when, as according to Michael Walzer, it is in response to acts "that shock the moral conscience of mankind."[559] This argument undoubtedly is more a philosophical debate than a legal one. However, it is worth noting that the international community acts not only when there is domestic pressure but also, more often than not, when there are strategic national and international interests involved, hence the reason why they engage in efforts in some countries and abandon others.

Humanitarian intervention has generated much discussion as a consequence of both the post-Cold War era debate surrounding human rights at the international level and the growing understanding of the relationship between international security and violations of human rights. The international legal scholar Fernando Teson puts forward the liberal argument of humanitarian intervention as the:

> proportionate international use or threat of military force, undertaken in principle by a liberal government or alliance, aimed at ending tyranny or anarchy, welcomed by the victims, and consistent with the doctrine of double effect.[560]

---

557   J.L. Holzgrefe, "The humanitarian intervention debate," in J.L. Holzgrefe and Robert O. Keohane (eds.), *Humanitarian Intervention. Ethical, legal, and Political Dilemmas*, Cambridge: Cambridge University Press (2003) at 18

558   Wil D. Verwey, "Humanitarian Intervention in the 1990s and Beyond: An International Law Perspective," in Jan Nederveen Pieterse (ed.), *World Orders in the Making*, London: Macmillan Press Ltd. (1998) at 180

559   Michael Walzer, *Just and Unjust Wars: A Moral Argument with Historical Illustrations*, 3rd Ed., New York: Basic Books (2000) at 107

560   Fernando R. Teson, "The liberal case for humanitarian intervention," in J.L. Holzgrefe and Robert O. Keohane (eds.), *Humanitarian Intervention. Ethical, legal, and Political Dilemmas*, Cambridge: Cambridge University Press (2003) at 94

The doctrine of double effect has its origins in the works of Saint Thomas Aquinas regarding ethical and moral criteria for evaluating the permissibility of certain acts:

> the nature of the act is itself good, or at least morally neutral; the agent intends the good effect and not the bad either as a means to the good or as an end itself; the good effect outweighs the bad effect in circumstances sufficiently grave to justify causing the bad effect and the agent exercises due diligence to minimize the harm.[561]

For Teson, human rights must prevail and the international legal system must be changed to allow for the implementation of human rights standards even if this means overriding conventional international law.

Daniel Joyner and other legal scholars reject Teson's argument, noting that if a law "can be circumvented at will then it is not law but rather a mere collection of recommendations."[562] Joyner forcefully argues against humanitarian intervention even in cases where customary international legal rules of humanitarian intervention are clearly established, as he claims nothing justifies the abrogation of the obligations of United Nations Charter Members and threats of actions against the territorial integrity or political independence of any state.[563] He argues that intervention by member states of the United Nations without the approval of the Security Council "is and should be a violation of international law."[564] Furthermore, according to Joyner, the Security Council is not in fact paralyzed, as some would argue, but is fulfilling its role as discretionary, governing a body of nations. He further notes that "[i]t should not be bypassed simply because its procedures lead to result in some cases unpalatable to a portion of its members."[565]

Joyner rejects the notion that failure by the international community to act in order to stop evil acts makes the international community complicit in these acts, for the international community is:

> far from being complicit in violence and terror, seeking to assure that those maladies do not afflict the international community on a far greater

---

561   T. A. Cavanaugh, *Double-Effect Reasoning: Doing Good and Avoiding Evil*, Oxford: Oxford University Press (2006) at 36

562   Daniel Joyner, "The Kosovo Intervention: Legal Analysis and a More Persuasive Paradigm," *European Journal of International Law*, Vol. 13. No. 3 (2002) at 609

563   Ibid.

564   Ibid. at 598

565   Ibid. at 608

level and scope and that a system of law is in place to keep this greater catastrophe from being realized as it has in the past.[566]

He concludes that the United Nations system:

> represents the legal and most prudential system for the governance of the entire area of internal use-of-force law, and that its obligations and strictures in this area should not be blithely circumvented in the hope of furthering the cause of humanitarian intervention in the short term.[567]

The General Assembly has also issued a declaration that:

> No State or group of States has the right to intervene, directly or indirectly, for any reason whatever, in the internal or external affairs of any other State. Consequently, armed intervention and all other forms of interference or attempted threats against the personality of the State or against its political, economic, or cultural elements, are in violation of international law.[568]

Michael Byers and Simon Chesterman recast the debate on humanitarian intervention by referencing the United Nations Charter, which prevails over all other treaties, particularly Article 2(4) of the Charter, which explicitly states that force across borders is not permitted. For Byers and Chesterman, the central argument is that international law cannot be changed by states who want to act to prevent human rights in part because of their own national interests:

> These ends are not served by distorting the international legal regime to validate retrospectively actions by one state or group of states, particularly when the cost of doing so may include the integrity of the legal order itself. ... The greatest threat to an international rule of law lies not in the occasional breach of that law—laws are frequently broken in all legal systems, sometimes for the best of reasons—but in attempts to mould that law to accommodate the shifting practices of the powerful.[569]

---

566 Ibid. at 617

567 Ibid. at 618

568 Declaration on Principles of International Law Concerning Friendly Relations and Cooperation Among States in Accordance with the Charter of the United Nations, General Assembly Resolution 2625, XXV (24 October 1970)

569 Robert O. Keohane, "Introduction," in J.L. Holzgrefe and Robert O. Keohane (eds.), *Humanitarian Intervention. Ethical, legal, and Political Dilemmas*, Cambridge: Cambridge University Press (2003) at 5-6

However, I would strongly argue that intervention is necessary in some cases, and that respect for human rights is the fundamental principal of the United Nations' existence. Article 1 of the UN Charter emphasizes promoting respect for human rights and justice as one of the fundamental missions of the organization. As well, Article 1(3) calls attention to the importance of respect for human rights and justice:

> [t]o achieve international cooperation in solving international problems of an economic, social, cultural, or humanitarian character, and in promoting and encouraging respect for human rights and for fundamental freedoms for all without distinction as to race, sex, language, or religion.[570]

Byers and Chesterman, pointing to Article 2(4), claim that all member states of the United Nations who "refrain from the threat or use of force," however, fail to take note of the importance of Article 1(3), "promoting and encoring respect for human rights," which needs to be balanced with the ensuing article.

Responsibility to Protect Doctrine

The central question from which has arisen much debate is what the response of the world community should be when human rights are consistently violated and where sovereign states are unwilling or unable to prevent mass murder.

Does the international community have a responsibility to act? In cases of genocide and mass atrocities in failed states where administrative institutions have collapsed, provisions for human rights are largely ineffective—with the state engaged in human rights violations or acting as a bystander and offering no more than peripheral protection—the answer would surely be yes, given the mandate of the UN Human Rights Charter and the international treaties that bind nations.[571]

The Responsibility to Protect doctrine took form as a direct result of the North Atlantic Treaty Organization intervention in Kosovo and the various opinions on the legality of NATO's actions and the failure of the Security Council to act. Canadian Minister of Foreign Affairs Lloyd Axworthy played a leading role in the establishing the International Commission on Intervention and State Sovereignty (ICISS)[572]

---

[570] Charter of the United Nations, signed on 26 June 1945 in San Francisco

[571] Daniel Thürer, *The 'Failed State' and International Law*, Geneva: International Review of the Red Cross, No. 836 (31 December 1999)

[572] *The Responsibility To Protect*, International Commission on Intervention and State Sovereignty (December 2001)

in December of 2001 in order to clarify some of these issues. The report was entitled "Responsibility to Protect," and the concept was endorsed by world leaders at the UN in the fall of 2005. The report set out four core principles for military intervention to adhere to when states fail to protect their own people,[573] leading some scholars to argue that the norm of the Responsibility to Protect has weakened the Westphalian system of absolute state sovereignty and, given that it was endorsed by the United Nations General Assembly, come to represent a new doctrine of international law. It should, however, be noted that the specific recommendations of the report were never endorsed.

The International Commission on Intervention and State Sovereignty was chaired by Gareth Evans and Mohamed Sahnoun and examined the central question, a serious dilemma, posed by Secretary-General Kofi Annan:

> [I]f humanitarian intervention is, indeed, an unacceptable assault on sovereignty, how should we respond to a Rwanda, to a Srebrenica—to gross and systematic violations of human rights that affect every precept of our common humanity?[574]

Annan's appeal to the international community was to try and find, once and for all, a "new consensus on how to approach these issues, to 'forge unity' around the basic questions of principle and process involved."[575] The Commission consulted broadly for opinions around the world and reported back to Annan. The title of the report, "Responsibility to Protect," reflects the notion that sovereign states have an obligation to offer protection to their citizens:

> from avoidable catastrophe—from mass murder and rape, from starvation—but that when they are unwilling or unable to do so, that responsibility must be borne by the broader community of states.[576]

The report was commissioned in the aftermath of events in Somalia, Bosnia, Kosovo and Rwanda. NATO's intervention in Kosovo in 1999

---

[573] Many of the ideas in the *Responsibility to Protect* were advance in the 5th century by Saint Augustine - *Bellum iustum* such as: war must occur for a good and just purpose rather than for self-gain; war must be waged by a properly instituted authority; peace must be a central motive even in the midst of violence. Saint Thomas Aquinas further developed Saint Augustine's arguments.

[574] *The Responsibility To Protect* at VII

[575] Ibid.

[576] Ibid. at VIII

brought the debate to the centre of attention of a divided Security Council. As well, during the genocide in Rwanda wherein three short months as many as 800,000 Tutsis were shot, burned, starved, tortured, stabbed, or hacked to death, the international community, especially the Security Council, did little if anything to stop the atrocities.[577]

The International Commission on Intervention and State Sovereignty, in its Responsibility to Protect report, advanced the notion of "sovereignty as responsibility." This notion was first introduced by Francis Deng, at the Brookings Institution in 1996 and challenged the established principle of absolute state sovereignty which recognized the sovereignty of a state regardless of whether that state committed serious human rights abuses against its own citizens.[578] The Commission's report also notes that:

> responsibility to protect resides first and foremost with the state whose people are directly affected. This fact reflects not only international law and the modern state system, also the practical realities of who is best placed to make a positive difference. The domestic authority is best placed to take action to prevent problems from turning into potential conflicts. When problems arise the domestic authority is also best placed to understand them and to deal with them. When solutions are needed, it is the citizens of a particular state who have the greatest interest and the largest stake in the success of those solutions, in ensuring that the domestic authorities are fully accountable for their actions or inactions in addressing these problems, and in helping to ensure that past problems are not allowed to recur.[579]

The Commission further added to the debate over what should be done if a state fails and is unable or unwilling to stop gross and systematic violations of human rights by noting that:

> ...if states do not live up to their responsibilities, it is the task of the more responsible members of the international community to intervene – for the sake not only of the beleaguered citizens, but also of wider international peace and security.[580]

---

[577] J.L. Holzgrefe, "The humanitarian intervention debate," in J.L. Holzgrefe and Robert O. Keohane (eds.), *Humanitarian Intervention. Ethical, legal, and Political Dilemmas*, Cambridge: Cambridge University Press (2003) at 17

[578] *W2I Mobilizing the Will to Intervene*, Montreal Institute for Genocide and Human Rights Studies, Concordia University (2010) at 3. Deng was appointed in 2012 as UN Special Adviser for the Prevention of Genocide.

[579] *The Responsibility To Protect* at 2.30

[580] Lars Engberg-Pedersen et al, *Fragile States on the International Agenda*, Copenhagen: Danish Institute of International Studies (2008) at 7

Both Fernando Teson and Allen Buchanan are strong supporters of what is referred to by some as the Responsibility to Protect doctrine. Teson and Buchanan advocate a paradigm shift in the notion of state sovereignty and the role of the United Nations as "[t]he perception is growing that the requirement of Security Council authorization is an obstacle to the protection of basic human rights in international conflicts."[581]

Other scholars observe that the drafters of the United Nations Charter did so in a post-Second World War context, likely envisioning situations where action would be required as a result of conflict between countries and not within states themselves. Ove Bring of Stockholm University argues in favour of a doctrine of humanitarian intervention formulated and built upon emerging international norms that give precedence to the protection of human rights over sovereignty in certain circumstances[582] For example, Bring and others argue that NATO's action in Kosovo has come to be accepted as reflective of the will of the international community. Given that there were serious human rights violations perpetrated against the citizens of Kosovo, international intervention was required. Bring further argues that regional organizations intervening in order to protect human rights in failed states should be included as part of international law.[583]

The intervention in Kosovo has been justified on the basis of the emerging doctrine of the Responsibility to Protect. As noted above, in many ways the International Commission on Intervention and State Sovereignty report was a response to both the international community's humanitarian intervention in Kosovo without Security Council approval and the United Nations lack of action in places like Rwanda; however, the report, while addressing the issue of humanitarian intervention, has left many other issues unresolved. It is legal fact that the United Nations Charter prohibits nations from attacking other states, as it violates Article 2(4). However, it should also be noted that Article 51 states that "[n]othing in the present Charter shall impair the inherent right of individual or collective self-defence if an armed attack occurs against a Member of the United Nations." Also, the Security Council may authorize the use of force under Chapter VII in order to maintain or restore international peace and security.

---

581   Allen Buchanan, "Reforming the international law of humanitarian intervention," in J.L. Holzgrefe and Robert O. Keohane (eds.), *Humanitarian Intervention. Ethical, legal, and Political Dilemmas,* Cambridge: Cambridge University Press (2003) at 131

582   Ove Bring, "Should NATO take the lead in formulating a doctrine on humanitarian intervention?," *NATO Review,* No.3 (Autumn 1999) at 24

583   Ibid. at 26

The United Nations realized the gravity of the situation in Kosovo when the Security Council established The International Tribunal for the Prosecution of Persons Responsible for Serious Violations of International Humanitarian Law Committed in the Territory of the Former Yugoslavia since 1991, more commonly referred to as the International Criminal Tribunal for the former Yugoslavia, to prosecute war crimes in the former Yugoslavia.

With respect to Kosovo, the Russian veto meant that no United Nations Security Council Resolution could succeed in authorizing the use of force to prevent ethnic cleansing. The Canadian Ambassador to the United Nations, Paul Heinbecker, pointed out that this intervention did in fact accurately represent the will of the international community. As well, international legal scholars such as Thomas Franck pointed out to the Canadian House of Commons Standing Committee on Foreign Affairs and International Trade in February of 2003 that a failed Russian attempt to condemn NATO's action amounted to a retrospective legal ratification for the intervention. According to Professor Franck:

> ...Russia took the ill-advised step of calling for a vote on the illegality of NATO recourse to force in the humanitarian intervention in Kosovo, and it lost that vote by, I think, 12 votes to 3, and ever since it's been firmly asserted by international lawyers, including myself, that that negative vote on the censure motion was the closest thing you needed to have to ratifying the recourse to force, even in the absence of an affirmative Security Council resolution.[584]

Those states that supported NATO's action maintain that a resolution tabled by Russia condemning the air campaign in Kosovo was defeated by the Security Council and, therefore, indirect support for the intervention was in fact given. Professor Thomas Franck argues that this development was the closest thing to ratification in the absence of an actual successful Security Council resolution for intervention.[585] Nicholas Wheeler also maintains that although the failure of the Russian veto did not constitute a retroactive authorization, it did add credence to the belief that there was a moral consensus among liberal states and some others about the right to intervention in extreme humanitarian emergencies.[586]

---

[584] Canadian House of Commons Standing Committee on Foreign Affairs and International Trade, *Minutes of Proceedings and Evidence*, Meeting No. 22 (27 February 2003)

[585] Ibid.

[586] Nicholas Wheeler, "The Legality of NATO intervention in Kosovo," in Ken Booth (ed.) *The Kosovo Tragedy: The Human Rights Dimensions*, Portland: Frank Cass (2001) at 156

However, as noted above, many legal scholars, including Professor Michael Reisman of Yale Law School have made the argument that states cannot be expected to remain idle while a great number of people die; the Charter was not a suicide pact.[587] It is worth noting that in the case of Libya, the Security Council did act promptly and, in addition, members of the Security Council used the language of the doctrine of the Responsibility to Protect although they did not refer to it in their final resolution. On March 17th, 2011, the United Nations Security Council, acting under the authority of Chapter VII, adopted the milestone Resolution 1973, calling for member states to take "all necessary measures ... to protect civilians and civilian populated areas under threat of attack in the Libyan Arab Jamahiriya, including Benghazi."[588] The Resolution is a significant step forward in support of the legality of the use of force in humanitarian intervention.

Protecting human rights and respecting the emerging norms of humanitarian intervention requires concrete definitions, thus some legal scholars have looked to the criteria set out in the doctrine of the Responsibility to Protect for humanitarian intervention to provide answers to unresolved questions. For example, the Responsibility to Protect report declares that there is no "better or more appropriate body than the United Nations Security Council to authorize military intervention for human protection purposes."[589] However, if the Security Council fails to act, the doctrine advances the notion that alternative options must be considered, including the referring of a matter to the General Assembly in an "Emergency Special Session under the 'Uniting for Peace' procedure"[590] and even the appeal to regional bodies to take action.

I would argue that "Uniting for Peace" Resolution 377 of the General Assembly[591] is now part of customary international law and therefore an effective tool to be used for the General Assembly to take legal action against those states that continue to perpetrate genocide and mass atrocities. In the case of the Rohingya people of Myanmar, it was clear that China would have voted against any military or economic sanction against Myanmar. However, the "Uniting for Peace" Resolution 377 should have

---

[587] Michael Reisman, "The Constitutional Crisis in the United Nations," *American Journal of International Law*, Vol. 87, No.1 (1993) at 89. Reisman borrows the term from American Jurist Oliver Wendell Holmes' argument about the United States Constitution.

[588] Security Council Resolution 1973 (17 March 2011)

[589] *The Responsibility To Protect* at 3(A)

[590] Ibid. at 3(E.I)

[591] A/RES/377 General Assembly (3 November 1950)

been used by the General Assembly to end the genocide, notwithstanding the fact that the veto power of the Security Council has never yet been rendered irrelevant and these measures by the General Assembly have been, to an extent, more symbolic than authoritative.[592] This is in spite of the fact that the five permanent Members of the Security Council have disproportionate influence in decision-making that influences peremptory norms of customary international law.

Michael Ignatieff, who was one of the authors of the Responsibility to Protect report, sees interventions as often hindered by the desire of interveners to remain neutral between competing factions. I would argue, along with Ignatieff, that the situation in Bosnia demonstrated the disastrous results of seeking to remain neutral between oppressor and victim. As Ignatieff pointed out, neutral intervention can also aid the aggressor, as we have seen in Afghanistan, and strengthen the various warlords, enabling them to fight for longer periods. Hence, Ignatieff argues for more vigorous and sustained intervention, as "the idea of a responsibility to protect also implies a responsibility to prevent and a responsibility to follow through."[593]

In the case of failed or failing states, failure to act inevitably poses a lethal threat to regional stability and international security. As the contemporary history of Iraq, Syria, Somalia, and Afghanistan demonstrates, failed states generate grave international security and humanitarian costs.[594] The emergence of piracy off the coast of Somalia is a good example of the disruptive effects of failed states. The International Maritime Organization reported that global piracy increased by 200% in 2008 compared to the previous year.[595] Gareth Evans has argued that states unwilling or unable to end atrocities within their own borders will be just as ineffective in stopping terrorism; the trafficking of arms, drugs and people; the circulation of health pandemics; and other global disasters.[596]

The Responsibility to Protect, as noted, advances the notion that state sovereignty is a "privilege and not a right, and is derived from a reciprocal

---

[592] Brendan I. Koerner, "Can You Bypass a U.N. Security Council Veto?," New York: *Slate* (12 March 2003)

[593] Michael Ignatieff, "State failure and nation-building," in J.L. Holzgrefe and Robert O. Keohane (eds.), *Humanitarian Intervention. Ethical, legal, and Political Dilemmas*, Cambridge: Cambridge University Press (2003) at 320

[594] *W2I Mobilizing the Will to Intervene*, Montreal Institute for Genocide and Human Rights Studies, Concordia University (2010) at 9

[595] Ibid. at 9

[596] Gareth Evans, "Towards a More Bound –Together World," Brussels: International Crisis Group (27 March 2009)

relationship of respect between the state and its citizens."[597] At the 2005 World Summit, the United Nations General Assembly agreed that if a state is unwilling or unable to protect its own citizens against gross and systematic violations of internationally recognized human rights, the international community must assume the responsibility to protect them. Under such circumstances, the international community has a duty to launch preventative, reactive and rebuilding measures that are aimed at protecting defenceless civilians from abuse by their own governments. The United Nations General Assembly World Summit Outcome Document singled out prevention as the most important element of the Responsibility to Protect. In addition, there is growing belief in sovereignty as an evolving principle, intrinsically linked to the security and protection of civilians.[598]

Notwithstanding the need for a paradigm shift that will persuade states to adopt the concept of state failure prevention as outlined previously, the reality is simply that the arguments in favour of the doctrine of Responsibility to Protect have been used by some states inconsistently. The advancing notion is that ignoring weak and failed states invariably leads to serious atrocities and civil conflict and poses both national and international threats. The Responsibility to Protect doctrine is just one tool that can be used by states and the international community in dealing with failed states. However, dealing with terrorist groups, mass atrocities, and failed states will of course require a broad spectrum of tools and, essentially, the political will of the international community.

United Nations Secretary-General Ban Ki-moon, speaking in October 2011, provided the examples of Côte d'Ivoire, when the incumbent president refused to stand down and began committing violence against his own people, and Libya, where the people of the country were being massacred, to illustrate that:

> The United Nations stood up for the will of the people—and for the 'responsibility to protect.' That new doctrine aims to ensure that people facing mass atrocity crimes are not alone when their own country cannot or will not protect them.[599]

The Charter gives the Security Council authority to act; however, the debate surrounding the legality of intervention when it takes place outside of a United Nations mandate is much more complicated.

---

[597] *W2I Mobilizing the Will to Intervene*, Montreal Institute for Genocide and Human Rights Studies, Concordia University (2010) at 3

[598] Ibid. at 3

[599] "Ban Urges Students to Help Build Rule of Law Institutions in Emerging Democracies," UN News, New York (4 October 2011)

Emergence of New Customary Law – Intervention

The legality of humanitarian intervention depends in great part upon who is interpreting the conventions. Legal realists endeavour to justify humanitarian intervention through a liberal understanding of Chapter VII: *Action with Respect to Threats to the Peace, Breaches of the Peace, and Acts of Aggression*, Article 39, which states that:

> The Security Council shall determine the existence of any threat to the peace, breach of the peace, or act of aggression and shall make recommendations, or decide what measures shall be taken in accordance with Articles 41 and 42, to maintain or restore international peace and security.[600]

Legal realists argue that Article 39 gives the Security Council "jurisdiction over any 'threat to the peace,' rather than over any threat to international peace, therefore permitting it to intervene in order to end human rights violations that lack trans-boundary effects."[601]

Notwithstanding the legal obligations of the Security Council to act when there is a threat to the peace, actions have had, to date, mixed success. During the civil war in the early 1990s in Somalia, the international community became alarmed by the spiral of violence and state failure. On December 3rd, 1992, the Security Council unanimously adopted Resolution 794, which "strongly condemned the violations of international law and demanded the cessation of all hostilities from all parties involved."[602] The Security Council further determined that the civil war was a threat to international peace and security, which was "further exacerbated by the obstacles being created to the distribution of humanitarian assistance."[603] Resolution 794 also authorized the creation of the Unified Task Force (UNITAF) for "establishing a secure environment for humanitarian relief operations."[604] It further authorized action under Chapter VII entailing the "deployment of the 3,500 personnel of the United Nations Operation in Somalia (UNOSOM)"[605] to aid in achieving the above objective.

---

[600] Charter of the United Nations, signed on 26 June 1945 in San Francisco

[601] J.L. Holzgrefe, "The humanitarian intervention debate," in J.L. Holzgrefe and Robert O. Keohane (eds.), *Humanitarian Intervention. Ethical, legal, and Political Dilemmas*, Cambridge: Cambridge University Press (2003) at 40

[602] Security Council Resolution 794 (3 December 1992)

[603] Ibid.

[604] Ibid.

[605] Ibid.

The Security Council approved several resolutions that attempted to deal with the situation in Somalia, but the killing of peacekeepers by Somali militia forces eventually led many states to withdraw their forces by the mid-1990s.

On November 4th, 1994, the Security Council adopted Resolution 954, recognizing:

> that the lack of progress in the Somali peace process and in national reconciliation, in particular the lack of sufficient cooperation from the Somali parties over security issues, has fundamentally undermined the United Nations objectives in Somalia and, in these circumstances, continuation of UNOSOM II beyond March 1995 cannot be justified.[606]

A secure environment has yet to be established despite the many human and financial resources that have been exhausted in Somalia by member states of the United Nations.

In the case of Rwanda, the Security Council adopted Resolution 935 on July 1st, 1994 concerning "continuing reports indicating that systematic, widespread and flagrant violations of international humanitarian law, including acts of genocide, have been committed in Rwanda."[607] Yet, despite the massacre of hundreds of thousands of Tutsis in a short period of time,[608] the Security Council did not express in its resolution that the reported genocide also constituted a threat to peace and security. Only on November 8th, 1994 did the Security Council adopt Resolution 955, which called the reported acts of genocide and violations of humanitarian law "a threat to international peace and security" and set out "to take effective measures to bring to justice the persons who are responsible for them."[609]

The failure of the Security Council to act quickly led Kofi Annan to state that "[t]he genocide in Rwanda showed us how terrible the consequences of inaction can be in the face of mass murder"[610] Also, in his well-known address to the Commission on Human Rights in 1999, Kofi Annan stated that "[a] United Nations that will not stand up for human rights is a United Nations that cannot stand up for itself."[611] He further remarked that:

---

[606]   Security Council Resolution 954 (4 November 1994)

[607]   Security Council Resolution 935 (1 July 1994)

[608]   "Rwanda: How the genocide happened," BBC News Africa (17 May 2011)

[609]   Security Council Resolution 955 (8 November1994)

[610]   Kofi A. Annan, "Two concepts of sovereignty," *The Economist* (18 September 1999)

[611]   "Secretary-General calls for renewed commitment in new century to protect rights of man, woman, child – regardless of ethnic, national belonging," UN News, New York (7 April 1999)

Emerging slowly, but I believe surely, is an international norm against the violent repression of minorities that will and must take precedence over concerns of State sovereignty. It is a principle that protects minorities—and majorities—from gross violations. ... No government has the right to hide behind national sovereignty in order to violate the human rights or fundamental freedoms of its peoples. ... This developing international norm will pose fundamental challenges to the United Nations.[612]

The focal point of Annan's address was that the purpose of the international community is not to stand still, a point which is made clear by his statement that:

the tragedy of East Timor, coming so soon after that of Kosovo, has focused attention once again on the need for timely intervention by the international community when death and suffering are being inflicted on large numbers of people, and when the state nominally in charge is unable or unwilling to stop it.[613]

Annan, acutely aware of the problems of inaction, is equally attentive to the important questions regarding the consequences of action without international consensus and clear legal authority, as well as the inability of the international community to reconcile these two compelling interests.[614]

The Security Council has been unwilling to deal with issues of state failure in Iraq, instead focusing on the terrorist groups which have destabilized the country. There is broad consensus among its members that the crimes committed by ISIS/ISIL include:

acts which may amount to war crimes, crimes against humanity or genocide, is part of the ideology and strategic objectives of ISIL (Da'esh), and used by ISIL (Da'esh) as a tactic of terrorism, and that holding ISIL (Da'esh) members accountable, particularly those who bear the greatest responsibility, including in terms of leadership, which can include regional or mid-level commanders, and the ordering and commission of crimes, will further expose this, and could assist in countering terrorism and violent extremism which can be conducive to terrorism, including by stemming financing and the continued flow of international recruits to the terrorist group ISIL (Da'esh).[615]

---

[612] Ibid.

[613] Kofi A. Annan, "Two concepts of sovereignty," *The Economist* (18 September 1999)

[614] Ibid.

[615] https://undocs.org/S/RES/2490(2019)

I would argue that the Genocide Convention, by enjoining its signatories to "prevent and punish" the "crime of genocide," may have made genocide the exceptional circumstance that warrants intervention. Many states are signatories to international treaties that recognize the fundamental respect for human rights, and most legal scholars would argue that the prohibitions on genocide and crimes against humanity have achieved the status of *jus cogens* and arguably of "peremptory norms from which in theory at least, no derogation is permitted."[616]

However, in the Genocide Convention, Article 8 declares that contracting parties may legally prevent acts of genocide by calling upon "the competent organs of the United Nations to take such action ... as they consider appropriate."[617] Arguably, this does not establish a right of unauthorized humanitarian intervention. It is a topic of great debate whether the source of international law and its conventions permit unauthorized humanitarian interventions.

NATO's intervention in Kosovo was not authorized by the Security Council; however, it received sympathy from most of the member states of the United Nations, including Secretary-General Kofi Annan,[618] even though it was inconsistent with international legal principles of "the sovereign equality of all its Members,"[619] and Article 2(4), which requires that all Members shall "refrain in their international relations from the threat or use of force against the territorial integrity or political independence of any states."[620]

The notion of use of force that violates the territorial integrity or political independence of a state for the purpose of humanitarian intervention is in the early stages of debate and may, over time, come to be considered as a customary norm supported by the majority of states. It should also be noted that the development of customary international law has long been a matter of debate and disagreement among legal scholars and states, especially the notion concerning state practice.[621] Scholars such as Anthony D' Amato, Mark Weisburd, and Karol Wolfke, have maintained that:

---

[616] Bartram S. Brown, "Humanitarian Intervention at a Crossroads," *William and Mary Law Review*, Vol. 41 (2000) at 1698

[617] *Convention on the Prevention and Punishment of the Crime of Genocide*, General Assembly Resolution 260 (III) (9 December 1948)

[618] Annan, Kofi A., "Speech to the General Assembly " (20 September 1999)

[619] United Nations Charter at Article 2.1

[620] Ibid. at Article 2.4

[621] Michael Byers and Simon Chesterman, "Changing the rules about rules? Unilateral humanitarian intervention and the future of international law," in J.L. Holzgrefe and Robert O. Keohane (eds.), *Humanitarian Intervention. Ethical, legal, and Political Dilemmas*, Cambridge: Cambridge University Press (2003) at 188

only physical acts count as state practice, which means that any state wishing to support or oppose the development or change of a rule must engage in some sort of act, and that statements or claims do not suffice.[622]

They would also be of the opinion that under a traditional understanding of international law, the only way that humanitarian intervention, as in the case of Kosovo, could be legal was if a right of unilateral humanitarian intervention had somehow achieved the status of *jus cogens*, thus overriding conflicting treaty provisions.

Allen Buchanan notes that there has not yet been a shift towards recognition of humanitarian intervention as a peremptory norm. He is equally critical of the different justifications for illegal interventions for the protection of human rights that are used by states. Buchanan lists three justifications used by states: First, there is the 'moral principle justification'; second, there is the 'illegal but necessary justification'; and third, there is the 'illegal-legal reform justification', which is used when humanitarian intervention is taken not only in response to human rights violations, but also in order to create a new norm of international law.[623]

Buchanan observes that there is no newly formed norm of humanitarian intervention:

> [A] new customary rule does not emerge by officially registering that they do not regard their behaviour as legally required thus thwarting satisfaction of the *opinio juris* condition... new customary norms do not emerge from a single action or even from a persistent pattern of action by one state or a group of states. Thus the initial effort to create a new customary norm is a gamble. A new norm is created only when the initial behaviour is repeated consistently by a preponderance of states over a considerable period of time and only when there is a shift in the legal consciousness of all or most states as to the juridical status of the behaviour.[624]

The issue remains at the centre of considerable debate, with many legal scholars disagreeing with Buchanan over whether a new norm of humanitarian intervention has been established and pointing instead to the example of the resolutions of the General Assembly on the matter of humanitarian assistance, including those adopted during the Kosovo War, as having contributed to customary international law and the role of humanitarian intervention.

---

[622] Ibid.

[623] Allen Buchanan, "Reforming the international law of humanitarian intervention," in J.L. Holzgrefe and Robert O. Keohane (eds.), *Humanitarian Intervention. Ethical, legal, and Political Dilemmas*, Cambridge: Cambridge University Press (2003) at 131-132

[624] Ibid. at 143

The view that a right of unauthorized humanitarian intervention possesses *opinio juris sive necessitatis* is complicated by the extensive list of United Nations General Assembly resolutions rejecting such a right.[625] Ultimately, as Scott Fairley emphasizes, "the use of force for humanitarian ends more often than not has become self-defeating, increasing the human misery and loss of life it was intended originally to relieve."[626] Fairley reasons that if humanitarian intervention were legal, "powerful states would receive an almost unlimited right to overthrow governments alleged to be unresponsive to the popular will or the goal of self-determination."[627] However, given that most violations are within states rather than between states, there is reasonable debate concerning the need for re-evaluating the role of the Charter in dealing with humanitarian intervention in an ever-evolving world.

The debate surrounding the legal regulations of humanitarian intervention has been reignited by the actions of states, Security Council resolutions, and decisions of the International Court of Justice relating to United Nations resolutions. In the 1986 *Nicaragua v United States of America*, the International Court of Justice accepted that a series of General Assembly resolutions played a role in the development of customary rules prohibiting intervention and aggression.[628]

In order for a legal principle to obtain the status of customary international law, *opinio juris*, it is required that there is a consistent practice that is also obligatory. The decision of the International Court of Justice in the *Nicaragua v United States of America* case noted that evidence of *opinio juris* may be gathered from treaties and non-binding instruments such as declarations and General Assembly resolutions.[629] As well, the International Court of Justice established that "the effect of consent to the text of such resolutions ... may be understood as an acceptance of the validity of the rule or set of rules declared by the resolution."[630] Evidently, the decision of the International Court of Justice in *Nicaragua v United States of*

---

[625] J.L. Holzgrefe and Robert O. Keohane, *Humanitarian Intervention. Ethical, legal, and Political Dilemmas*, Cambridge: Cambridge University Press (2003) at 47

[626] Scott H. Fairely, "State Actors, Humanitarian Intervention and International Law: Reopening Pandora's Box," *Georgia Journal of International and Comparative Law*, Vol. 10, No. 1 (1980) at 63

[627] Oscar Schachter, "The Legality of Pro-democratic Invasion," *American Journal of International Law* Vol. 78 (1984) at 649

[628] *Case Concerning the Military and Paramilitary Activities in and Against Nicaragua (Nicaragua v. United States of America)*, International Court of Justice, Summary of the Judgment (27 June 1986)

[629] Ibid. at para. 188

[630] Ibid.

America has, *inter alia*, added to the debate over the acceptance of General Assembly resolutions as *opinio juris* and of the existence of a new rule of customary international law.

Nevertheless, one of the most powerful members of the Security Council, the United States, has resisted any effort to recognize resolutions by the General Assembly as state practice, noting that NATO's 1999 intervention in Kosovo does not mention any relevant General Assembly resolutions, including the 1970 *Declaration on Principles of International Law concerning Friendly Relations and Co-operation among States.*

Article 103 of The United Nations Charter states explicitly that it prevails over all other treaties:

> In the event of a conflict between the obligations of the Members of the United Nations under the present Charter and their obligations under any other international agreement, their obligations under the present Charter shall prevail.[631]

Article 103 of the Charter is comprehensive and binds all member states of the United Nations. In 1992, the International Court of Justice, the UN's principal judicial organ, decided in the Lockerbie case (*Libya v United Kingdom*)[632] on the crucial issue of whether the obligations of member states of the United Nations under Resolution 748 (1992) and other Chapter VII resolutions prevailed over Members' obligations under the 1971 *Montreal Convention on Aircraft Sabotage.*[633] In 1992, the Court decided that in:

> [a]ccordance with Article 103, the obligations to carry out decisions of the Security Council prevail over obligations of any other treaty, including the Montreal Convention, and therefore that the prima facie the Charter obligations extend to Resolution 748.[634]

---

[631] United Nations Charter at Article 103

[632] Questions of Interpretation and Application of the 1971 Montreal Convention arising from the Aerial Incident at Lockerbie, International Court of Justice, *Libyan Arab Jamahiriya v. United Kingdom* (27 February 1998) Preliminary Objections – Judgment – General List No. 88

[633] Anthony Aust, *Modern Treaty Law and Practice*, Cambridge: Cambridge University Press (2002) at 219

[634] Questions of Interpretation and Application of the 1971 Montreal Convention arising from the Aerial Incident at Lockerbie, International Court of Justice, *Libyan Arab Jamahiriya v. United Kingdom* (27 February 1998) Preliminary Objections – Judgment – General List No. 88

Given the primacy of the United Nations Charter, it is important to consider, as noted above, that it makes clear that "member States have pledged themselves to achieve, in co-operation with the United Nations, the promotion of universal respect for and observance of human rights and fundamental freedoms,"[635] and obligates member states of the United Nations to act to fulfil these rights, as "a common understanding of these rights and freedoms is of the greatest importance for the full realization of this pledge."[636]

There is no consensus among international legal scholars as to whether the NATO intervention in the Federal Republic of Yugoslavia constituted a violation of customary international law. However, it could be argued that a new and evolving international practice has developed that recognizes that in certain circumstances a humanitarian crisis is so grave that a moral and legal justification for intervention exists. Several legal scholars, such as Thomas Franck, note that international law "has begun gingerly to develop ways to bridge the gap between what is requisite in strict legality and what is generally regarded as just and moral."[637] Franck points to the Independent International Commission on Kosovo (Goldstone Commission on Kosovo), which concluded that NATO's action, "while not strictly legal, was legitimate."[638] The Commission concluded that international legal interpretation should be more compatible with "an international moral consensus."[639]

India's intervention in East Pakistan in 1971 in reaction to Pakistan's immense human right violations, the Tanzanian 1979 intervention in Uganda which led to the overthrow of the dictatorial and murderous regime of Idi Amin, and the Vietnamese intervention in 1978 against Pol Pot's genocidal regime in Cambodia have all been alluded to as humanitarian interventions in response to human rights violations, yet all were all without United Nations Security Council approval.[640]

In this regard, the linkage between violations of human rights and international armed conflicts which pose a threat to international peace

---

[635] United Nations Charter at Preamble

[636] Ibid.

[637] Thomas Franck, "Interpretation and change in the law of humanitarian intervention," in J.L. Holzgrefe and Robert O. Keohane (eds.), *Humanitarian Intervention. Ethical, legal, and Political Dilemmas*, Cambridge: Cambridge University Press (2003) at 214

[638] Ibid. at 215

[639] Ibid. at 215-216 and Independent International commission on Kosovo, *Kosovo Report: Conflict, International Response, Lessons Learned*, Oxford: Oxford University Press (2000) at 4 and 163

[640] Allen Buchanan, "Reforming the international law of humanitarian intervention," in J.L. Holzgrefe and Robert O. Keohane (eds.), *Humanitarian Intervention. Ethical, legal, and Political Dilemmas*, Cambridge: Cambridge University Press (2003) at 130

and security could provide a space in which humanitarian intervention would be possible. Serious violations of human rights in failed states create inroads in the traditional perceptions of state sovereignty,[641] leading some scholars, such as Alexandros Yannis, to suggest that there has been a shift away from state-centred consideration and towards the individual.[642] However, even states that have intervened in order to end dreadful human rights abuses have been reluctant to invoke a customary right of unauthorized humanitarian intervention to defend their actions. India's justification of its invasion of East Pakistan was self-defence, Vietnam argued that it was reacting to an aggressive war, and Tanzania defended its actions as a response to Uganda's invasion of Kagera.[643]

NATO defended the 1999 air bombing of the former Yugoslavia as justified and consistent with Security Council resolutions 1160, 1199, and 1203.[644] With the exception of Belgium, the other members of NATO did not "appeal to a right of unauthorized humanitarian intervention to legitimate their actions."[645]

The examination of international law by legal scholars such as Franck is:

> part of an evolving discourse similar to how states that have a tradition of common law and that each organ of the United Nations is authorized to interpret the Charter's mandate for itself, and must do so to prevent the emergence of a large gap between law and a 'common sense of values.'[646]

Such a gap would threaten the legitimacy of international law and international organizations.

The 1949 Corfu Channel Case (*United Kingdom of Great Britain and Northern Ireland v. Albania*) was the first major International Court of Justice decision on self-defence under the newly created United Nations Charter. The United Kingdom argued that the unilateral minesweeping did not violate Albania's territorial integrity and political independence and

---

[641] Alexandros Yannis, "State Collapse and its Implications for Peace-Building and Reconstruction," in Jennifer Milliken (ed.), *State Failure, Collapse & Reconstruction*, Oxford: Blackwell Publishing (2003) at 69

[642] Ibid. at 69-70

[643] J.L. Holzgrefe, "The humanitarian intervention debate," in J.L. Holzgrefe and Robert O. Keohane, *Humanitarian Intervention. Ethical, legal, and Political Dilemmas*, Cambridge: Cambridge University Press (2003) at 48-49

[644] Ibid. at 48

[645] Ibid. at 49

[646] Ibid. at 6

that it was justified given that "nobody else was prepared to deal with the threat, mines planted in an international strait."[647] The United Kingdom argued that it acted for reasons of self-defence to safeguard evidence, the *corpora delicti*. The International Court of Justice rejected these arguments. As well, the Court rejected the notion of 'self-help' in gathering evidence located in another state's territory, considering it a violation of international law:

> The Court cannot accept this line of defence. The Court can only regard the alleged right of intervention as a policy of force, such as has, in the past, given rise to the most serious abuses and such as cannot, whatever be the present defects in international organization, find a place in international law. As regards the notion of self-help, the Court is also unable to accept it: between independent States the respect for territorial sovereignty is an essential foundation for international relations.[648]

In its decision, the International Court of Justice adopted "an expansive view of the prohibited uses of force under the United Nations Charter, and a broad principle of non-intervention."[649]

There is an emerging practice based on the responsibility of human protection. A vision of this is contained in the International Commission on Intervention and State Sovereignty report, which contains the following:

> The debate on military intervention for human protection purposes was ignited in the international community essentially because of the critical gap between, on the one hand, the needs and distress being felt, and seen to be felt, in the real world, and on the other hand the codified instruments and modalities for managing world order. There has been a parallel gap, no less critical, between the codified best practice of international behaviour as articulated in the UN Charter and actual state practice as it has evolved in the 56 years since the Charter was signed. While there is not yet a sufficiently strong basis to claim the emergence of a new principle of customary international law, growing state and regional organization practice as well as Security Council precedent suggest an emerging

---

[647] Michael Byers and Simon Chesterman, "Changing the rules about rules? Unilateral humanitarian intervention and the future of international law," in J.L. Holzgrefe and Robert O. Keohane (eds.), *Humanitarian Intervention. Ethical, legal, and Political Dilemmas*, Cambridge: Cambridge University Press (2003) at 182

[648] *Corfu Channel (United Kingdom of Great Britain and Northern Ireland v. Albania)* International Court of Justice (9 April 1949) Merits, Judgment

[649] Max Planck, *Institute for Comparative Public Law and International Law*, Oxford: Oxford University Press (2001) at 4

guiding principle—which in the Commission's view could properly be termed 'the responsibility to protect.'[650]

This principle is demonstrated by the fact that:

> The Security Council itself has been increasingly prepared in recent years to act on this basis, most obviously in Somalia, defining what was essentially an internal situation as constituting a threat to international peace and security such as to justify enforcement action under Chapter VII of the UN Charter. This is also the basis on which the interventions by the Economic Community of West African States (ECOWAS) in Liberia and Sierra Leone were essentially justified by the interveners, as was the intervention mounted without Security Council authorization by NATO allies in Kosovo.[651]

A number of legal sources provide a framework for the emerging principle, which favours military intervention in situations where human protection is required. These sources:

> exist independently of any duties, responsibilities or authority that may be derived from Chapter VII of the UN Charter. These legal foundations include fundamental natural law principles; the human rights provisions of the UN Charter; the Universal Declaration of Human Rights together with the Genocide Convention; the Geneva Conventions and Additional Protocols on international humanitarian law; the statute of the International Criminal Court; and a number of other international human rights and human protection agreements and covenants.[652]

The International Commission on Intervention and State Sovereignty argues that there should be increased flexibility when considering military intervention, in spite of the Charter's predisposition against such action. It states that:

> The degree of legitimacy accorded to intervention will usually turn on the answers to such questions as the purpose, the means, the exhaustion of other avenues of redress against grievances, the proportionality of the riposte to the initiating provocation, and the agency of authorization. These are all questions that will recur: for present purposes the point is simply that there is a large and accumulating body of law and practice which supports the notion that, whatever form the exercise of that

---

650   *The Responsibility to Protect* at 2.24

651   Ibid. at 2.25

652   Ibid. at 2.26

responsibility may properly take, members of the broad community of states do have a responsibility to protect both their own citizens and those of other states as well.[653]

Several world leaders who spoke at the United Nations General Assembly in September 2011 spoke in favour of the doctrine of the Responsibility to Protect, including Belgium's Deputy Prime Minister Steven Vanackere who stated that sovereignty cannot stop intervention that aims to put an end to human rights abuse:

> Belgium will not stand idly by when people claim a future free of coercion and terror … Instead of non-interference, Belgium believes in non-indifference. Sovereignty is no longer a wall leaders can use as an excuse to violate the rights of their citizens.[654]

Italian Foreign Minister Franco Frattini expressed a similar view at the General Assembly and gave the example of Libya, suggesting that the only way to prevent a massacre of the Libyan people was to invoke the principle of the Responsibility to Protect:

> By helping to implement this decision in military, diplomatic and, and humanitarian terms, we shifted from a culture of sovereign impunity to one of responsible sovereignty, rooted in national and international accountability for the most serious violations of human rights.[655]

Secretary-General Ban Ki-moon also stressed the importance of the principle of the Responsibility to Protect in his address:

> This is a critical moment in the life of the Responsibility to Protect. In the six short years since its endorsement by the World Summit, this doctrine has gone from crawling to walking to running...Let us do our utmost to ensure that this umbrella of protection covers all who need it.[656]

The Secretary-General noted the onset of the principle in the international community's collective actions in Côte d'Ivoire and Libya as well as in its diplomatic efforts. He further pointed out that:

---

[653] Ibid. at 2.27

[654] "Belgium's Deputy Prime Minister Steven Vanackere address to the General Assembly," UN News, New York (26 September 2011)

[655] "Italy's Foreign Minister Franco Frattini address to the General Assembly," UN News, New York (26 September 2011)

[656] "Responsibility to Protect Principle Must Cover All Who Need It," UN News, New York (23 September 2011)

Our challenge now is to keep all [UN] Charter-based options open, and all of our collective tools sharp...We need to strengthen ties with our regional, sub-regional and civil society partners...We need to share information and assessments about States under stress. Effective prevention requires early, active and sustained engagement...No government questions the principle. Tactics, however, will – and should – be the subject of continuing scrutiny.[657]

Statements by various governments and the Secretary-General at the General Assembly in 2011 demonstrate the importance of humanitarian intervention in failed states by the United Nations.

Establishing Accountability – Ending Impunity

Strengthening institutions that provide greater transparency and deliver public goods, security, rule of law and judicial independence is imperative to regaining the trust of the people and restoring the accountability of the state. Accountability is indispensable and "means working to limit corruption, especially by making it easy for private parties to complain against officials."[658] The absence of accountability, the failure of state institutions to put an end to the culture of impunity, and the burden of self-serving leaders have all contributed to weak and failed governance.

Haiti is a perfect example,[659] having several structural competency failures and a lack of national minded leadership; as a result, "it has remained perpetually weak, often teetering on the brink of failure. If Haiti is to become stronger it needs better leadership as well as long-term foreign assistance."[660] Notwithstanding the reconstruction needs of Haiti following the disastrous earthquake of January 2010, the Haitian parliament has created a stalemate by rejecting newly elected President Michel Martelly's two nominees for the post of Prime Minister, impeding the ability of the new government to function since the May 2011 election. His third choice, Garry Conille, was eventually elected by the Senate as Prime Minister on October 4th, 2011, but he resigned

---

[657] Ibid.

[658] René Lemarchand, "The Democratic Republic of the Congo: From Failure to Potential Reconstruction," in Robert I. Rotberg (ed.), *State Failure and State Weakness in a Time of Terror,* Washington D.C.: Brookings Institution Press (2003) at 35

[659] M. Gélin-Adams and D. Malone, "Haiti: A Case of Endemic Weakness," in Robert I. Rotberg, (ed.), *State Failure and State Weakness in a Time of Terror,* Washington D.C.: Brookings Institution Press (2003) at 299

[660] Ibid. at 301

in February 2012, creating even further uncertainty in the troubled country.[661]

Adama Dieng, United Nations Under-Secretary-General and Registrar of the International Criminal Tribunal for Rwanda, defines impunity as "the act of not being punished, hiding from or escaping punishment either due to circumstances or to the law."[662] He notes that the question that is most often asked is "how to punish those who commit serious violations at a time when a State sets out to democratize public life."[663] He indicates that it is important to ask, in considering reconciliation in a nation with a history of political violence, "[w]hat should be done with those responsible for serious violations of human rights?"[664] In discussing this critical concern, Dieng points out that:

> The human rights map shows that the African political environment is characterised by violence at the top most level. The states which have achieved a degree of political stability are crumbling, conventional armies have been replaced by militias and guerrilla groups that specialize in looting and political assassinations, warlords enlist children in their armies for some of the most horrendous tasks, and the despots who torment their people enrich themselves by pillaging their meagre resources. Impunity stifles and criminalizes public life.[665]

To credibly fight impunity, he notes, it is not only punishment that is important, but also a proper identification of the perpetrators of the crime and an investigation that is detailed and unbiased. To Dieng, this:

> [c]asts doubt as to States' international commitment to respect fundamental rights and to punish those responsible for violating them, and is an issue in several African States where security forces have overthrown legally constituted governments or refuse to submit to the civilian authorities. For a long time, crimes were committed under the aegis of government and, in many cases, those responsible for such crimes were not prosecuted and the crimes generally fell into official oblivion.[666]

---

661 "Haiti senate approves president's 3rd pick for prime minister, ends stalemate," *Washington Post* (October 5, 2011)

662 Adama Dieng, Registrar of the International Criminal Tribunal for Rwanda, "Clarification on the Concepts: Justice, Reconciliation and Impunity," ICTR (24 May 2002) at 4

663 Ibid.

664 Ibid.

665 Ibid.

666 Ibid.

The lack of accountable institutions and regimes that for political reasons refuse to investigate and punish, is major obstacle, according to Dieng, to achieving peace in post conflict Africa.[667]

Owing to several of these reasons, leaders who are guilty of committing crimes against their people are evasive players in international efforts towards peace. The true weight of such serious human rights violations is diminished when governments are not engaged in ending impunity. State reconstruction is further encumbered when criminal impunity increases; inevitably, this leads to more violence, and, as suggested by Dieng, this blatant reality in Africa leads to a rise in corruption, economic inequality and plundering of national resources by elites as well as widening the disparity between rich and poor.[668] Dieng argues that such conduct should be:

> characterized as a crime against humanity. The danger in the link between corruption and organized crime in Africa is the institution of all-encompassing corruption. The negative aspects of corruption and criminal impunity are two issues that cannot be reconciled with democratic principles. It is necessary to find efficient methods of prevention, suppression and prosecution, both internationally and internally. The two phenomena are closely connected.[669]

Impunity should not be addressed in vague terms as this inevitably leads to the refusal to address the problem openly. Dieng suggests that in reconstruction efforts, it is not possible to rely solely on the local judicial system as it is too often deeply infected with the virus of impunity. He notes that "African judges, in the main, can only enjoy relative independence with some chinks of apparent impartiality."[670] While in Iraq, as noted above, the chosen model was the establishment of a national court to deal with past incidents of gross and systematic violations of human rights, Dieng has advocated for an international tribunal to address the concerns of impunity in Africa. Dieng points to the example of Sierra Leone, noting that in response to an initial agreement with the Revolutionary United Front rebels:

> the Special Representative of the United Nations Secretary General expressed very specific reservations in respect of the impunity guaranteed to the rebels in the agreement. The battle against impunity is in essence a dynamic process inasmuch as criminals are forever seeking new strategies to discreetly pursue their activities.[671]

---

[667] Ibid. at 5

[668] Ibid.

[669] Ibid.

[670] Ibid. at 6

[671] Ibid. at 6

The United Nations has, as part of its reconstruction objectives for post-conflict failed states, assisted several states with efforts to hold accountable those who are guilty of past violations of human rights. The United Nations, for example, has backed the tribunal in Cambodia that deals with mass killings and other crimes committed between April 1975 and January 1979 under the Khmer Rouge. It is reported that over 1.7 million people were killed during this time.[672] However, the process of bringing those responsible to trial is slow, with the Extraordinary Chambers in the Courts of Cambodia for the Prosecution of Crimes Committed during the Period of Democratic Kampuchea (ECCC) only being set up in 2006. The international community provides support through the United Nations Assistance to the Khmer Rouge Trials (UNAKRT).[673] The tribunal is made up of both Cambodian and foreign judges, who have raised several concerns of interference by the Government of Cambodia.[674] Thus far, only one of the five people indicted by the Court for genocide, crimes against humanity and war crimes has been convicted, and his sentence is now under appeal.[675]

With respect to Africa, in reference to the International Criminal Tribunal for Rwanda:

> The Judgements pronounced by the Tribunal have had an important impact on the entire Continent, characterized as it was for several decades by a culture of impunity. Indeed, the 1999 Lusaka Accords, regarding the conflict in the Democratic Republic of Congo, went as far as to provide for the surrender for trial before the Arusha Tribunal, of belligerents suspected of having taken part in the genocide.[676]

The establishment of the International Criminal Court, which is governed by *the Rome Statute*, has been an important step towards helping to eliminate impunity for those committing crimes and gross and systematic human rights violations. There exists an integral link between security and legitimacy that must be taken into account when considering the elements necessary to nation-building:

---

[672] "UN-Backed Cambodia Genocide Tribunal Begins Fitness Hearing for Accused," UN News, New York (29 August 2011)

[673] Ibid.

[674] "In Cambodia, UN Legal Chief Warns on Interference in Work of Genocide Tribunal," UN News, New York (20 October 2011)

[675] Composite Chronology of the Evolution and Operation of the Extraordinary Chambers in the Courts of Cambodia, available at www.cambodiatribunal.org

[676] Adama Dieng, Registrar of the International Criminal Tribunal for Rwanda, "Clarification on the Concepts: Justice, Reconciliation and Impunity," ICTR (24 May 2002) at 6

Building a legitimate and functioning state is central to maintaining peace and stability and to achieving development outcomes in post-conflict and transitional situations. Establishing human security is essential to strengthening state legitimacy. A government's legitimacy is eroded when significant areas of a county or social groups continue to challenge the state's authority (e.g. Côte d'Ivoire) or when state security forces act with impunity against their own citizens (e.g. Nepal). In periods of transition, a key role for development partners may therefore be to monitor and reinforce the peace and to provide a security guarantee for the transition process (e.g. peace keeping operations Kosovo, Liberia, Sierra Leone and Timor-Leste). Over time, however, the state's own security forces, police and justice system must be able to gain control of, if not a monopoly of the use of force.[677]

The gradual transition from sovereign impunity to accountability, both national and international, has seen many successes, resulting from efforts by both the United Nations and NGOs. It is these international norms and instruments, such as the International Criminal Court and the *Convention on the Prohibition of the Use, Stockpiling, Production and Transfer of Anti-Personnel Mines and on Their Destruction* (Ottawa Convention), which have advanced the importance of state conduct in respect to violations of human rights and accountability.[678]

The Responsibility to Protect report notes that "[j]ust as the substance of human rights law is coming increasingly closer to realizing the notion of universal justice—justice without borders—so too is the process."[679] Given that the history of failed states is noticeably afflicted by the absence of rule of law, lack of accountability, and impunity, it is important that reconstruction efforts do not fail to address these issues. In the following subsection, the issue of the establishment of security as an important component in the reinforcement of reconstruction efforts will be analysed.

Establishing Security

Security is a key prerequisite to stabilizing and rebuilding a state. A main component in state-building is the restoration of national security not just in the capital city but also throughout the state; this inevitably requires the support of the international community in order to combat issues that may be present, such as trafficking in drugs and arms. This new challenge to

---

[677] *The applicability of the Paris Declaration in fragile and conflict-affected situations: Thematic Study*, Oxford: IDL Group (August 2008) at 33

[678] *The Responsibility to Protect* at 2.18

[679] Ibid. at 2.18

international collective security must be confronted with efforts to disarm groups, facilitate humanitarian operations, and protect civilians, with the aim of bringing about stability and security.[680]

Establishing security can be at times more complicated than ending conflicts[681] as:

> [a]lmost half of all post-conflict states fall back into violent conflict within a decade. Yet this is not unavoidable: experience shows that there are ways to rebuild the fabric of society and create institutions that enhance sustainable peace.[682]

In establishing security, there exists the need to work with the police force and the military as well as with paramilitary units. This requires civilian oversight as "[u]naccountable, corrupt and/or subversive security forces are major barriers to state legitimacy, impede the restoration of basic services and often contribute to reigniting conflict."[683]

The various civil wars in Central America fundamentally affected every institution of the state, with massive human rights violations, ruined infrastructure and collapsed economies. However, since the end of the civil war in Guatemala in 1996 and the signing of the Peace Accords, the transition to demilitarization has gone relatively well. Both sides made concessions, and the guerrillas received land in exchange for arms. The signing of the Peace Accords for El Salvador in 1992 also helped to establish conditions for peace and security in that country. Civil war in Nicaragua ended in a compromise, with the electoral defeat of the Sandinista government in 1990.[684] Daniel Ortega was eventually returned to power by democratic means, and the transition has been relatively peaceful.

The security situation for the newest member of the United Nations has also been complicated, with reports of increased violence in parts of the country. The leader of the United Nations Mission in South Sudan (UNMISS), Hilde Johnson, expressed at a news conference in Juba her

---

680   Stephen K. Pichat, "Peacekeeping, Disarmament and International Force: A Circular Proposition," *Disarmament Forum* (2000) at *13*

681   Derick W. Brinkerfoff, "Rebuilding Governance in Failed States and Post-Conflict," *Public Administration and Development*, Vol. 25, No. 1 (2005) at 6

682   Simon Mason, "Failed States, Post-Conflict States and Reconstruction," Zurich: Center for Security Studies (April 2007) at 102

683   Derick W. Brinkerfoff, "Rebuilding Governance in Failed States and Post-Conflict," *Public Administration and Development*, Vol. 25, No. 1 (2005) at 6

684   Jack Spence, *War and Peace in Central America*, Brookline: Hemisphere Initiatives (November 2004) at Summary

serious concerns regarding security and violence in the country. Two months following the birth of the new state in 2011, more than 600 people have been killed in ethnic clashes. UNMISS was deployed to assist in defusing tensions and, according to the United Nations envoy, bringing about "stop-gap measures and trying to get processes in place that can help resolve the issues over time."[685] Neither Sudan nor South Sudan have met their obligations and commitment to withdraw their forces from the disputed area of Abyei, creating a "serious deterioration in tensions between migrating herders and displaced farmers returning to plant their crops ... The withdrawal is essential to facilitate the return of the displaced, create conditions for a peaceful Misseriya migration and build confidence among the parties."[686] Without a doubt, there is a need for further resources and police training by the United Nations; however, there are challenges in training a police force in human rights standards when 80% of the police force is illiterate.[687]

In order for the state to meet human security needs, there are certain tasks which need to be performed and understood. The tendency of development partners is to primarily assist in the areas of security, including disarmament and demobilisation and issues surrounding justice reform. This is understandable given that without security it is impossible to assist failed states in tackling the issues surrounding structural competency failures and assisting in their transition to a functioning state. However, there is a need to work across all levels, tackling not just security but also the social and economic needs of the local population. In the reconstruction of Afghanistan and Iraq, for example, billions of dollars have been disproportionately spent on military, while minimal attention has been given to the infrastructure and social needs of the population.

Another prime example is Liberia, in which unresolved security issues contributed to the re-emergence of conflict and a dramatic 80% downturn in its economy. Under-Secretary-General for Peacekeeping Operations Hervé Ladsous noted that "[i]neffective and poorly governed security sectors can become decisive obstacles to stability, poverty reduction, sustainable development and peacebuilding." He emphasized that security is necessary for "early recovery from conflict, economic development and

[685] "World is Watching How South Sudan Builds New Nations, Says UN Envoy," UN News, New York (28 September 2011)

[686] "UN Warns of Further Tension as Sudan and South Sudan Maintain Troops in Disputed Area," UN News, New York (6 October 2011)

[687] "World is Watching How South Sudan Builds New Nations, Says UN Envoy," UN News, New York (28 September 2011)

sustainable peacebuilding, as well as regional stability and international peacekeeping."[688] The United Nations has also undertaken several security and development initiatives, from Burundi, Liberia, Somalia and Côte d'Ivoire to the Democratic Republic of the Congo and Guinea-Bissau, to name a few.[689] As well, given the ongoing conflict in parts of Africa, the Security Council "reiterates the link between security sector reform and socio-economic development, and underlines that such reform efforts should be situated within the broader and more comprehensive spectrum of peacebuilding."[690] It has also asked for local participation in establishing security.

Although establishing security is an important undertaking, it has been suggested that it should not be done at the expense of other commitments, such as to rule of law, education and health. Clearly, there is a need to address these various structural competencies in order to rebuild a state. Post-conflict failed states also present the need for disarmament, as will be discussed in the next subsection.

Universal Jurisdiction

Universal jurisdiction allows states or international organizations to claim criminal jurisdiction over an accused person regardless of where the alleged crime was committed, and regardless of the accused's nationality, country of residence, or any other relation with the prosecuting entity. Crimes prosecuted under universal jurisdiction are considered crimes against all, too serious to tolerate jurisdictional arbitrage.

Certain crimes pose so serious a threat to the international community as a whole that states have a logical and moral duty to prosecute an individual responsible; therefore, no place should be a safe haven for those who have committed genocide, crimes against humanity, extrajudicial executions, war crimes, torture and forced disappearances.

The United Nations Security Council Resolution 1674, adopted by the United Nations Security Council on April 28th, 2006, "reaffirm[ed] the provisions of paragraphs 138 and 139 of the 2005 World Summit Outcome Document regarding the responsibility to protect populations from genocide, war crimes, ethnic cleansing and crimes against humanity" and commits the Security Council to action to protect civilians in armed conflict.

---

688   "Security Sector Reform in African Countries Emerging From Conflict Vital, UN Says," UN News, New York (12 October 2011)

689   Ibid.

690   Ibid.

State Failure – Internal and External Factors

State failure, whether narrowly or broadly defined, has significant consequences for the international community. The terminology of state failure varies and is often subject to when and where it is applied. State failure ranges in degree from weak, failing to fully failed state.

State failure can be attributed *inter alia* to historical factors such as colonialism and also to exclusively internal considerations of the state. The author presents ten broad categories by which state failure is to be defined. These are comprised of the essential structural competency areas. They are: (1) absence of rule of law; (2) political instability and lack of legitimacy; (3) economic and social instability directly contributing to poverty; (4) lack of security and/or the presence internal conflict; (5) authoritarian rule and clan loyalty; (6) impunity and an ineffective justice system; (7) loss of internal territorial control (*de jure* and *de facto* sovereignty); (8) gross and systematic violations of human rights; (9) loss of social cohesion and development; and (10) corruption and weak institutions. The last factor would include for example a weak or weakening bureaucratic structure.

There are indeed competency gaps that are specific in nature. Failed states are characterized by an implosion of structural competencies as well as instability that creates a vacuum for various groups including armed factions. These situations create refugee flows and as a result extend instability to neighbouring states. It is essential that these component facts be recognized so that the causes and conditions of state failure are understood. The notion of state failure does not have one definitive meaning but in fact states evolve thorough various stages ultimately leading to full failed state status.

The reality of state failure is in fact an accumulation of structural competency gaps that evolve over a period of time that result in failed state status and all that this encompasses including but no exclusive to internal and regional instability.

Failed states are characterized by poverty, authoritarian rule, corruption lack of economic security, political instability and a lack of legitimacy. Often, the catalyst for the evolution of the process of state failure can be found in external intervention in a state such as the overthrow of a regime by another power. The process of state failure often then begins as a result of the elimination of a state structure and the nurturing of competency gaps.

Failing states should be viewed in the context of the absence of core structural competency as defined above, affecting their stability and thereby creating a host of security concerns for the international community. It is understandable that there be broad interest in and concern about failed states given their proliferation since the conclusion of the Second World

War, concurrent with the many challenges presented to these troubled emerging states. In order to secure a more comprehensive understanding of the evolution of state failure, it is necessary to examine structural competency and the prevailing literature associated with the subject.

Failed states result from temporary or prolonged loss of the structural competency of the state to provide security and basic political goods. Adding to the seemingly overwhelming misery of the situation is widespread poverty, rampant corruption and a loss of social cohesion and development.

The characteristics of state failure are not homogeneous and vary from region to region. Failure is attributed to the structural incompetency of the state and its genesis is to be found in the historical realities of both Cold War politics and the effects of colonialism. Leaders who have lost the legitimacy to govern and who provide for no social and economic development, using clan and elite sections of society to maintain power, have also undoubtedly paved the way for state failure.

By way of example of the forgoing, in Zaire (now the Democratic Republic of the Congo), President Mobutu Sese Seko's three decades of authoritarian rule annihilated the infrastructure of the state. This was also the situation in Sierra Leone during President Siaka Stevens rule from 1967 to 1985 as well as in Somalia during the tenure of President Mohamed Siad Barre from 1969 to 1991. Their seemingly insatiable greed and blatant disregard for the security and well being of their people was a preordaining factor in the almost inevitable destruction of their states.[691]

According to Stephen Walt of Harvard University, "[w]hen governments collapse, the resulting anarchy often triggers large-scale migration, economic chaos, and mass violence."[692] These humanitarian and national security challenges in states that have failed, such as Sierra Leone, Liberia, Rwanda, Afghanistan and Somalia, create instability, mass migration and terrorism. State failure in these countries not only constitutes an undeniable threat to the lives of the people living within them but also poses a considerable threat to world peace as has been demonstrated by the conflicts that followed 9/11.[693]

In order to define state failure, it is essential that one comprehend the pattern of state formation in both a contemporary and historical context as well as the way in which the state is characterized.

---

[691]   Robert I. Rotberg, "Failed States in a World of Terror," *Foreign Affairs*, Vol. 81, No.4 (July/August 2002)

[692]   Stephen M. Walt, "Beyond bin Laden: Reshaping U.S. Foreign Policy," *International Security*, Vol. 26, No. 3 (Winter 2001/02) at 62

[693]   Robert I. Rotberg, "Failed States in a World of Terror," *Foreign Affairs*, Vol. 81, No. 4 (July/August 2002)

Robert Rotberg's book, *When States Fail: Causes and Consequences*,[694] resulted from a five year project by Harvard University's World Peace Foundation Program on Intrastate Conflict, involving more than forty collaborators. The study sought to address all aspects of state failure in its research. For Rotberg, states exist as a means of delivering political goods:

Political goods are those intangible and hard to quantify claims that citizens once made on sovereigns and now make on states. They encompass indigenous expectations, conceivably obligations, inform the local political culture, and together give content to the social contract between ruler and ruled that is at the core of regime/government and citizenry interactions.[695]

Rotberg and his colleagues state that strong states perform well in all levels of competency. They control their territories and provide security as "[c]itizens depend on states and central governments to secure their persons and free them from fear."[696] Strong states or functioning states provide for political freedom and respect human rights, the rule of law and the delivery political goods. As well, these states create physical and commercial infrastructure, which establishes a set of criteria according to which states may be judged strong, weak, failed and collapsed.[697]

Strong states perform well by international indicators such as the Human Development Index, which is prepared by United Nations Development Programme. The Index (HDI)[698] ranks countries by levels of human development, measuring life expectancy, literacy, education and standards of living. The Index notes that functioning states provide peace and order while failed states are unsuccessful in delivering both.[699] State failure, however, is not necessarily a result of violence or civil war,

---

[694]   Robert I. Rotberg, (ed.), *When States Fail Causes and Consequences*, Princeton: Princeton University Press (2004)

[695]   Ibid. at 2 – 3 (See also reference for political goods J. Roland Pennock, "Political Development, Political Systems, and Political Goods," *World Politics*, Vol. *XVIII* (1966) at 420 – 26, 433

[696]   Robert I. Rotberg, (ed.), *When States Fail Causes and Consequences*, Princeton: Princeton University Press (2004) at 6

[697]   Robert I. Rotberg, (ed.), *State Failure and State Weakness in a Time of Terror*, Washington D. C.: Brookings Institution Press (2003) at 4

[698]   For further information see: HDI-trends 1970-2010, Human Development Report, United Nations Development Programme (2011). Available at:< http://hdr.undp.org/en/data/trends/hybrid/> accessed 19 March 2012

[699]   Robert I. Rotberg, (ed.), *State Failure and State Weakness in a Time of Terror*, Washington D.C.: Brookings Institution Press (2003) at 4

although such violence certainly constitutes at least a failure in some basic sub-components of state function in the provision of peace and security throughout the state.[700] States fail for a host of reasons, as outlined above, stemming from a failure to meet structural competency levels of a functioning state resulting, *inter alia*, in a loss of security and legitimacy. The inability to provide security and political goods is, according to Rotberg, what leads to failure. Rotberg is seen by many observers as the pre-eminent authority on the subject of state failure, and he expands the meaning of the failed state by establishing a hierarchy of political goods, the most critical of these being the supply of security, particularly human security, that serves:

> to prevent cross-border invasions and infiltrations, and any loss of territory; to eliminate domestic threats to or attacks upon the national order and social structure; to prevent crime and any related dangers to domestic human security; and to enable citizens to resolve their differences with the state and with their fellow inhabitants without recourse to arms or other forms of physical coercion.[701]

Rotberg enunciates several characteristics of failing states from endemic civil wars, inability to control peripheral regions, increased criminal violence and lawlessness and rampant corruption to dramatically declining economic growth and loss of political legitimacy.[702]

The performance criteria of the nation state is measured and ranked by Rotberg and his team to encompass the principles of strong, weak, failed or collapsed states which he describes as a rare and extreme version of a failed state.[703] He classifies weak states as those that may be inherently weak due to geographical or economic constraints. It has been generally noted that failed states are predominantly ruled by despots who support various forms of divisiveness, such as on ethnic, linguistic or religious differences.[704] Many scholars stress the importance of the symptoms of

---

[700] Jonathan Di John, *Conceptualising The Causes And Consequences of Failed States: A Critical Review of the Literature*, London: Crisis States Working Papers Series No. 2, London School of Economics (January 2008) at 10

[701] Robert I. Rotberg (ed.), *When States Fail Causes and Consequences*, Princeton: Princeton University Press (2004) at 3

[702] Stewart Patrick, "'Failed' States and Global Security: Empirical Questions and Policy Dilemmas," *International Studies Review*, Vol. 9, No. 4 (2007) at 646

[703] Robert I. Rotberg (ed.), *When States Fail Causes and Consequences*, Princeton: Princeton University Press (2004) at 9

[704] Robert I. Rotberg (ed.), *State Failure and State Weakness in a Time of Terror*, Washington D. C.: Brookings Institution Press (2003) at 4

violence, civil war and the growth of terrorist organizations as critical to state failure.[705] Accordingly, Rotberg and his associates incorporate security as the benchmark for state success and failure, observing that failed states are "tense, deeply conflicted, dangerous, and bitterly contested by warring factions. In most failed states, government troops battle armed revolts led by one or more rivals."[706]

Both Rotberg and Erin Jenne note that North Korea with its authoritarian regime, Iraq under Saddam Hussein and even Libya before Resolution 1973 do not fall readily into any category, given that these states enjoy a monopoly on the use of force and were at least capable of controlling at one point in some cases their territories.[707][190]

In the case of Libya, the analysis provided by Rotberg and Jenne was made prior to the 2011 United Nations Security Council Resolution 1973. The events in Libya during the 2011/2012 civil strife, as well as the human rights abuses, eventually led to instability, popular uprising and loss of territorial control, which would easily classify it as a failed state. However, notwithstanding the failed state categorization that was present during the period of the popular uprising against Gaddafi that eventually contributed to his removal from power, the Libyan National Transitional Council quickly established a number of structural competencies and was given a seat at the United Nations Security Council on September 16th, 2011. The General Assembly, as well, adopted a motion to extend to the National Transitional Council, formed seven months earlier in the wake of popular protests, successor rights to represent Libya at the General Assembly with full voting privileges.[708] As evidenced in Libya, these authoritarian states can easily slide from weak to failed but, as has been noted earlier in this paper, the characteristics of failed states can be broad, and some remain in this defined state for a relatively short period.

On September 12th, 2019, the Security Council unanimously adopted the motion to extend the mandate of the United Nations Support Mission in Libya (UNSMIL):

---

[705] Jonathan Di John, *Conceptualising The Causes And Consequences of Failed States: A Critical Review of the Literature*, London: Crisis States Working Papers Series No. 2, London School of Economics (January 2008) at 4

[706] Robert I. Rotberg (ed.), *When States Fail Causes and Consequences*, Princeton: Princeton University Press (2004) at 5

[707] [190] Erin K. Jenne, "Sri Lanka: A Fragmented State," in Robert I. Rotberg (ed.), *When States Fail Causes and Consequences*, Princeton: Princeton University Press (2004) at 219

[708] General Assembly seats National Transitional Council of Libya as country's representative at sixty-sixth General Assembly Plenary, GA/11137 (16 September 2011)

as an integrated special political mission to support an inclusive political process in Libya and continued implementation of the Libyan Political Agreement. Mission is to support the consolidation of the Government of National Accord as well as a possible ceasefire and subsequent phases of the Libyan transition process, including the constitutional process and the organization of elections.

The Council further decided that the Mission, within operational and security constraints, should offer assistance to key Libyan institutions, support—on request—the provision of essential services and delivery of humanitarian assistance, undertake human rights monitoring and reporting, extend support for securing uncontrolled arms and related material, and assist efforts led by the Government of National Accord to stabilize post-conflict zones, including those liberated from Islamic State in Iraq and the Levant (ISIL/Da'esh).[709]

In Sri Lanka, the internal conflict in the northern and eastern parts of the country endured for 26 years until the defeat of the Liberation Tigers of Tamil Eelam in May 2009. Secretary-General Ban Ki-moon has stressed the need for a "credible national accountability process"[710] following the conclusion of the strife in Sri Lanka. To this day, Sri Lanka has not come to terms with the crimes committed by the government in its fight against the Tamil Tigers.

A United Nations panel of experts on accountability have found credible reports that both government forces and the LTTE committed war crimes during the final months of the war.[711] The conflict was due in part to the discriminatory policies of the Sri Lanka government.[712]

State weakness is the erosion of the state's capacity to govern effectively. Taken to the extreme, the result is a complete collapse of state power and function.[713]

There have been differing references in several works with regard to the fact that failed states suffer from an enduring character of violence, with dissonance between communities and rulers that prey on their own people.

---

[709]   https://www.un.org/press/en/2019/sc13948.doc.htm

[710]   "Sri Lanka: Ban Stresses Need for Accountability Process Over End to Civil War," U.N. News Service,
New York (24 September 2011)

[711]   Ibid.

[712]   Erin K. Jenne, "Sri Lanka: A Fragmented State," in Robert I. Rotberg (ed.), *When States Fail Causes and Consequences*, Princeton: Princeton University Press (2004) at 221

[713]   Liana Sun Wyler, "Weak and Failing States: Evolving Security Threats and U.S. Policy," CRS Report for Congress (28 August 2008) at 4

Failed states "exhibit flawed institutions ... deteriorating or destroyed infrastructures ... [and] corruption flourishes." A nation-state "also fails when it loses legitimacy"[714] and is able to provide only "limited quantities of other essential political goods."[715]

In Rotberg's description of violence in failed states he maintains that it is not "the absolute intensity of violence that identifies a failed state. Rather, it is the enduring character of that violence."[716] In places such as Sierra Leone, the Democratic Republic of the Congo, Chad, and Sudan, where the state does not have the competency to provide any safety net of security for its people, there is an inevitable loss of legitimacy in the view of their people as "[t]he social contract that binds inhabitants to an overarching polity becomes breached."[717] Immense profits are often realized by the ruler and a select few in failed states while corruption spreads like wildfire and thrives on an unusually destructive scale.[718]

In many cases of state failure legitimacy is lost and individuals turn to clan leaders or warlords for assistance; it is under these circumstances that "terror can breed along with the prevailing anarchy that naturally accompanies state breakdown and failure."[719]

Some scholars have argued that the inability of state leaders to achieve predominant presence in large areas of their countries relates directly to the:

> capacity of the state (or incapacity, as the case may be), especially the ability to implement social policies and to mobilize the public, relates to the structure of society. The ineffectiveness of state leaders who have faced impenetrable barriers to state predominance has stemmed from the nature of the societies they have confronted-from the resistance posed by chiefs, landlords, bosses, rich peasants, clan leaders.[720]

Others, such as Michael Ignatieff, have adopted a more narrow understanding of state failure, stating that it occurs when "the central government loses the monopoly of the means of violence."[721] Ignatieff, Simon

---

[714]   Robert I. Rotberg (ed.), *When States Fail Causes and Consequences*, Princeton: Princeton University Press (2004) at 7-9

[715]   Ibid. at 6

[716]   Ibid. at 5

[717]   Ibid. at 9

[718]   Ibid. at 8

[719]   Ibid. at 9

[720]   Joel Migdal, *Strong States and Weak Societies: State-Society Relations in the Third World*, Princeton: Princeton University Press (1988) at 33

[721]   Michael Ignatieff, "Intervention and State Failure," *Dissent*, Vol. 49, No. 1 (Winter 2002) at 118

Chesterman, and Ramesh Thakur have noted that one of the most important conditions of making states work is the creation of:

> apolitical bureaucratic structures (civil service, judiciary, police, army) supported by an ideology that legitimate the role of neutral state authority in maintaining social order through prescribed procedures and the rule of law.[722]

Professor Ira William Zartman uses the term "state collapse" in referencing state failure as a "deeper phenomenon than mere rebellion, coup, or riot. It refers to a situation where the structure, authority (legitimate power), law, and political order have fallen apart and must be reconstituted in some form, old or new."[723] Zartman adopts Hobbes' narrative of the social contract theory, noting that state failure occurs when the basic functions of authority, law and political order have failed and the state no longer performs its requirements.[724] Zartman further observes that states fail when:

> the basic functions of the state are no longer performed ... as the decision-making center ... order is not preserved. ... As a territory, it is no longer assured security and provisionment by a central sovereign organization. ... [I]t has lost its legitimacy, which is therefore up for grabs, and so has lost its right to command and conduct public affairs.[725]

Both Zartman and Rotberg approach state formation as the creation of a provider of public goods and make a distinction between the various services they provide, such as security, infrastructure and social services. Several scholars have presented an alternative view to that of Zartman and Rotberg, arguing that these authors define state function and failure in terms that are simply too narrow to be useful.

Laura Tedesco, by way of example, views Zartman's and Rotberg's analysis as lacking any historical account and maintains that it merely constitutes a label that encourages cosmetic solutions,[726] while others, such as

---

[722] Simon Chesterman, Michael Ignatieff and Ramesh Thakur (eds.), *Making States Work*, Tokyo: United Nations University Press (2005) at 2-3

[723] William Zartman (ed.), *Collapsed States: The Disintegration and Reinstitution of Legitimate Authority*, Boulder: Lynne Rienner (1995) at 1

[724] Jonathan Di John, *'Failed States' in Sub-Saharan Africa: A Review of the Literature*, Madrid: Real Instituto Elcano (14 January 2011)

[725] William Zartman (ed.), *Collapsed States: The Disintegration and Reinstitution of Legitimate Authority*, Boulder: Lynne Rienner (1995) at 5

[726] Laura Tedesco, "The Latin American State: 'failed' or evolving?," Fundación para las Relaciones Internacionales y el Diálogo Exterior, Madrid: Working Paper 37 (May 2007) at 2

Nelson Kasfir, comment that state failure is used as a means to override sovereignty.[727]

As previously noted, a failed state that "exhibits a vacuum of authority,"[728] such as Somalia, Bosnia, Lebanon, Afghanistan, Nigeria and Sierra Leone,[729] is noted for sub-state actors seizing control over regions that were once part of the state. Their conduct is generally characterized by the establishment of their own security forces.

Additionally, international relations are characterized by disorder and the presence of criminal enterprises such as arms and drug trafficking that operate in conjunction with external terrorist networks.[730] However, there are scholars who have cautioned that these designations are neither static nor terminal, as demonstrated by examples such as Lebanon, Nigeria, and Tajikistan, all of which recovered from collapse and are now categorized as weak. Neither weakness nor failure is inevitable, rather it is the structural competency flaws of a weak and failed state and the imprudent decisions that are taken by those in positions of authority that are the root of the problem.

Even states that inherited weaknesses at the onset of their independence from colonial rule often manage to succeed in spite of the many challenges. The common denominator associated with such success is the presence of political will and exceptional leadership. Botswana presents a suitable example of this phenomenon. [731] In contrast, Zimbabwe is an example of a once strong African state that has as a result of President Robert Mugabe's autocratic rule and abuse of power fallen into failure, with massive poverty, hunger, loss of legitimacy and rampant violence.[732] Mugabe was eventually removed from office and died in 2019, but his legacy of incompetence and authoritarian rule continues to affect the lives of Zimbabweans today.

While several scholars have subscribed to the importance of the security paradigm in analysing state failure, others such as Lisa Chauvet and Paul Collier define failed states in economic terms:

---

[727] Nelson Kasfir, "Domestic Anarchy, Security Dilemmas, and Violent Predation," in Robert I. Rotberg, (ed.), *When States Fail Causes and Consequences*, Princeton: Princeton University Press (2004) at 57

[728] Robert I. Rotberg, (ed.), *State Failure and State Weakness in a Time of Terror*, Washington D.C.: Brookings Institution Press (2003) at 9

[729] Robert I. Rotberg, (ed.), *When States Fail Causes and Consequences*, Princeton: Princeton University Press (2004) at 10

[730] Ibid. at 10

[731] Robert I. Rotberg, "Failed States, Collapsed States, Weak States: Causes and Indicators," in Robert I. Rotberg (ed.), *State Failure and State Weakness in a Time of Terror*, Washington D.C.: Brookings Institution Press (2003) at 19

[732] Ibid. at 15

[A] failing state is a low-income country in which economic policies, institutions and governance are so poor that growth is highly unlikely. The state is failing its citizens because even if there is peace they are stuck in poverty ... Through various routes the state may become a hazard to its neighbours and conceivably to the world.[733]

Chauvet and Collier note the example of Equatorial Guinea which in the application of their criteria is not considered to have failed due to the high income levels enjoyed from oil revenues.[734] This position is problematic to say the least given that wealth is in no way equitably or evenly distributed and the overwhelming majority of the Equatorial Guinea's residents live in poverty. Equatorial Guinea was ranked 117th among world nations by the UNDP Human Development Index.[735] In a study regarding corruption, Transparency International, which ranks 180 countries, listed Equatorial Guinea at the bottom of their rankings, in 168th place.[736]

Robert Kaplan presents a number of African states as excellent examples of 'the coming anarchy' and suggests that the path to state failure is to be found within the chaos that emerges in the face of a fading central government and the consequent ascendancy of tribal domains which, due to scarcity, crime, overpopulation, tribalism, and disease, are rapidly destroying the social fabric.[737] Kaplan provides an overview of the discourse on failed states by issuing a warning to Western governments with respect to the regressive developments in West Africa of "the withering away of central governments, the rise of tribal and regional domains, the unchecked spread of disease, and the growing pervasiveness of war."[738] He concludes that state failure and collapse are manifested by "disease, overpopulation, unprovoked crime, scarcity of resources, refugee migrations, the increasing erosion of nation-states, irrational borders, and the empowerment of private armies, security firms, and international drug cartels."[739]

---

733 Lisa Chauvet and Paul Collier, "What are the preconditions for turnarounds in failing states?," Centre for the Study of African Economies, Oxford University (January 2007) at Introduction. Available at: <http://users.ox.ac.uk/~econpco/research/pdfs/WhatPreconditionsForTurnaround.pdf> accessed March 19, 2012

734 Ibid. at 13

735 HDI-Human Development Index 2010, United Nations Development Programme. Available at: <http://hdr.undp.org/en/> accessed March 19, 2012

736 Transparency International Corruption Perceptions Index 2009, available at: <http://www.transparency.org/policy_research/surveys_indices/cpi/2009/cpi_2009_table > accessed 20 March 2012

737 Robert D. Kaplan, "The Coming Anarchy," *The Atlantic Magazine* (February 1994)

738 Ibid.

739 Ibid. at 44

There have been a number studies and task forces charged with examining the issue of state failure, including the 1994 State Failure Task Force that was commissioned by the United States government at the request of Vice President Al Gore.[740] The Task Force established a panel of distinguished academic social scientists, experts in data collection, and consultants in statistical methods. The Task Force was chaired by Ted Robert Gurr, an authority on political instability. It noted that state failure consists of:

> sustained military conflicts between insurgents and central governments, aimed at displacing the regime...sustained policies by states or their agents and, in civil wars, by contending authorities that result in the deaths of a substantial portion of members of communal or political groups...major, abrupt shifts in patterns of governance, including state collapse, periods of severe regime instability, and shifts toward authoritarian rule.[741]

The Task Force also identified 136 instances of state failure between 1995 and 1998 in countries with populations in excess of 500,000 people. It further defined state failure as a "range of severe political conflicts and regime crises"[742] and as categorized by a "total or near-collapse of central political authority."[743] Included in the analysis were four types of events that lead to state failure:

Revolutionary wars. Episodes of sustained violent conflict between governments and politically organized challengers that seek to overthrow the central government, to replace its leaders, or to seize power in one region.

Ethnic wars. Episodes of sustained violent conflict in which national, ethnic, religious or other communal minorities challenge governments to seek major changes in status.

Adverse regime changes. Major, abrupt shifts in patterns of governance, including state collapse, periods of severe elite or regime instability, and shifts away from democracy toward authoritarian rule.

---

[740] The Task Force used a number of different techniques to generate data and identify factors most closely associated with state failure, including logistic regression analysis, neural network analysis, and expert surveys. Currently referred to as the Political Instability Task Force (PITF)

[741] Daniel C. Esty et al, "The State Failure Project: Early Warning Research for U .S. Foreign Policy Planning," in John L. Davies and Ted Robert Gurr (eds.), *Preventive Measures: Building Risk Assessment and Crisis Early Warning Systems,* Lanham: Rowman and Littlefield (1998) at 27 – 38

[742] Liana Sun Wyler, "Weak and Failing States: Evolving Security Threats and U.S. Policy," CRS Report for Congress (28 August 2008) at 26

[743] Ibid.

Genocides and politicides. Sustained policies by states or their agents, or, in civil wars, by either of the contending authorities that result in the deaths of a substantial portion of a communal or political group.[744]

Of the four categories that the Task Force identified, adverse regime change emerged as the most prevalent causal factor of state failure, followed by ethnic war, revolutionary war, and then genocide.[745] The Task Force also identified partial democracy, trade closure and poor economic well being as indicated by high infant mortality rates as contributing primary causes of state failure.[746]

In addition to this Task Force, the United States government maintains a commission sponsored by the Centre for Global Development that seeks to address issues associated with weak states. The Commission on Weak States recognizes many of the assumptions of failed states enunciated by the previously noted Task Force and defines weak states as those with:

> governments unable to do the things that their own citizens and the international community expect from them: protecting people from internal and external threats, delivering basic health services and education, and providing institutions that respond to the legitimate demands and needs of the population.[747]

---

[744] Jack A. Goldstone et al, *State Failure Task Force Report: Phase III Findings*, McLean: Science Applications International Corporation (30 September 2000) at V

[745] Ibid. at IV, V, 3-5. The State Failure project was commissioned by the Central Intelligence Agency in 1994 and was carried out by a task force composed of individuals from universities and consulting companies. All of the data presented by the project are unclassified, and the findings of the project are those of the members of the task force, not the U.S. government or any of its agencies. The State Failure Task Force defines "adverse regime change" as "major, abrupt shifts in patterns of governance, including state collapse, periods of severe elite or regime instability, and shifts away from democracy toward authoritarian rule." There were fewer than twenty cases of state failure narrowly defined as the collapse of authority structures for several years. The Task Force consisted of: Jack A. Goldstone; Ted Robert Gurr; Barbara Harff; Marc A. Levy; Monty G. Marshall; Robert H. Bates; David L. Epstein; Colin H. Kahl; Pamela T. Surko; John C. Ulfelder Jr. and Alan N. Unger.

[746] Gary King and Langche Zeng criticize the methodology of the State Failure project even though they find that most of its conclusions, especially the empirical link between high infant mortality and partial democracy, are supported. Gary King and Langehe Zeng, "Improving Forecasts of State Failure," *World Politics*, Vol. 53, No. 4 (July 2001) at 623-658

[747] Liana Sun Wyler, "Weak and Failing States: Evolving Security Threats and U.S. Policy," CRS Report for Congress (28 August 2008) at 26

The Commission's 2004 report also classifies fifty to sixty countries as weak states based on their failure to provide physical security, social welfare, and legitimate institutions.

Each year, the Fund for Peace releases its Failed States Index, which is found in *Foreign Policy* magazine. The 2011 report is very comprehensive, measuring 177 countries across 12 indicators to determine the rating for each state. The 12 indicators include: (1) democratic pressures; (2) refugees and internally displaced persons; (3) group grievance; (4) human flight; (5) uneven development; (6) economic decline; (7) delegitimization of the state; (8) public service; (9) human rights; (10) security apparatus; (11) factionalized elites; and (12) external intervention.[748]

The Failed States Index grades states in direct correlation to their susceptibility to political instability and violence, using computer software that scans news articles, United States State Department reports, independent studies and corporate financial filings, noting the number of positive and negative 'hits' for each country.[749] In the Failed States Index, a higher value denotes a higher level of state weakness and failure, while lower values represent a more functional state. Although the Failed States Index precludes the inclusion of significant factors associated with the rule of law along with impunity in regard to structural competency failures of a state, which are in fact major causes of state failure, it is still an important undertaking with respect to understanding the causes and impact of failed states. Yemen topped the list in 2019 as a result of the civil war:

> Yemen's top ranking is the result of its rapid worsening over the past decade, with a brutal civil war which has been compounded by regional instability and power plays for which its population are unspeakably suffering.[750]

The United Kingdom's Department for International Development and the OECD retain complementary definitions of fragile states, which also focus on service entitlements. The Department defines fragile states as places where the government is unwilling or unable to deliver core functions to the majority of its citizens, particularly the poorest of its residents. It is noted that "[t]he most important functions of the state

---

[748] The Fund for Peace, "Failed States Index 2011," *Foreign Policy* (2011)

[749] Stewart Patrick, "'Failed' States and Global Security: Empirical Questions and Policy Dilemmas," *International Studies Review*, Vol. 9, No. 4 (2007) at 646

[750] https://fragilestatesindex.org/2019/04/10/fragile-states-index-2019-released-venezuela-and-brazil-most-worsened-countries-in-2019/

for poverty reduction are territorial control, safety and security, capacity to manage public resources, delivery of basic services, and the ability to protect and support the ways in which the poorest people sustain themselves."[751] Once again, the definition is premised upon the fundamental structural competency failure of states and is not specifically related to the performance of the functions necessary to subscribe to the basic expectations of statehood. The Centre for Research on Inequality and Social Exclusion also defines fragile states as "failing or at risk of failing, with respect to authority, comprehensive service entitlements or legitimacy."[752]

Recognizing the complexity and the constricted view present when using the term 'failed states,' the Crisis States Research Centre at the London School of Economics (LSE) lists three categories of state vulnerability and effectiveness as fragile, crisis and failed. Accordingly, a fragile state is significantly more susceptible with respect to institutional arrangements which embody and preserve the conditions of crisis during the period in which it is under acute stress. In such a situation the reigning institutions must contend with serious contestation and are potentially unable to manage conflict and shocks.

Finally, a failed state, according to LSE Research Centre, is in a condition of state collapse when it can no longer perform its basic security and development functions and has lost control of its territory and borders.[753] It has been suggested that the term 'failing state' is a more appropriate categorization than 'failed state', as the former is more flexible, allowing for different degrees of failure along a continuum as the state governing capacity weakens.[754] Human rights groups now increasingly favour the much broader terminology of 'fragility'. The challenge with respect to these approaches is that they nuance the complexity of the situation associated with state failure and delay any possible response that may be required from the international community.

In the post-Cold War era, many researchers have approached the phenomenon of state failure from a 'Third World' perspective; this was mainly attributed to the sheer number of weak states in Africa:

---

[751] *Why We Need to Work More Effectively in Fragile States,* London: U.K. Department for International Development (January 2005) at 7

[752] Frances Stewart and Graham Brown, "Fragile States," CRISE Working Paper No. 51 (January 2009) at 3

[753] Jonathan Di John, *Conceptualising The Causes And Consequences of Failed States: A Critical Review of the Literature,* London: Crisis States Working Papers Series No. 2, London School of Economics (January 2008) at 10

[754] Ibid.

Thirty-four years after 1960, the symbolic year of 'Africa's independence' many African countries continue to experience serious difficulty in the process of consolidation of their statehood ... Some African nations have in the past few years reduced themselves to a state of 'suspended state-hood' in which there may still be recognized frontiers, but everything inside has become anarchy and lawlessness.[755]

There is concern in the capitals of many Western nations that the potential exists ever increasingly that failed states will transform to transnational threats. A 2003 report prepared by the European Security Strategy identifies the "alarming phenomenon" of state failure as one of the main threats to the European Union.[756] The European Security Strategy is the document that is referenced by the European Union to clarify its security strategy and which defines state failure as "[c]ivil conflict and bad governance—corruption, abuse of power, weak institutions and lack of accountability—corrode States from within."[757] The report notes that a failed state leads to a "collapse of state institutions" and "undermines global governance and adds to regional instability."[758]

Similarly, state failure has been portrayed "as the Achilles' heel of collective security."[759] United Nations Secretary-General Kofi Annan declared in his 2005 report, *In Larger Freedom*, that "if states are fragile, the peoples of the world will not enjoy the security, development, and justice that are their right"[760] In 2006, member States of the United Nations endorsed the

---

[755]   Alexandros Yannis, "State Collapse and its Implications for Peace-Building and Reconstruction," in Jennifer Milliken (ed.), *State Failure, Collapse & Reconstruction*, Oxford: Blackwell Publishing (2003) at 64

[756]   Stewart Patrick, "Failed' States and Global Security: Empirical Questions and Policy Dilemmas," *International Studies Review*, Vol. 9, No. 4 (2007) at 646. In Great Britain, the Prime Minister's Strategy Unit (PMSU) has advocated a new, government-wide effort to help prevent failed states from generating pathologies like crime, terrorism, disease, uncontrolled migration, and energy insecurity (PMSU 2005). Similarly, Canada's International Policy Statement of 2005 (Government of Canada 2005) and Australia's recent white paper on overseas programs (Australian National Aid Agency 2006) advocate cross-departmental collaboration to forestall state collapse and its associated negative consequences.

[757]   "A Secure Europe in a Better World," *European Security Strategy*, Brussels (12 December 2003)

[758]   Ibid.

[759]   Stewart Patrick, "Failed' States and Global Security: Empirical Questions and Policy Dilemmas," *International Studies Review*, Vol. 9, No. 4 (2007) at 646

[760]   *In Larger Freedom, Towards Security, Development and Human Rights for All*, Report of the Secretary-General of the United Nations, for decision by Head of State and Government (September 2005)

creation agency known as the Peace Building Commission[761] to ensure that war-torn states do not collapse once again into failure.[762] Further review of conflict prevention and development in the context of the primary challenges they present to peace-building will be undertaken in this study.

In the post-Cold War period, the terms "failed states" and "state collapse" have commonly and often interchangeably been utilized to describe the failure to meet structural competencies, which is invariably the product of a "collapse of the power structures providing political support for law and order, a process generally triggered and accompanied by "anarchic" forms of internal violence."[763] UN Secretary-General Boutros Ghali described this situation accordingly when he wrote:

> A feature of such conflicts is the collapse of state institutions, especially the police and judiciary, with resulting paralysis of governance, a breakdown of law and order, and general banditry and chaos. Not only are the functions of government suspended, but also its assets are destroyed or looted and experienced officials are killed or flee the country. This is rarely the case in inter-state wars. It means that international intervention must extend beyond military and humanitarian tasks and must include the promotion of international reconciliation and the re-establishment of effective government.[764]

In March 1995, the United Nations Congress on Public International Law was convened with the theme, "Towards the Twenty-first Century: International Law as a Language for International Relations." It brought together approximately 600 lawyers from 125 countries who, in their summary paper, maintained that the issue of failed states was a:

> significant challenge to the juridical conception of the State is the problem of States that fail to provide minimum social order and are unable to meet the basic needs of their peoples. The challenge posed by so-called failed States arises, inter alia, from the problems of defining the rights

---

[761] *The Peacebuilding Commission*, Resolution adopted by the General Assembly (A/RES/60/180) (30 December 2005)

[762] Stewart Patrick, "'Failed' States and Global Security: Empirical Questions and Policy Dilemmas," *International Studies Review*, Vol. 9, No. 4 (2007) at 646. Also the major donors of the OECD (2005) have pursued a 'Fragile States' initiative in partnership with the World Bank (2006) Low Income Countries under Stress (LICUS) program.

[763] Daniel Thürer, *The 'Failed State' and International Law*, Geneva: International Review of the Red Cross, No. 836 (31 December 1999)

[764] Boutros Boutros Ghali, "Towards the Twenty-First Century: International Law as a Language for International Relations ," United Nations Congress on Public International Law (13-17 March 1995) at 9

and obligations of other States or international organizations in dealing with the breakdown of the social order or with the unmet needs of the people of the failed State.[765]

When the basic functions of the state are debilitated and there exists a lack of structural competency in respect of the provision of basic political goods, a state is not able to create and enforce laws that provide for social cohesion, nor is it able to assure the security of its territory. As well, its political institutions defer all legitimacy.[766]

As a consequence, a view of state failure must consider the conflicts that have provoked the collapse of the social contract.[767] As indicated by several scholars and institutions, state failure has multiple attributes as well as key indicators that address an expansive range of elements of structural competency. From loss of control of territory and security, to erosion of legitimate authority and the inability to provide public goods and services, "states can fail at varying rates through explosion, implosion, erosion, or invasion over different time periods."[768]

Finally, it is important to note that structural indicators as well as designations of state failure are not necessarily terminal, as demonstrated historically by examples of state failure in places such as Colombia, El Salvador, Lebanon and Tajikistan, which, although weak have in fact recovered.

Absence of Rule of Law

Rule of law is an established principle of international law and a fundamental foundation upon which the good governance of a state can be determined. In order to fully comprehend the spectrum of state failure, the fundamentals of rule of law must be addressed.

In contemporary thought it is reasonably argued that strong institutions with a legal framework are essential to stability, legitimacy in the minds of citizens of a state and economic growth.[769] Rule of law is not

---

[765] *International Law as a Language for International Relations Report,* The Hague: Kluwer Law International (1996) at 577

[766] William Zartman (ed.), *Collapsed States: The Disintegration and Reinstitution of Legitimate Authority,* Boulder: Lynne Rienner (1995) at 5

[767] Laura Tedesco, "The Latin American State: 'failed' or evolving?," Fundaciun para las Relaciones Internacionales y el Dialogo Exterior, Madrid: Working Paper 37 (May 2007) at 9

[768] Fund for Peace, Failed States Index: Frequent asked question

[769] Claire Vallings and Magi Moreno-Torres, "Drivers of Fragility: What Makes States Fragile?," London: Department for International Development (2005) at 14

solely a legal principle; however, some legal scholars have proposed a series of features that are common to the concept, including:

> 1) Powers exercised by officials must be based upon authority conferred by law. 2) The law itself must conform to certain standards of justice, both substantial and procedural. 3) There must be a substantial separation of powers between the executive, the legislature and the judicial function.[770]

Rule of law is conferred legitimacy when it is based upon justice and respect for human rights. States that exhibit weakness and failure harass civil society as they do not respect rule of law, have no independent judicial system and are frequently ruled by despots.[771] Several of these autocratic rulers control dissent, lack legitimacy and in extreme cases such as in North Korea permit their people to starve. Cambodia under Pol Pot and Iraq under Saddam Hussein also qualify, as do contemporary Belarus, Turkmenistan, and Libya ruled by Gaddafi. Many would argue legitimately that Syria under Bashar al-Assad falls into this category.

In recent times, the list of states that are fundamentally weak but appear to be strong is ever more extensive.[772] States that provide predictable and systematic means of resolving disputes and regulating the behaviour and values of a society with an enforceable body of law and an effective judicial system are the antithesis of state failure.[773]

It is important to take account of failed states that seemingly operate with flawed institutions and broker no democratic debate while maintaining a strong executive along with a judiciary that exists in name only:

> The Judiciary is derivative of the executive rather than being independent, and citizens know that they cannot rely on the court system for significant redress or remedy, especially against the state.[774]

In Haiti, for example, political, economic and social rights, along with the rule of law, are all tenuous and were so long before the earthquake that took place there in 2010. Along with the tragic loss of over 200,000 people, most of the state infrastructure that did exist was destroyed by the earthquake.

---

[770] Ian Brownlie, *The Rule of Law in International Affairs*, The Hague: Kluwer Law International (1998) at 213

[771] Robert I. Rotberg (ed.), *State Failure and State Weakness in a Time of Terror*, Washington D.C.: Brookings Institution Press (2003) at 4

[772] Ibid.

[773] Ibid. at 3-4

[774] Ibid. at 6 -7

Furthermore, Haiti has yet to ratify the *International Covenant on Economic, Social and Cultural Rights*. According to United Nations independent expert Michel Forst, ratification of the *Covenant* would be a clear signal to Haitians that their government is in fact determined to combat social and economic inequalities, seek international and bilateral technical assistance and make a commitment to co-operation to "provide universal access to education, a viable health-care system, drinking water and sanitation services, adequate housing as well as guaranteed employment income and training."[775]

The Forst report outlines six human rights concerns with respect to Haiti including the country's penitentiary situation and prison overcrowding, violence against women, lynching, human trafficking, deportation and the lack of economic, social and cultural rights.

Forst also expressed concern, in his 2011 report, about the reinstatement of police officers with questionable records of conduct and the restoration of a problematic penal system:

> [I]n the midst of the cholera epidemic, latrines in several prisons are no longer emptied, and that the supply of food is almost no longer assured. ... This is profoundly shocking, not to mention the risk of an explosion of violence that the inaction of the state entails when inmates no longer receive food.[776]

Haiti has commenced its commitment to confronting appalling levels of violence against women by ratifying important regional and international treaties as well as establishing domestic laws to address this issue. Irrespective of this fact, although rape and indecent assault may be dealt with under provisions of the Haitian Criminal Code, there is concern that sexual harassment is in practice tolerated by society in general and the state in particular.

Many victims are dissuaded from reporting such incidents by the perpetrator, the perpetrator's family, or even by their own family members who fear reprisals.[777] Many instances of so-called vigilante justice have been reported, often in the form of the murder of those who are accused of

---

[775] Michael Forst, "*Technical Assistance and Capacity-Building: Report of the Independent Expert on the Situation of Human Rights in Haiti*," Geneva: United Nations Human Rights Council (26 March 2009)

[776] "Haiti: UN Expert Welcomes Declaration on Rule of Law, Awaits Implementation," UN News, New York (2 September 2011)

[777] Michael Forst, "Technical Assistance and Capacity-Building: Report of the Independent Expert on the Situation of Human Rights in Haiti," Geneva: United Nations Human Rights Council (26 March 2009)

committing theft, murder, kidnapping, witchcraft and other criminal acts. The application of extra-judicial punishment originates from the profound lack of confidence in the police force and justice system generally found amongst Haitians.[778]

Human trafficking is another significant problem, especially in the border regions between Haiti and the Dominican Republic. Children are especially at risk. Many births in the region go unregistered, exacerbating issues such as kidnapping, adoption and forced child labour.[779]

A system of domestic servitude also exists, which the United Nations considers a "modern form of slavery."[780] Establishing the rule of law in Haiti is a necessary precursor to improving human security. It is only when this occurs that it will be possible to contemplate the country's sustainable development and in so doing initiate the required reform of the police force and the judiciary. It is essential that reforms in these two areas be implemented equitably and that neither takes precedence over the other.[781] The most significant failures of the Haitian Government in terms of public security derive in many respects from a traditionally weakened structural competency which has been ineffective in addressing the country's needs.[782]

Any efforts at precluding state failure will be enormously challenging in the absence of institutional accountability, promotion of the rule of law, security, and provision of the most basic human needs. It should be understood that "[t]he promotion and construction of legality and bureaucracy are the most important tasks in state formation after state failure."[783] The restoration, or indeed creation of the rule of law is critical to state formation after state failure as it represents both a barometer, so to speak, of what can be reasonably expected from the state and an aura of badly needed legitimacy.

It also must be recognized that the development of administrative institutions is a minimum requirement for state formation, as the absence

---

778 Ibid.

779 Ibid.

780 Ibid.

781 Patrick Bellegarde-Smith, *Haiti: The Breached Citadel,* Boulder: Westview Press (1990) and Marlye Gelin-Adams and David M. Malone, *"Haiti: A Case of Endemic Weakness,"* in Robert I. Rotberg (ed.), *"State Failure and State Weakness in a Time of Terror,"* Washington D.C.: Brookings Institution Press (2003) at 289. Security Council Resolution 1840 (2008) states: "Recognizing the interconnected nature of the challenges in Haiti, reaffirming that sustainable progress on security, the rule of law and institutional reform, national reconciliation and development are mutually reinforcing."

782 Mario Silva, "Island of Distress: State Failure in Haiti," *Florida Journal of International Law,* Vol. 23 (2011) at 63

783 Jens Meierhenrich, "Forming States after Failure," in Robert I. Rotberg (ed.), *When States Fail Causes and Consequences,* Princeton: Princeton University Press (2004) at 156

of these is one of the principal contributors to state failure. The rule of law imposes limits on the political regime and indeed upon the state itself.[784] It is also to be remembered that the legal systems and their agents within failed states protect neither individual nor property rights; however, the law can represent a commitment to the reduction of violence and exploitation [785]

A lack of the rule of law within failed states, as well as prevailing political instability, often results in armed revolts and/or civil unrest.[786] Civil wars that characterize failed states generally originate with inter-communal differences, such as those based on ethnicity, religion or language. However, the failure of states cannot be attributed singularly to such differences, nor can these explain the oppression of minority groups by a given majority, although they may well be an important contributing factor.[787] Citizens depend upon the state to insulate them from arbitrary violations of their personal security.

When states neither provide minimum services nor meet the core structural competencies of ensuring the rule of law and security, they fail to fulfil the matrix of a nation state. By way of a practical example of the foregoing, the UNDP's Rule of Law and Security Programme (ROLS) in Somalia notes that "the absence or weakness of the state is at the root of Somalia's endemic conflict."[788] The government is unable to exercise authority, which is made worse as the total "collapse of those

---

[784] Susan Rose-Ackerman, "Establishing the Rule of Law" in Robert I. Rotberg (ed.), *When States Fail Causes and Consequences*, Princeton: Princeton University Press (2004) at 183

[785] Ibid. at 209

[786] Robert I. Rotberg, "Failed States, Collapsed States, Weak States: Causes and Indicators," in Robert I. Rotberg (ed.), *State Failure and State Weakness in a Time of Terror*, Washington D.C.: Brookings Institution Press (2003) at 5

[787] Ibid.

[788] UNDP Newsroom, *Rule of Law & Security (ROLS)*, UNDP in Somalia (October 2011). The Three ROLS projects provide a development approach to rule of law and security, addressing simultaneously the institutional (top down) and community (bottom up) aspects of rule of law and security:

- Access to justice – The project is not only seeking to train and build the capacity of the legal profession, it also works on providing access to justice for most vulnerable communities, especially those living in areas with no functioning state institutions.
- Law enforcement – UNDP considers police work to be a service to the community.
- Community safety – (DDR/AVR) – Community safety recognizes the role of communities in ensuring their wellbeing and reducing armed violence at the local level, in partnership with local authorities.

structures designed to administer justice, including law enforcement and the protection of human rights, continues to hamper progress towards the establishment of formal mechanisms for the rule of law."[789]

Walter Clarke and Robert Gosende ponder how it is that Somalia with its strongly cohesive culture, language, and religion could reach the point of collapse. Perhaps "it never constituted a single coherent territory, having been part of the colonial empires of two suzerains, with other Somalis living outside the boundaries of the two colonies."[790] Somalia has always had a strong clan system, and it is important to note that a strong central government was never able to mature. Rather, the rulers pandered to the clan and sub-clan system and indeed utilized it to support their power. This conduct inevitably set in motion the failure of the Somali state, as far as it existed.

In states such as Burundi, the majority-minority war has impeded its capacity to perform as a state, and for a decade it has been fatally crippled by majority-backed insurgencies against autocratic minority-led governments.[791]

Burundi and Somalia are still experiencing many challenges to the rule of law, with traditional justice systems that predate the colonial era still operating today, regardless of their seeming ineffectiveness. For instance, "[i]n Burundi, the *bashingantahe* system deals mainly with civil matters, whereas in Somalia, the *xeer* system is used to regulate inter-clan relationships."[792] These types of informal justice systems[793] fail to meet international human rights law standards. The Islamic Courts Union, a group of Sharia Courts united as a political group to form a rival administration to the Transitional Federal Government in Somalia, deploy a comparatively harsh interpretation of Sharia law. All factors have combined alongside the continuing insurgency to create increased alienation from the local population.[794]

Failed states are beset by weak national institutions that undermine the legitimacy of state.[795] In Sri Lanka, the violent civil war was in part due to:

---

[789]   Ibid.

[790]   Robert I. Rotberg, "Failed States, Collapsed States, Weak States: Causes and Indicators," in Robert I. Rotberg (ed.), *State Failure and State Weakness in a Time of Terror*, Washington D.C.: Brookings Institution Press (2003) at 13

[791]   Ibid.

[792]   Kristina Thorne, "Rule of Law through imperfect bodies? The informal justice systems of Burundi and Somalia," Peace-Justice Conference report (November 2005) at 3

[793]   Ibid.

[794]   Jason McLure, "The Troubled Horn of Africa: Can the War-torn Region Be Stabilised?," *3 CQ Global Researcher* (2009) at 167-68

[795]   Seth D. Kaplan, *Fixing Fragile States A New Paradigm For Development*, Westport: Praeger Security International (2008) at 37

community fragments as one or more identifiable groups no longer recognizes the legitimacy of the central state. A violent struggle ensues in which different groups contest either control of the central state or the right to secede from it. The state fails in the sense that insurrections prevent it from enforcing its authority and laws over a significant proportion of its territory. The central state may, however, remain strong in the regions under its control, which it may continue to administer strenuously. Indeed, in longstanding civil wars, the central state is usually relatively healthy, except for its ability to control some (large) part of the country.[796]

It is especially troubling that corrupt autocratic regimes operate with neither strong legal norms nor an independent judiciary. The rule of law has two fundamentally different ways of setting legal limits in both the civil and political realms. Although the rule of law is not the only necessary component for stability, it is clear that without the existence of such a paradigm, the state potentially disintegrates rather rapidly.[797]

States that fail to establish legal limits and that are in essence weak or unable to control violence and destruction, permit those in power to act with impunity. These states rapidly come to realize that such circumstances lead to further violence and create a fragile democratic state that can be undermined by its failure to limit private lawlessness. This can certainly result in state failure. Establishing rule of law will entail either a strengthening of state capacity or a weakening of state power.

The scholar Rotberg argues that there is a hierarchy of political goods. None of these is more critical than the supply of human security in preventing threats to the state, enforcing the rule of law and preventing crime and domestic threats or attacks. This is because they enable the delivery of a range of other desirable political goods.[798] In essence then, the rule of law is necessary in order to avoid violence and chaos. It is essential to take note of the fact that weak and failed states and corrupt leaders who ignore the rule of law create political instability which inevitably leads to a loss of legitimacy in the eyes of the people. This will be explored in more detail in the next sub-section.

---

[796] Nicolas Van De Walle, "The Economic Correlates of State Failure," in Robert I. Rotberg (ed.), *When States Fail Causes and Consequences*, Princeton: Princeton University Press (2004) at 94

[797] Susan Rose-Ackerman, "Establishing the Rule of Law," in Robert I. Rotberg (ed.), *When States Fail Causes and Consequences*, Princeton: Princeton University Press (2004) at 182

[798] Robert I. Rotberg, "Failed States, Collapsed States, Weak States: Causes and Indicators," in Robert I. Rotberg (ed.), *State Failure and State Weakness in a Time of Terror*, Washington D.C.: Brookings Institution Press (2003) at 1-3

Lack of Internal Security

The linking of security and development to the notion of failed states has since 9/11 come to establish the overall framework for debate on weak and failed states. It is argued that security is needed in order to reduce poverty and that poverty and conflict in one part of the world will create problems of insecurity and instability in other regions.[799] This overlapping relationship of security and development is often referred to as the 'security-development nexus', which:

> provides the overall framework for the fragile states debate. It reflects a dual claim, on the one hand, that security is fundamental for reducing poverty; and on the other hand, that a lack of development causes conflict...one cannot be pursued in isolation from the other.[800]

This has been the predominant view adopted by many NATO countries in order for them to justify their mission in Afghanistan to their respective populations. Many liberal democracies argue that human security also requires democratic reform and support of human rights. Fragile states, as argued by many, have difficulty in fulfilling these values and therefore become failed states. State fragility is caused by bad governance, and integrated approaches are required to deal with both the causes and effects of such fragility.[801]

Many regimes in African countries fail to provide political goods, although they do have some supporters to whom they provide exclusive benefits.[802] Ranging from Sierra Leone to the Democratic Republic of the Congo, all African countries rank low in the UNDP's Human Development Index, with severe poverty despite vast natural resources. In the Democratic Republic of the Congo, "most of the country was reduced to subsistence living,"[803] despite the fact that it has valuable deposits of diamonds, gold, cobalt, coltan, and copper.[804] It was, and still is, difficult to have development without security, given that before "the economy could grow, the conflict had to end and inflation needed to be brought under control."[805]

---

799   Lars Engberg-Pedersen et al, *Fragile States on the International Agenda*, Copenhagen: Danish Institute of International Studies (2008) at 10

800   Ibid.

801   Ibid.

802   Ibid. at 76

803   **James Dobbins et al, *Europe's Role in Nation-Building: From the Balkans to Congo*, Santa Monica: Rand Corporation (2008) at 102**

804   Ibid.

805   Ibid.

Most weak and failed states:

> share bleak socioeconomic indicators-from GDP per capita levels typically half that of low-income countries; child mortality rates twice as high as other low income-countries; mortality rates plummeting by up to thirty years as HIV afflicts over 42 million; and over 200 million lacking access to improved water and sanitation. Fragile states are the main barrier impeding international efforts to meet the United Nations' Millennium Development Goals-which include eradicating hunger, reducing child mortality, and achieving universal primary education-by 2015.[806]

In Afghanistan, for example, al-Qaeda took advantage of a weak government, finding sanctuary in ungoverned territory; "[t]he lack of institutional mechanisms to deal with crises suggests that the costs of terrorism are greater in fragile states—a conclusion too obvious to debate."[807] The lack of internal security provides an explanation of how Afghanistan became a failed state.

Throughout the Cold War period many weak and failed states were propped up in order to maintain their allegiances. However, in the post-Cold War period the need for allegiance vanished as did much of the concern for the less fortunate. Today, Western governments are not to a great extent concerned in putting in place regimes that are potential allies but rather those that can govern well, promote economic development and safeguard human rights within their territory.

The lack of internal security that leads to anarchy renders the state incapable of providing security to individuals. These security dilemmas are:

> constructed out of units that can act upon the fears of their members.... The nature of state failure may produce new and less accepted groups that supplant pre-existing entities, or permit new illegitimate warlords with access to arms to replace culturally sanctioned leaders.[808]

Often, these prolonged internal conflicts create economic stagnation, decaying national infrastructure and the erosion of all state institutions and authority. Michael Klare argued that it is possible for an:

---

[806] Seth D. Kaplan, *Fixing Fragile States: A New Paradigm For Development*, Westport: Praeger Security International (2008) at 4

[807] Lars Engberg-Pedersen et al, *Fragile States on the International Agenda*, Copenhagen: Danish Institute of International Studies (2008) at 11

[808] Nelson Kasfir, "Domestic Anarchy, Security Dilemmas, and Violent Predation," in Robert I. Rotberg (ed.), *When States Fail Causes and Consequences*, Princeton: Princeton University Press (2004) at 71

effective leader or leadership group to reverse the process and avert full state collapse; even without such leadership, an ailing state can remain in a weakened condition for many years without slipping into total disarray. But a state's capacity to resist failure can decline rapidly when armed militias emerge or the official security forces break up into semi-autonomous bands. Once established, these bands and militias tend to compete with one another for control of territory, population, and resources-thereby subjecting the country to recurring bouts of violence and disorder. Under these circumstances, the transition from failing to failed state is usually irreversible.[809]

The state has a duty to protect its population from violence, and when it is unwilling or unable to provide such protection, when it loses its monopoly over the legitimate use of violence, or when its authority is weakened, then failure and decline are to be expected.[810] The emergence of semi-autonomous militia in a fragile and divided state only leads to an increase in violence, a considerable decline in state authority and the distribution throughout society of small arms and light weapons.[811]

Once paramilitary groups emerge in a country of this sort and acquire substantial stocks of arms and ammunition, that country is destined to face severe stress and trauma. The government involved may be able to avert total failure, but it is almost certain to lose control of significant areas of the countryside.[812] In the Democratic Republic of the Congo, anarchy and violence are rampant, resulting in shocking human loss and the killing of millions of people.[813]

From the end of the twentieth century and continuing into the beginning of this century, states such as Côte d'Ivoire, Liberia, Sierra Leone, Somalia, Rwanda, the Democratic Republic of the Congo and Sudan have all endured protracted conflicts. In Sierra Leone, the struggle and brutal violence of the Revolutionary United Front (RUF) wreak terror on a defenceless population. Since the independence of many of these colonial states, problems such as wealth disparities between rich and poor, lack of education, impoverishment, and inadequate security and development have

---

[809] Michael T. Klare, "The Deadly Connection Paramilitary Bands, Small Arms Diffusion, And State Failure," in Robert I. Rotberg (ed.), *When States Fail Causes and Consequences*, Princeton: Princeton University Press (2004) at 116

[810] Ibid. at 117

[811] Ibid. at 121

[812] Ibid. at 125

[813] René Lemarchand, "The Democratic Republic of the Congo: From Failure to Potential Reconstruction," in Robert I. Rotberg (ed.), *State Failure and State Weakness in a Time of Terror*, Washington D.C.: Brookings Institution Press (2003) at 29

never been properly addressed. In a 2011 meeting with the United Nations Secretary-General, President Alassane Ouattara of Côte d'Ivoire discussed the potential of United Nations support in addressing the fragile, ongoing security situation and the cross-border threats from Liberia, as heavily armed militiamen had crossed over and attacked and killed civilians.[814]

In the 1990s, Sierra Leone produced 300 to 450 million dollars' worth of diamonds annually, almost all of which were smuggled through Liberia and Côte d'Ivoire.[815] Sierra Leone's inability to provide for the structural competency in security and the delivery of political goods stems from the fact that "rulers intentionally destroyed state capacity to provide public goods."[816]

The Truth and Reconciliation Commission for Sierra Leone, which was established in 2002 in the aftermath of the conflict, acknowledged the important role that diamonds played in the conflict, as they yielded tremendous revenues that were used to buy weapons and that led to the enslavement of individuals to work in the mines.[817]

In the same way in Angola, powerful members of the elite have grown wealthy from diamond trafficking, while in Afghanistan and Colombia it is the profit from illegal drug trafficking by warlords and paramilitary groups that prolongs the conflict and instability. Sierra Leone, one of the poorest countries on earth, has had its economy devastated by the conflict. The gruesome attacks on civilians and the overwhelming destruction of property was accentuated by diamond sales, as the quantity mined was high and rebels had no trouble selling them.[818]

Charles Taylor, who served from 1997 to 2003 as president of Liberia, was on trial before the Special Court for Sierra Leone for his involvement in crimes committed in backing the Revolutionary United Front reign of terror by supplying arms in exchange for diamonds.[819] In April 2012 Taylor

---

[814] "Côte d'Ivoire: UN Has Key Role in Strengthening Democracy, President Says," UN News, New York (22 September 2011)

[815] John L. Hirsch, *Diamonds and the Struggle for Democracy*, Boulder: Lynne Reinner Publisher (2001) at 25

[816] William Reno, "Sierra Leone: Warfare in a Post-State Society," in Robert I. Rotberg (ed.), *State Failure and State Weakness in a Time of Terror*, Washington D. C.: Brookings Institution Press (2003) at 71

[817] Iryna Marchuk, "Confronting Blood Diamonds in Sierra Leone: The Trial of Charles Taylor," *Yale Journal of International Law*, Vol. 4, No. 2 (Spring Summer 2009) at 88

[818] James Dobbins et al, *Europe's Role in Nation-Building: From the Balkans to Congo*, Santa Monica: Rand Corporation (2008) at 31

[819] Iryna Marchuk, "Confronting Blood Diamonds in Sierra Leone: The Trial of Charles Taylor," *Yale Journal of International Law*, Vol. 4, No. 2 (Spring Summer 2009) at 89

was sentenced for his role in arming rebels in Sierra Leone in return for so-called "blood diamonds" during the country's ten year civil war which claimed the lives of 120,000 people. It was the first judgement lodged against a national leader since the Nuremburg Trials in 1946.[820]

External actors and states also play a role in destabilizing the security and development of another state. The lack of security and development was experienced by many youth who viewed themselves as victims of corrupt political elites and who were further victimized by the armed conflict, many being forced to become child soldiers. The social damage of state failure with no alternative vision creates:

> a class of unemployed, desperate youth who have been abandoned by elite political classes, who see joining armed gangs as one the few remaining ways to improve their personal situations, and who then become the means of advancing the interests of organizers, who pursue their own objectives.[821]

Secretary General Kofi Annan, in his speech to the Security Council, acknowledged the importance of addressing the issue of child soldiers when he stated that:

The question of children and armed conflict is an integral part of the United Nations' core responsibilities for the maintenance of international peace and security, for the advancement of human rights and for sustainable human development.[822]

There are several legal frameworks that spell out the rights of children in armed conflict and in peacetime. The 1989 *Convention on the Rights of the Child*, the *Optional Protocol to the Convention on the Rights of the Child* was adopted by the General Assembly on May 25th, 2000 and clearly sets the minimum age for compulsory recruitment. This objective is clear in Article 1 of the Optional Protocol that "states Parties shall take all feasible measures to ensure that members of their armed forces who have not attained the age of 18 years do not take a direct part in hostilities."[823]

---

[820] Admiral Doenitz, who succeeded Hitler as head of state of the Third Reich in April 1945, was indicted, tried and convicted by the International Military Tribunal.

[821] William Reno, "Sierra Leone: Warfare in a Post-State Society," in Robert I. Rotberg (ed.), *State Failure and State Weakness in a Time of Terror*, Washington D. C.: Brookings Institution Press (2003) at 96

[822] Annan, Kofi A., speech to the Security Council (26 July 2000)

[823] Optional Protocol to the Convention on the Rights of the Child on the involvement of children in armed conflict, Adopted and opened for signature, ratification and accession by General Assembly resolution A/RES/54/263 (25 May 2000) entry into force 12 February 2002

As well, The 1998 *Rome Statute of the International Criminal Court*, Article 8(2)(b)(xxvi) defines such conscription as the enlistment of children under fifteen by national armed forces or armed groups in order to use them to participate in hostilities as a war crime. The recruitment of children is also prohibited by the Additional Protocol I of the Geneva Convention and Article 4.3.c of Protocol II, which states that "children who have not attained the age of fifteen years shall neither be recruited in the armed forces or groups nor allowed to take part in hostilities."[824]

In 2006, Thomas Lubanga Dyilo, former leader of a militia group at war in the North Eastern Ituri district of the Democratic Republic of the Congo, was charged by the Prosecutor of the ICC with enlisting and conscripting children under the age of fifteen and using them to participate actively in hostilities. This was the first time that an individual had been brought before an international court solely on the basis of these crimes.[825]

Failed states are tense, conflicted, and dangerous with shared characteristics such as high levels of criminal and political violence, loss of sovereignty, civil war, the use of terror against their own citizens, high levels of corruption and poverty.[826] Endemic civil conflicts undermine the "accountability, capacity and legitimacy of the state,"[827] leading weak states to failure and loss of control over their territory. In Haiti, for example, the government has been associated with deep failures in public security services—failures that are derived in "large part from a traditionally weak Haitian state incapable of effectively addressing the country's needs."[828] The trafficking of narcotics has been a serious problem in Haiti since the 1980s, with the government either unwilling or unable to prevent the smuggling of drugs.[829] Moreover, the prevailing political turmoil and poor economic conditions have caused an increase in crime and violence, which the police and judiciary have been unable to tackle

---

[824] Protocol II, additional to the Geneva Conventions of 12 August 1949 at 4.3.c

[825] "Child soldier charges in the first International Criminal Court case," ICC Press release (2006)

[826] Robert I. Rotberg, "Failed States in a World of Terror," *Foreign Affairs*, Vol. 81, No. 4 (July/August 2002)

[827] *The applicability of the Paris Declaration in fragile and conflict-affected situations: Thematic Study*, Oxford: IDL Group (August 2008) at 9

[828] Patrick Bellegarde-Smith, *Haiti: The Breached Citadel*, Boulder: Westview Press (1990) and Marlye Gélin-Adams and David M. Malone, "*Haiti: A Case of Endemic Weakness,*" in Robert I. Rotberg (ed.) *State Failure and State Weakness in a Time of Terror*, Washington D.C.: Brookings Institution Press (2003) at 287

[829] Robert I. Rotberg, (ed.), *When States Fail Causes and Consequences*, Princeton: Princeton University Press (2004).

effectively.[830] Despite over US$2 billion spent on international efforts to develop an independent police force in Haiti, this goal has yet to be achieved.[831] Haiti's failure in public security has long hampered development. Haiti's weak institutions and political paralysis has resulted in high crime rates, violence, drug trafficking, unemployment and poverty.[832]

In Equatorial Guinea, civil conflict led to the deaths of an estimated 80,000 people out of a population of 300,000.[833] The country has experienced several coups, including a 2004 attempt carried out by mercenaries to replace the President.[834] A 2011 United Nations panel report on mercenaries in Equatorial Guinea called for greater regulation of mercenaries and private military groups:

Outsourcing security creates risks for human rights...The report on Equatorial Guinea noted that the 2004 coup attempt was the most widely reported incident clearly involving mercenaries, some of them employees or former employees of private military and security companies from several countries, illustrating 'possible close and disturbing links' between mercenaries and such companies.[835]

The panel report recommended that all mercenaries be held accountable for their actions.

The Security Council has also expressed concerns over the lack of security in the Central African region, particularly in respect to the flow of illicit small arms, border security and the threat posed by Lord's Resistance Army (LRA). The LRA is listed by the United States as a terrorist organization that now operates beyond northern Uganda and is a regional problem, operating in countries such as South Sudan, Central African Republic and the Democratic Republic of the Congo.[836] The majority

---

830   Patrick Bellegarde-Smith, *Haiti: The Breached Citadel*, Boulder: Westview Press (1990) and Marlye Gélin-Adams and David M. Malone, *"Haiti: A Case of Endemic Weakness,"* in Robert I. Rotberg (ed.), *"State Failure and State Weakness in a Time of Terror,"* Washington D.C.: Brookings Institution Press (2003) at 298

831   Ibid. at 297

832   Marlye Gélin-Adams & David M. Malone, "Haiti: A Case of Endemic Weakness," in Robert I. Rotberg, (ed.), *State Failure and State Weakness in a Time of Terror*, Washington D.C.: Brookings Institution Press (2003) at 287

833   Kim Sengupta, "Coup plotter faces life in Africa's most notorious jail," *The Independent* (11 May 2007)

834   Ibid.

835   "Outsourcing to Private Security Contractors Threatens Human Rights, UN Panel Warns," UN News, New York (14 September 2011)

836   "LRA: A Regional Strategy Beyond Killing Kony," *Africa Report*, N°157, International Crisis Group (28 April 2010) at I

of the atrocities carried out by the LRA took place in northern Uganda in the 1990s. However, remnants of the LRA continued their attacks on civilians in the Central African Republic and the Democratic Republic of Congo as well as in South Sudan. Since 2019, more than 445,000 people are reported to have been displaced from their homes, and the majority of these displacements occurred as a result of violent actions by the LRA.[837]

In the absence of a functioning state it is virtually impossible to provide for either security or development as such environments are not conducive to the growth of economic opportunity. The achievement of human development, human rights and human security are related by a range of structural competencies of the state. Unfortunately, most failed states are ruled by autocratic regimes or leaders whose only concern is retaining power.

Impunity and Ineffective Justice Systems

Failed states demonstrate flawed institutions with almost no safety nets for their people and are either unwilling or unable to perform the essential functions of a nation-state. The legislative and judicial branches of government have no independence from the executive, and while the armed forces may not be as dysfunctional, they are often highly politicized.[838] In extreme cases, failed states are characterized by a vacuum of authority, such as in Somalia.

The preamble of the *Rome Statute of the International Criminal Court*, establishes that State Parties to this Statute affirm:

> that the most serious crimes of concern to the international community as a whole must not go unpunished and that their effective prosecution must be ensured by taking measures at the national level and by enhancing international cooperation. Determined to put an end to impunity for the perpetrators of these crimes and thus to contribute to the prevention of such crimes.[839]

Bringing to trial those who have committed serious crimes is an important endeavour, essential to the re-establishment of the rule of law and the facilitation of national reconciliation in a post-reconstruction failed state.

---

[837] "Ban Urges Support for Central African Efforts to End Lord's Resistance Army Threat," UN News, New York (14 Jun 2012)

[838] Robert I. Rotberg, "Failed States, Collapsed States, Weak States: Causes and Indicators," in Robert I. Rotberg (ed.), *State Failure and State Weakness in a Time of Terror*, Washington D.C.: Brookings Institution Press (2003) at 6

[839] *Rome Statute of the International Criminal Court*, U.N. Doc. A/CONF.183/9, entered into force on 1 July 2002

However, the road to reconciliation and justice is complicated, even more so for those who are attempting to restore a sense of normalcy to the failed state. As Adama Dieng, Registrar of the International Criminal Tribunal for Rwanda, stated:

Impunity has political, juridical and moral aspects when the offences committed are of a serious nature. It prevents peaceful co-existence between national communities, and constitutes a major obstacle to the evolution of democracy. Gone are the days when people believed in wiping the slate and starting anew.[840]

The establishment of the International Criminal Court in 2002 has allowed, for the first time in history, a permanent court to have universal jurisdiction over instances of leadership criminality in failed states. Consequently, leaders who commit genocide, crimes against humanity, war crimes, and crimes of aggression are now actually being prosecuted for their crimes. United Nations Secretary-General Kofi Annan articulates the significant historical and monumental role the establishment of the International Criminal Court can play in "the promise of universal justice."[841]

The Nuremberg and Tokyo trials, the *Convention on the Prevention and Punishment of the Crime of Genocide* and the establishment of the International Criminal Tribunal for the former Yugoslavia (ICTY) have all helped in fundamentally advancing the pursuit of international criminal justice, the forming of extemporized tribunals, and the creation of an accountability paradigm and *the Rome Statute for the International Criminal Court*. The ICTY has become a fundamental component of post-conflict peace-building in the former Yugoslavia.

There have been several detentions to date of individuals who were implicated in the atrocities of several failed states, the most notable being Thomas Lubanga, Germain Katanga, Mathieu Ngudjolo Chui, Jean-Pierre Bemba, Callixte Mbarushimana and Liberian President Charles Taylor, who has been tried the International Criminal Court. In addition to the International Criminal Court, there has also been the establishment of the International Criminal Tribunal for the former Yugoslavia and the International Criminal Tribunal for Rwanda.

Many legal scholars have been critical of involving senior officials who committed crimes against their people in the process of implementation of a peace accord.[842] The focus on reconciliation with too weak an effort in

---

[840]   Adama Dieng, *Clarification of concepts: Justice, reconciliation, and impunity*. Arusha: United Nations International Criminal Tribunal for Rwanda (24 May2002) at 1-2

[841]   The International Criminal Court, CBC News Online (9 July 2004)

[842]   Rena L. Scott, "Moving from Impunity to Accountability in Post-War Liberia: Possibilities, Cautions, and Challenges," *International Journal of Legal Information*, Vol. 33

prosecuting those who have committed such crimes has been criticized. This criticism was especially evident after the signing of the *Comprehensive Peace Accord* (CPA) in Liberia when it appeared that the perpetrators of these crimes were not going to be held accountable:

> Liberia's present CPA does precisely that; it focuses exclusively on reconciliation. Ultimately, positive change is far more likely in Liberia through the use of judicially punitive mechanisms such as prosecution in a hybrid Special Court of law.[843]

However, as of late, the situation in Liberia has improved, especially after the election in Liberia of the first female president on the African continent, Ellen Johnson Sirleaf,[844] and the indictment of Taylor in 2003 by the Special Court for Sierra Leone prosecution on eleven counts for war crimes and crimes against humanity committed during the conflict in Sierra Leone.

Holding those who commit crimes against their people responsible is necessary for any effort to put to an end the culture of impunity. Rwanda's 'culture of impunity' has been cited for years as one of the central causes of the 1994 genocide. The International Criminal Tribunal for Rwanda (ICTR) mentioned the 'culture of impunity' as one of the causes of genocide:

> African countries must absorb the lessons of the Rwanda genocide in order to avoid a repetition of the ultimate crime" on the continent. Weak institutions in many African countries have given rise to a culture of impunity, especially under dictatorships that will do anything to cling to power.[845]

The International Criminal Tribunal for Rwanda also has defined impunity as "the failure to punish violations of established norms."[846]

Rwanda's Prosecutor General Gerald Gahima stated in an interview that:

(Winter 2005) at 363

[843]   Ibid. at 417

[844]   Ellen Johnson Sirleaf won the Nobel Peace Price on the 7th of October 2011 and was re-elected as President of Liberia on January 16, 2012

[845]   International Criminal Tribunal for Rwanda, General Information. Available at ICTR website: <http://unictr.org/AboutICTR/GeneralInformation/tabid/101/Default.aspx> accessed March 20, 2012

[846]   Adama Dieng, *Clarification of concepts: Justice, reconciliation, and impunity.* Arusha, Tanzania: United Nations International Criminal Tribunal for Rwanda (24 May2002) at 4

genocide was possible in part because of a culture of impunity that had taken root in our society since 1959, so after the genocide in 1994, by and large our society felt that there had to be accountability for the genocide if we [wanted] to end this culture of impunity, [but] you could not have accountability oblivious to this involvement of large numbers of members of our society. So we started, back then in 1995, thinking about this problem: how to have accountability, but at the same time, in a manner that would help to bring about stability and reconciliation and peace. Because if you dealt with it strictly as a legal matter, you'd create more instability, more conflict.[847]

Despite the challenges associated with ending impunity, on September 29th, 2011 the appeals chamber of the United Nations International Criminal Tribunal for Rwanda (ICTR) upheld twenty-five-year jail terms imposed on Lieutenant Colonel Ephrem Setako and Yussuf Munyakazi for crimes of genocide.

Opposition to the culture of impunity necessitates strong determination from the international community and the reinforcement of judicial instruments. In Haiti, one of the unfavourable circumstances leading to impunity is that the judicial branch remains inaccessible to large segments of the population and is lacking in resources, credibility, and competence, as judges who are often threatened with assassination in many cases elect to protect themselves rather than uphold the law.[848] The incapacity of the legal system to tackle crime and provide legal redress has often led to mob justice and increased cycles of violence, testing the inability of an already weak state.[849]

In Pakistan, blasphemy laws relating to the desecration or denigration of holy personages, items and places of the Islamic faith have widely been misused to harass and victimize minorities.[850] Attempts to reform or repeal the blasphemy laws have been met by repression and, in extreme cases, murder, such as the assassination of Punjab Governor Salmaan Taseer. The perpetrators of these offences, particularly Mumtaz Qadri, who was employed as a bodyguard for Governor Taseer when he

---

[847]   Catherine Honeyman et al, "Establishing Collective Norms: Potentials for Participatory Justice in Rwanda," *Peace and Conflict: Journal of Peace Psychology*, Vol. 10, No.1 (2004) at 4

[848]   Marlye Gélin-Adams and David M. Malone, "Haiti: A Case of Endemic Weakness," in Robert I. Rotberg, (ed.), *State Failure and State Weakness in a Time of Terror*, Washington D.C.: Brookings Institution Press (2003) at 299

[849]   Ibid.

[850]   Mario Silva, "Pakistan's State Failure: Impunity and the Rise of Militancy," *International Journal of Rights and Security*, Vol.1.1 (2012) at 61

committed the assassination, have been greeted with adulation instead of condemnation.

In fact, during Qadri's court appearance, there were loud cheers and rose petals thrown at him.[851] As well, when Member of Parliament Sherry Rehman attempted to put forward a motion at the National Assembly to repeal the blasphemy law, she was forced to withdraw it after being harassed and having her life threatened.[852] Others, such as Shahbaz Bhatti, Pakistan's first Federal Minister for Minorities, were highly critical of Pakistan's blasphemy law; he was assassinated on March 2nd, 2011.

Pakistan's blasphemy law prohibits and punishes anyone who speaks against Islam, with sentences ranging from prison terms to the death penalty. Thousands of Christians, Ahmadi Muslims, and other religious minorities remain in custody, charged with violations of the blasphemy laws. More than 1,000 religious minorities have been charged under blasphemy laws between 1986 and 2011, and thirty-two have been killed extra-judicially by angry mobs and individuals.[853] Although religious minorities represent only a small fraction of Pakistan's population, they account for more than 50% of prosecutions under blasphemy laws. [854]

The culture of impunity in Pakistan has been seriously condemned by several leading human rights organizations. The Jinnah Institute, for example, has asked that Pakistan:

[r]emove impunity in a systematic manner for prayer leaders in mosques, particularly those controlled by the state and under the respective provincial and federal Auqaf departments, for incitement to hatred on the basis of religious affiliation.[855]

In addition, the Institute has asked for parliamentarians to create a consensus for "regulating madrassas and mosques to prevent their use for the promotion and propagation of anti-minority propaganda and hate speech against non-Muslims."[856]

---

[851] Babar Dogar, "Muslim scholars praise killer of Pakistan governor," *Associated Press* (5 January 2011)

[852] Declan Wash, "Pakistan MP Sherry Rehman drops effort to reform blasphemy laws," *The Guardian* (3 February 2011)

[853] *A Question of Faith: A Report on the Status of Religious Minorities in Pakistan*, Karachi: Jinnah Institute (2011) at 40

[854] Ibid.

[855] Ibid. at 8

[856] Ibid.

Leading organizations such as the Asian Human Rights Commission (AHRC) have also expressed their concern about the endemic nature of human rights violations in Pakistan.[857] The AHRC refers to the reports of thousands of people being tortured and suffering forced disappearance by law enforcement agencies. In the Balochistan province between 2002 and 2005, more than 4,000 people were detained, yet less than 200 were presented before the courts, with the remaining detainees held incommunicado.[858] As well, honour killing is still prevalent, with reports of up to 500 women being killed per year, as many as 20% of whom are minors.[859]

Other states have been embroiled in a bitter and destructive civil war. The civil war in Sri Lanka, between the majority Sinhala government and the Tamil minority, eventually led to the killing of the rebel leader of the LTTE. Several reports by various human rights organizations, including the Office of the High Commissioner for Human Rights, have been critical of the lack of judicial independence in Sri Lanka.[860] Impunity for those who committed gross and systematic violations of human rights will make it impossible to achieve the reconciliation that is needed between the Sinhalese and the Tamil communities.

Sovereignty implies legal autonomy and constitutional independence, and when states fail in their ability to control their territory, it certainly poses a challenge to the effective pursuit of justice.

Gross and Systematic Violations of Human Rights
Some human rights advocates argue that the state is the problem. The state is the principal defender of human rights, and failed states pose a threat to this responsibility. One of enduring attributes of failed states is the level of gross and systematic violence committed by both state and non-state actors, including sexual violence, murder, extra-judicial killing, and, in extreme cases, war crimes, crimes against humanity, and other breaches of international humanitarian and human rights law. William Schabas has maintained that, in the hierarchy of crimes, genocide "belongs at the apex

---

[857] *Pakistan: The Human Rights Situation in 2006 An overview,* Hong Kong: Asian Human Rights Commission (2006)

[858] Ibid.

[859] Ibid.

[860] Kishali Pinto-Jayawardena, "The Rule of Law in Decline, Study on Prevalence, Determinants and Causes of Torture and Other Forms of Cruel, Inhuman or Degrading Treatment or Punishment in Sri Lanka," Copenhagen: The Rehabilitation and Research Centre for Torture Victims (2009) at 81

of the pyramid."[861] These violations of human rights inevitably lead to the internal displacement of people and entire communities as well as refugee flows to neighbouring states. Professor Payam Akhavan views with merit Schabas' observation and goes on to address in his book the simple but overlooked question of whether genocide is in fact the 'ultimate crime', pointing to "the ongoing debate over whether atrocities committed by the Sudanese government in Sudan constitute genocide,"[862] in order to illustrate the relevance of such a question.

It has also been noted that sexual violence continues to be a problem in several of the world's major conflicts, presenting a challenge for international efforts to eradicate it. Just over ten years ago, the Security Council of the United Nations adopted what was meant to be a landmark Resolution 1325 requiring parties in conflict situations to respect women's rights and to participate in peace negotiations.[863] In 2008, the Security Council adopted Resolution 1820, which recognized sexual violence as a tactic of war and stated its intent to consider sanctions against responsible parties. The Security Council Resolution notes that:

> civilians account for the vast majority of those adversely affected by armed conflict; that women and girls are particularly targeted by the use of sexual violence, including as a tactic of war to humiliate, dominate, instil fear in, disperse and/or forcibly relocate civilian members of a community or ethnic group; and that sexual violence perpetrated in this manner may in some instances persist after the cessation of hostilities; Recalling its condemnation in the strongest terms of all sexual and other forms of violence committed against civilians in armed conflict, in particular women and children.[864]

The Security Council demanded the "immediate and complete cessation by all parties to armed conflict of all acts of sexual violence against civilians"[865] and expressed "its deep concern that, despite repeated condem-

---

861   William Schabas, *Genocide in International law, The Crime of Crimes (2nd ed.)*, Cambridge: Cambridge University press, 2009) at 10-11

862   Payam Akhavan, *Reducing Genocide to Law*, Cambridge: Cambridge University Press (2012) at 135

863   Security Council Resolution 1325, adopted unanimously on October 31, 2000. The Security Council resolution also called for the adoption of a gender perspective that included the special needs of women and girls during repatriation and resettlement, rehabilitation, reintegration and post-conflict reconstruction.

864   Security Council Resolution 1820, SC/9364 (19 June 2008)

865   "Security Council Demands Immediate and Complete Halt to Acts of Sexual Violence Against Civilians in Conflict Zones, Unanimously Adopting Resolution

nation, violence and sexual abuse of women and children trapped in war zones was not only continuing, but, in some cases, had become so widespread and systematic as to reach appalling levels of brutality."[866] In 2009, the Security Council expanded its scope of influence regarding children in armed conflict to include the killing, maiming or raping of children.[867]

Earlier that year, another resolution called for substantive action by the Secretary-General, including the establishment of a Special Representative on Sexual Violence in Conflict and the creation of a team of rule of law experts that could be sent to assist weak states in combating sexual violence. The Council requested the Secretary-General to provide detailed reports on parties suspected of committing acts of sexual violence against which the Council could then impose sanction.[868]

Eleven years after its adoption, Landmark Security Council Resolution 1320 has yielded very few results for women and children in many failed states. It is known that in Sudan "rape has long been identified as a weapon of war in Darfur,"[869] and although the Darfur peace negotiations contributed to a decrease in violence, "clashes that did continue between the government and various rebel factions have been accompanied by cases of rape, gang rape and other physical assaults thought to be carried out by all sides."[870]

Additionally, in the last couple of months, in light of South Sudan's independence, there has been an upshot in violence in Darfur. Adding to this:

[h]umanitarian agencies have been denied access to areas between North and South Darfur, and IDP populations—especially women and children—are thought to be particularly vulnerable.[871]

1820 (2008)," UN News, New York (19 June 2008)

[866] Ibid.

[867] Security Council, Resolution 1882 (4 August 2009)

[868] Security Council Resolution 1861 (14 January 2009)

[869] "Darfur: Rape as a weapon of War, Sexual Violence and its consequences, "Amnesty International (17 July 2004) also in Jennifer Leaning et al, "Nowhere to turn: Failure to protect, support and assure justice for Darfuri Women," Cambridge: Physicians for Human Rights & Harvard Humanitarian Initiative (1 June 2009) at 52

[870] "Report of the Secretary-General on the African Union-United Nations Hybrid Operation in Darfur," New York, S/2010/213 (28 April 2010) at11 and S/2010/382 (14 July 2010) at11

[871] "Sudan: New Attacks on Civilians in Darfur," Human Rights Watch report (28 January 2011) at Executive Summary. For reference to vulnerable IDP populations see "2011 UNHCR country operations profile – Sudan" at 2 and on government camp raids see CrisisWatch Sudan (north) entry (1 February 2011)

The situation in Sudan is aggravated by the systematic denial of the government of the extent, or even of the existence of widespread sexual violence. The government is prone to accuse international NGOs of fabricating a problem that they then use to obtain funding from their western donors for whom this is a popular cause.[872]

Louise Arbour, President of the International Crisis Group, noted in her presentation to the Canadian House of Commons Human Rights Committee in which I was the vice chair in 2011 that, notwithstanding the Comprehensive Peace Agreement between the North and South, one recent study suggested "that women continue to suffer rape and other forms of gender-based violence. Sexual violence is carried out with impunity by the police and armed forces since soldiers feel a sense of entitlement as liberators above the law."[873] Specifically, in the towns of Juba and Torit, a number of females in the marketplaces are victims of rape and sexual assault at the hands of security forces.[874] Furthermore, the deadly attacks in Jonglei in March and April of 2009 are evidenced to have been specifically intended to harm women and children.[875]

Gender equality and gender rights must be viewed as more critical in order to prevent such human rights abuses. The government of Afghanistan, along with its international supporters, is unable to secure and protect the equal rights of women (and girls) as outlined in the Afghan constitution. Their inability to do so must be viewed critically, as "[t]hese shortfalls can't be scrubbed away by reference to Afghan cultural norms. They should be seen in the context of an American-led international intervention in which justice and meaningful efforts to build rule of law institutions have been largely absent."[876] Similar circumstances can be found:

---

872   "Gender-Based Violence in Southern Sudan: Justice for Women long overdue," New Haven: Allard K. Lowenstein International Human Rights Clinic at Yale Law School, (25 January 2011) at10-15

873   Louise Arbour, President & CEO International Crisis Group, "Study on Sexual Violence in Conflict States," Canadian House of Commons Subcommittee on International Human Rights (10 February 2011)

874   "There is no protection: Insecurity and Human Rights in Southern Sudan," Human Rights Watch (2009) at 30

875   "Gender-Based Violence in Southern Sudan: Justice for Women long overdue," New Haven: Allard K. Lowenstein International Human Rights Clinic at Yale Law School, (25 January 2011) at 14 and also in at1

876   Louise Arbour, President & CEO International Crisis Group, "Study on Sexual Violence in Conflict States," Canadian House of Commons Subcommittee on International Human Rights (10 February 2011)

In Haiti, Sudan and Afghanistan, as well as in the eastern provinces of the Democratic Republic of Congo, entrenched patterns of abuse against women intersect with newer trends emerging from social breakdown associated with armed conflict.[877]

It is very important to consider that work concerning sexual violence is often subcontracted to civil society or humanitarian organizations, and while this is often times perceived as necessary, either because the state refuses to take part in resolving such concerns or is itself implicated in such crimes, "law enforcement and justice are basic public goods and, therefore, the preserve of state actors. The extent to which they can be contracted out to civil society groups is limited. NGOs can open clinics but not courts."[878] It is necessary to take into account that:

> [w]hile civil society groups—or peacekeepers—may be able to provide short term protection and assistance to victims, their work must be complemented by longer term development of state capacity to prevent sexual violence and punish perpetrators. And this is of course part and parcel of a larger effort at building state institutions in the justice sector, broadly defined.[879]

In Haiti, for example, sexual violence was pervasive:

> ... even before the earthquake and the subsequent humanitarian disaster, as the rule of law was weak and years of development efforts had failed to construct a functioning criminal justice system. The crisis has further increased the vulnerability of many women and girls. Data is unreliable, but widespread abuse and rape has been reported in the 1,200–1,300 IDP camps in the capital which house over one million residents.[880]

A United Nations report on South Sudan alleges that violations of international law, crimes against humanity and war crimes are being committed in the Kordofan state and attributes this to Sudanese Armed Forces (SAF). The reported alleges violations included:

> extrajudicial killings, arbitrary arrests and illegal detention, enforced disappearances, attacks against civilians, looting of civilian homes and destruction of property...a series of extrajudicial killings targeted at

---

877 Ibid.

878 Ibid.

879 Ibid.

880 Ibid.

people who were affiliated with the SPLA-N and SPLM, most of whom allegedly were from the Nuba communities. [881]

As noted above, failed states create instability for the international community as people become displaced or become refugees as a result of gross and systematic human rights violations. Individuals become victims of state oppression when international treaties are not respected. In Sudan, human rights agencies have charged that the government supports and participates in slavery as well as in attacks against its own people.[882]

A report published in 2011 by a coalition of human rights groups warned of rising levels of violence in Darfur. The conflict has been going on for a number of years. In 2006, the Darfur Peace Agreement was signed by the Sudan Liberation Movement and the government, which called for the disarmament and demobilization of the Janjaweed militia. The Agreement has since been supplanted by the Doha Agreement of 2011. A coalition, which included Human Rights Watch, African Centre for Peace and Justice Studies, and The Enough Project, insists that the situation is getting worse and has urged the United Nations Security Council to "insist on regular public reports on the humanitarian and human rights situation in Darfur and throughout Sudan in order to monitor the situation on the ground adequately."[883]

In Sierra Leone, state failure has led to the establishment of a class of downtrodden youths who see joining armed gangs as one of the only ways to improve their own lives.[884] In Chad, rebel forces are destabilizing the country, creating hundreds of thousands refugees and internally displaced persons (IDP).[885] The list of human rights violations in failed states is too excessive to be fully and effectively analyzed in this book.

---

[881] "UN Urges Inquiry Into Alleged War Crimes in Sudan's Southern Kordofan State," UN News, New York (15 August 2011)

[882] Gérard Prunier and Rachel M. Gisselquist, "The Sudan: A Successfully Failed States," in Robert I. Rotberg (ed.), *State Failure and State Weakness in a Time of Terror*, Washington D.C.: Brookings Institution Press (2003) at 106

[883] *Sudan: Deteriorating Situation in Darfur*, Human Rights Watch Report (8 January 2011) and

[884] William Reno, "Sierra Leone: Warfare in a Post-State Society," in Robert I. Rotberg (ed.), *State Failure and State Weakness in a Time of Terror*, Washington D. C.: Brookings Institution Press (2003) at 96

[885] Chad country profile, Fund For Peace (October 2011). Available at: <http://www.fundforpeace.org/global/states/ccppr11td-countryprofile-chad-10u.pdf> accessed 15 March 2012

Violations of human rights occur when any state or non-state actor breaches any of the treaties that exist in international human rights and humanitarian law. The violations of human rights and security in failed states inevitably lead, as will be examined in the next subsection, to the loss of social cohesion and development.

Practice of the Security Council – Opinio Juris

Although not always consistently, the Security Council has acted under the Chapter VII mandate and developed several approaches to various situations arising out of serious violations of human rights in failed states.[886] Under Chapter VII, Article 39:

> The Security Council shall determine the existence of any threat to the peace, breach of the peace, or act of aggression and shall make recommendations, or decide what measures shall be taken in accordance with Articles 41 and 42, to maintain or restore international peace and security.[887]

As well, under Article 42, the Security Council may take action:

> by air, sea, or land forces as may be necessary to maintain or restore international peace and security. Such action may include demonstrations, blockade, and other operations by air, sea, or land forces of Members of the United Nations.[888]

In the case of Somalia, the Security Council adopted Resolution 794, a milestone resolution under Chapter VII, which held that "the magnitude of the human tragedy caused by the conflict" was sufficient in itself to constitute a threat to peace within the meaning of Article 39 of the Charter.[889]

In late 1992, the United States led a coalition of states in Operation Restore Hope in Somalia with 36,000 peacekeeping forces. It was later replaced by the United Nations Operations Mission in Somalia (UNOSOM II) established under Security Council Resolution 814 of March 26th, 1993. On October 3rd, 1993, there came a turning point in United States involvement when eighteen soldiers lost their lives and seventy-five were

---

[886] Daniel Thürer, "An internal challenge: partnerships in fixing failed states," *Harvard International Review*, Vol. 29, No.4 (Winter 2008)

[887] UN Charter

[888] Ibid.

[889] Daniel Thürer, *The 'Failed State' and International Law*, Geneva: International Review of the Red Cross, No. 836 (31 December 1999)

wounded and subjected to humiliating treatment.[890] Soon afterwards, the United States announced its intention to withdraw.[891]

United Nations Secretary-General Boutros Boutros-Ghali has suggested that international intervention in failed states should include attempts at reconciliation and the re-establishment of effective government, given that the effects of such internal conflicts are usually much more devastating and far-reaching than in the case of inter-state conflicts.[892] The General Assembly has also taken action through the 'Uniting for Peace' resolution; however, the Security Council does not want to be rendered incapable of action and supplanted by the General Assembly.

In concern to Haiti, the Security Council decided in February 2004 that the armed rebellion that overthrew President Aristide of Haiti represented a threat to peace under Article 39 of the Charter.[893] In the case of Libya, the Security Council did act militarily to prevent breaches of human rights when state authority had broken down. The Security Council is empowered to intervene to restore order in failed states where there has been a threat to peace as defined in Article 39 of the Charter. In such circumstances, the Security Council does not require the state's consent.[894] In cases such as those of Bosnia-Herzegovina, Somalia and other failed states the Security Council has acted accordingly.[895]

On March 17th, 2011, the Security Council demanded an immediate ceasefire in Libya and imposed a no-fly zone upon adopting Resolution 1973.[896] The resolution, which called on member states to take "all necessary measures" to protect the people of Libya from the Gaddafi regime, was adopted with the support of the five permanent members of the Security Council, while in the case of Kosovo NATO's military intervention was undertaken without the sanction of a United Nations Security Council resolution, mainly due to the inability of all five permanent veto members to agree on a resolution.

---

[890] William Zartman (ed.), *Collapsed States: The Disintegration and Reinstitution of Legitimate Authority*, Boulder: Lynne Rienner (1995) at 228

[891] Ibid. at 229

[892] Boutros Boutros Ghali, "Towards the Twenty-First Century: International Law as a Language for International Relations ," United Nations Congress on Public International Law (13-17 March 1995) at 9

[893] Daniel Thürer, *The 'Failed State' and International Law*, Geneva: International Review of the Red Cross, No. 836 (31 December 1999)

[894] Ibid.

[895] Ibid.

[896] "Security Council Approves 'No-Fly Zone' over Libya, Authorizing 'All Necessary Measures' to Protect Civilians," UN News, New York (17 March 2011)

The Security Council has interpreted its mandate broadly:

> In various cases—most notably Cambodia—the Security Council has taken peace-building action in the form of far-reaching civil measures that range from the demobilization of armed forces to the reform of governmental and constitutional structures. Like Somalia, Cambodia was an instance in which the charge of the international community to take over complex administrative and political tasks in failed states was clearly evident. It would appear that at least in connection with the situation of failed states, a door has opened allowing the measures envisaged in Chapter VI of the Charter for inter-state relations to be used in the internal affairs of states as well.[897]

In the *Prosecutor v Duško Tadić* decision on October 2nd, 1995, the Appeals Chamber of the International Criminal Tribunal for the Former Yugoslavia stated in their decision on the defence motion for interlocutory appeal on jurisdiction that:

> It would be a travesty of law and a betrayal of the universal need for justice, should the concept of State sovereignty be allowed to be raised successfully against human rights. Borders should not be considered as a shield against the reach of the law and as a protection for those who trample underfoot the most elementary rights of humanity.[898]

The ICTY looked at the practice of the Security Council when it classified under Chapter VII "internal armed conflict" as constituting a "threat to the peace." It noted that:

> it can thus be said that there is a common understanding, manifested by the 'subsequent practice' of the membership of the United Nations at large, that the 'threat to the peace' of Article 39 may include, as one of its species, internal armed conflicts.[899]

The ICTY examined the range of measures under Chapter VII, and noted that:

> Once the Security Council determines that a particular situation poses a threat to the peace or that there exists a breach of the peace or an act of

---

[897] Daniel Thürer, *The 'Failed State' and International Law*, Geneva: International Review of the Red Cross, No. 836 (31 December 1999)

[898] *Prosecutor v. Duško Tadić* , IT-94-1-A, Decision on the Defence Motion for Interlocutory Appeal on Jurisdiction, ICTY **(2 October 1995)** at para 58

[899] Ibid. at para. 30

aggression, it enjoys a wide margin of discretion in choosing the course of action... it can either continue, in spite of its determination, to act via recommendations, i.e., as if it were still within Chapter VI ('Pacific Settlement of Disputes') or it can exercise its exceptional powers under Chapter VII. In the words of Article 39, it would then 'decide what measures shall be taken in accordance with Articles 41 and 42, to maintain or restore international peace and security.'[900]

The International Tribunal for the Prosecution of Persons Responsible for Serious Violations of International Humanitarian Law Committed in the Territory of the Former Yugoslavia since 1991 has greatly contributed to the jurisprudence of humanitarian intervention.

The Security Council has also engaged in various multifaceted operations in various failed states, and "[i]t would appear that at least in connection with the situation of failed states, a door has opened allowing the measures envisaged in Chapter VI of the Charter for inter-state relations to be used in the internal affairs of states as well."[901][790]

As indicated above, there has been a movement in favour of the emerging doctrine of the Responsibility to Protect given the serious human rights and security consequences that have emerged as a result of state failure. Adding to this responsibility is the role that the international community is playing in the reconstruction efforts, assisting failed states to strengthen their structural competencies, as will be examined in Chapter 5.

---

[900]   Ibid. at para. 31

[901]   [790] Daniel Thürer, "An internal challenge: partnerships in fixing failed states," *Harvard International Review*, Vol. 29, No.4 (Winter 2008) at 42

Conclusion

Following the recent genocides in Rwanda, Darfur, and Myanmar, and the disappearing Christian and Yazidi communities of the Middle East, there is urgent need to raise the consciousness of genocide as a threat to world peace and security. The international community must take a more proactive role in educating the populace and developing systems to recognize early warning signs of mass killing to help to prevent it from occurring in the first place. The examples of failing states such as Afghanistan, Somalia, the Democratic Republic of the Congo, Iraq, and Syria complicate the situation as many Western developed nations have been faced with the prospect of a lack of global institutional capacity to address such situations.

In addition, the failure to attain consensus among the five permanent members of the United Nations Security Council exemplifies the deep and persistent nature of the challenges of internationally coordinated action in these areas. The actions of the UNSC have been characterized by division, inconsistency, and a serious divergence in opinion with respect to the most effective approach to the events.

Under international human rights and humanitarian law, states are obligated to protect their citizens and ensure that their human rights are respected. While the United Nations Charter clearly outlines the point at which intervention under Chapters VII is to be considered, there is an emerging paradigm to be found within the Responsibility to Protect doctrine which asserts that sovereignty can be breached. The conditions under which such breaches are to be considered include the need to protect people who are under threat. The international community in such circumstances has an obligation to respond effectively as most states are signatories to United Nations human rights covenants and treaties and are thus bound by international law to protect both individual sovereignty and state sovereignty. It seems that this re-definition of the modern state is a reality that some states continue to be reticent to accept.

Following the Second World War, the United Nations was created for the purpose of a commitment to human rights and to maintain international peace and stability. In 1948, one of the first conventions that was drafted was the Convention on Genocide, with the principle of protecting the innocent from repeating the murderous and heinous acts committed during the Holocaust. Unfortunately, recent events do not bode well for the United Nations' capacity to prevent genocide in the twenty-first century.

For humanity's sake, it is important that the world community come together to prevent and respond to humanitarian crises in a timely manner. State failure and genocide is preventable if the UNSC acts quickly. The failure of the international community to deal with issues such as the Rohingya or Darfur genocides is stark evidence of the need for more robust action.

The contemporary reality of the modern world is plagued with the scars of violent wars, hate crimes, and genocides. Since the beginning of the twenty-first century, mass murderers, terrorism, and genocide have occurred, despite the United Nations action plan to prevent these atrocities. Today's conflicts are creating havoc for civilians, and the efficiency with which hatred is now propagated thanks to the Internet and social media has only exacerbated the problem.

It was hoped that the dawn of the twenty-first century would see the manifestation of the statement made by the international community on June 25th, 1993, by adopting the Vienna Declaration and Programme of Action that "[a]ll human rights are universal, indivisible and interdependent and interrelated."[902] The World Conference on Human Rights was deeply concerned about human rights violations "during armed conflicts, affecting the civilian population, especially women, children, the elderly and the disabled."[903] It was hoped that the promises of progress, development, all-inclusiveness, global integrity, and global peace would be adhered to by the member states that signed on to the declaration. But to the world's disappointment, what we continue to witness is humanity at its worst: with the deterioration of parts of the Middle East, Africa, and other parts of the world, it is clear that the modern world is deeply infected with the evils of war, violence, and genocide.

Genocide should have been confined to the murderous acts of the last century, but it is still a vivid and disturbing reality. With its devastating

---

[902]   https://www.ohchr.org/en/professionalinterest/pages/vienna.aspx

[903]   https://www.ohchr.org/en/professionalinterest/pages/vienna.aspx

presence, the genocide of the twenty-first century reminds us that along with other forms of progress and development, it is equally important to sow the seeds of humanity, peace, and justice. Finally, we must never be party to genocide denial, and must speak out whenever and wherever it occurs.

Appendix 1

Classification of Genocide

In 1996, Dr. Gregory H. Stanton, President of the International Alliance to End Genocide presented a briefing paper on the genocidal processes including what he identified as the eight stages of genocide and how to prevent genocide during each stage. These stages include:

1. CLASSIFICATION: All cultures have categories to distinguish people into "us and them" by ethnicity, race, religion, or nationality: e.g., German and Jew, Hutu and Tutsi. Bipolar societies that lack mixed categories, such as Rwanda and Burundi, are the most likely to have genocide. The main preventive measure at this early stage is to develop universalistic institutions that transcend ethnic or racial divisions, that actively promote tolerance and understanding, and that promote classifications that transcend the divisions. Promotion of a common language in countries like Tanzania has also promoted transcendent national identity. This search for common ground is vital to early prevention of genocide.

2. SYMBOLIZATION: We give names or other symbols to the classifications. We name people "Jews" or "Gypsies," or distinguish them by colours or dress, and apply the symbols to members of groups. Classification and symbolization are universally human and do not necessarily result in genocide unless they lead to the next stage, dehumanization. When combined with hatred, symbols may be forced upon unwilling members of pariah groups: the yellow star for Jews under Nazi rule, the blue scarf for people from the Eastern Zone in Khmer Rouge Cambodia. To combat symbolization, hate symbols can be legally forbidden (swastikas) as can hate speech. Group marking like gang clothing or tribal scarring can be outlawed, as well. The problem is that legal limitations will fail if unsupported by popular cultural enforcement. Though Hutu and Tutsi were forbidden words in Burundi until the 1980s, code-words replaced them. If widely supported, however, denial of symbolization can be powerful, as it was in Bulgaria, where the government refused to supply enough yellow badges and at least 80% of Jews did not wear them, depriving the yellow star of its significance as a Nazi symbol for Jews.

3. DEHUMANIZATION: One group denies the humanity of the other group. Members of the target group are equated with animals, vermin, insects, or diseases. Dehumanization overcomes the normal human revulsion against murder. At this stage, hate propaganda in print and on the radio is used to vilify the victim group. In combating this dehumanization, incitement to genocide should not be confused with protected speech. Genocidal societies lack constitutional protection for countervailing speech, and should be treated differently than democracies. Local and international leaders should condemn the use of hate speech and make it culturally unacceptable. Leaders who incite genocide should be banned from international travel and have their foreign finances frozen. Hate radio stations should be shut down, and hate propaganda banned. Hate crimes and atrocities should be promptly punished.

4. ORGANIZATION: Genocide is always organized, usually by the state, often using militias to provide deniability of state responsibility (e.g., the Janjaweed in Darfur.) Sometimes organization is informal (e.g., Hindu mobs led by local RSS militants) or decentralized (e.g., terrorist groups.) Special army units or militias are often trained and armed. Plans are made for genocidal killings. To combat this stage, membership in these militias should be outlawed. Their leaders should be denied visas for foreign travel. The UN should impose arms embargoes on governments and citizens of countries involved in genocidal massacres, and create commissions to investigate violations, as was done in post-genocide Rwanda.

5. POLARIZATION: Extremists drive the groups apart. Hate groups broadcast polarizing propaganda. Laws may forbid intermarriage or social interaction. Extremist terrorism targets moderates, intimidating and silencing the centre. Moderates from the perpetrators' own group are most able to stop genocide, so are the first to be arrested and killed. Prevention may mean security protection for moderate leaders or assistance to human rights groups. Assets of extremists may be seized, and visas for international t5 Polarization Extremists drive the groups apart. Hate groups broadcast polarizing propaganda. Laws may forbid intermarriage or social interaction. Extremist terrorism targets moderates, intimidating and silencing the center. Moderates from the perpetrators' own group are most able to stop genocide, so are the first to be arrested and killed. ravel denied to them. Coups d'état by extremists should be opposed by international sanctions.

6. PREPARATION: Victims are identified and separated out because of their ethnic or religious identity. Death lists are drawn up. Members of victim groups are forced to wear identifying symbols. Their property is expropriated. They are often segregated into ghettoes, deported into concentration camps, or confined to a famine-struck region and starved. At this stage, a Genocide Emergency must be declared. If the political will of the great powers, regional alliances, or the UN Security Council can be mobilized, armed international intervention should be prepared, or heavy assistance provided to the victim group to prepare for its self-defence. Otherwise, at least humanitarian assistance should be organized by the UN and private relief groups for the inevitable tide of refugees to come.

7. EXTERMINATION begins, and quickly becomes the mass killing legally called "genocide." It is "extermination" to the killers because they do not believe their victims to be fully human. When it is sponsored by the state, the armed forces often work with militias to do the killing. Sometimes the genocide results in revenge killings by groups against each other, creating the downward whirlpool-like cycle of bilateral genocide (as in Burundi). At this stage, only rapid and overwhelming armed intervention can stop genocide. Real safe areas or refugee escape corridors should be established with heavily armed international protection. (An unsafe "safe" area is worse than none at all.) The UN Standing High Readiness Brigade, EU Rapid Response Force, or regional forces should be authorized to act by the UN Security Council if the genocide is small. For larger interventions, a multilateral force authorized by the UN should intervene. If the UN is paralyzed, regional alliances must act. It is time to recognize that the international responsibility to protect transcends the narrow interests of individual nation states. If strong nations will not provide troops to intervene directly, they should provide the airlift, equipment, and financial means necessary for regional states to intervene.

8. DENIAL is the eighth stage that always follows a genocide. It is among the surest indicators of further genocidal massacres. The perpetrators of genocide dig up the mass graves, burn the bodies, and try to cover up the evidence and intimidate the witnesses. They deny that they committed any crimes, and often blame what happened on the victims. They block investigations of the crimes, and continue to govern until driven from power by force, when they flee into exile. There they remain with impunity, like Pol Pot or Idi Amin, unless they are captured and a tribunal is established to try them. The response to denial is punishment by an international tribunal or national courts. There the evidence can be heard, and the perpetrators punished. Tribunals like the Yugoslav or Rwanda Tribunals, the international tribunal to try the Khmer Rouge in Cambodia, or the International Criminal Court, may not deter the worst genocidal killers. But with the political will to arrest and prosecute them, some may be brought to justice.[904]

---

[904] http://www.genocidewatch.org/aboutgenocide/8stagesofgenocide.html

Index